WOMEN'S WAR MEMOIRS

Women in Military Service Memorial   in Washington, D.C.
Original art by Jilia Fulton.

WOMEN'S WAR MEMOIRS

by

ROSEMARY ECKROAT BACHLE

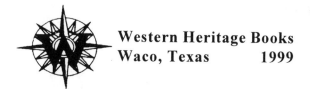

To Julia Williams

Memories are forever

Rosemary Eckroat Bachle

Western Heritage Books
Waco, Texas   1999

© 1999
Rosemary Eckroat Bachle

ISBN: 0-86546-095-7

All rights reserved. No part of this book may be reproduced or utilized in any form or by any means, electronic or mechanical, including photocopying and recording, or by any informational storage and retrieval system, without permission from the publisher.

Manufactured in the United States of America.

DEDICATION

To each life
forever changed—

To our daughters and sons, our grandchildren and great-grandchildren, that by bringing our war memoirs to life helps us rediscover the past so that we may influence their future, and it is hoped that we will leave a mark in the dust of time.

FOREWORD

by
Cathy Keating
First Lady of the State of Oklahoma

World War II was the first truly modern conflict. It involved attacks on civilian populations. It was a war of technology, from the codebreakers whose work helped win battles to the development of new weapons like the jet airplane and the atomic bomb. And it was the first war to significantly involve women as members of the military.

Our World War II veterans of both sexes (as well as those who waited for them on the home front) are gradually leaving the stage. It has been more than half a century since the war ended, and each day's obituary page bears the biographies of those who served. Often the photo is not of the man or woman of 75 or 80, but of the young, eager Army Air Corps pilot or infantryman or WAC, overseas cap cocked jauntily, ready to win the battle for freedom. As the World War 11 generation leaves us, many historians are suddenly realizing that these Americans—who grew up in the Depression, won the war, and came home to build our modern nation—represent a vast treasure of memories and recollections. Each story is unique, adding its share to a collective history.

Rosemary Eckroat Bachle was there. Now she has collected the first-person accounts of women who shared that enormous experience. Some were far from the fighting. Others were right in the middle of the greatest war in human history. There were women prisoners of war, women who ferried military aircraft to the fronts, women who courageously endured long separations and the London blitz, women who cared for the wounded and helped bury the dead. Some of them lost their own lives in a war where women were supposed to be "non-combatants."

This volume adds much to our understanding of those years and of the vital, central role women played in winning. Thanks, Rosemary, for helping tell these tales. They are part of America's story.

A WORD OF APPRECIATION
by
Major General Fred A. Daugherty (Retired)

It has been my pleasure to read many war books—especially books about World War II and the Korean War.

Reading *Women's War Memoirs* leaves me with the belief that women do not have to be members of the military to be soldiers serving our country in time of war! From my combat experience in World War II and the Korean War, the nurse has been my lasting impression of the woman soldier.

This is still my feeling, for they were near the front lines and even closer with the MASH units in the Korean War. For the first time in this war, our country's casualties were quickly moved from the front by helicopters equipped with metal closed beds affixed over each skid to doctors and nurses who gave them immediate medical attention with excellent facilities. Many lives were saved, and our injured soldiers had much better recoveries.

But in reading *Women's War Memoirs*, by Rosemary Eckroat Bachle, my views and impressions have been widened, and I now realize and appreciate that women at home and abroad were, in large measure, our fellow soldiers fighting our wars in so many essential and important ways.

After all, it takes the efforts of both men and women to make our country a great country.

INTRODUCTION

Women's War Memoirs is just that, a memory book, rather than one of hard fact and precise statistic. In recalling an epoch, more than 50 years ago, the women experienced pain in some instances, exhilaration in others. Often it was a fusing of both. A hesitancy, at first, was followed by a flow of memories, long-ago hurts and small triumphs, honors and humiliations. There was laughter, too. And that is what I experienced as I recorded the memories of the women thrown, hugger-mugger together fighting the Civil War all over again in their dorms; and of those men, women, and children on the home front who knew or did not know what the shouting was all about and of a moment in history, as recalled by the women at Los Alamos where each life was forever changed. They are precious memories.

Some of the stories take us back to our high school and college days in World War II when blackouts were a real scare for the U.S. on both the East and West coasts, and how the boys decided to enlist and how some of them died. Some bring us to the realization that World War II, the "Good War," wasn't the war to end all wars; since then there was the Korean Conflict, the Vietnam War, and women in the Desert Shield Operation.

But for those of us in the middle of the country—Oklahoma City, Oklahoma—the blackouts were less of a threat. It wasn't until the atomic bomb was dropped that we became more conscious of what might happen, and it just didn't seem possible that we were at war. But the war went on, and when we heard that President Roosevelt had died someone said, "Jesus Christ! We grew up with that man practically. We're behind the new President. Carry on till victory." And carry on we did. All of us.

The past becomes a mosaic blur of feelings and apparitions.

I remember how frightened I was when I drove my husband to the induction station at the Shrine Temple in Oklahoma City in June

1945. In the back seat of our Rio Flying Cloud our two-week-old baby girl, Elaine, was in a wicker bassinet, and our three-year-old daughter, Rosellen, snoozed on my husband's lap in the front seat. The war in Europe was about over, but men with two or more children were still drafted. I wondered what was in store for all of us in the coming months. I would soon be both mother and father to two little girls.

Patriotism was strong. "Don'cha know there's a war on?" were the catchwords for the day. We were all asking the same questions. What's gonna happen when it's finally over? What's the world gonna be like? All of us sending cookies, saving tinfoil, toothpaste tubes, or tin cans; and then wondering if we helped in some small way to make it possible for our children and grandchildren to have a safer, better life in the years to come.

And then there was rationing.

Rationing was already part of our everyday living. It would be easier for me now since my husband was drafted into the Army, and I would be eligible to purchase supplies from the PX (Post Exchange) at Tinker Field in Oklahoma City.

The first thing I did was read the ration reminders in the daily paper to find out what stamps were good that day. The colors of the stamps corresponded to certain foods, and stamps were only good on designated days of the week or month. Then I read the "Keep Up With Aunt Susan" column in the daily paper. I still have the recipe for "Conservation Supper" made with beef chunks, hominy, bacon, chili powder, onion, and tomato juice. Potatoes disappeared intermittently, and women substituted macaroni and rice. Thank goodness for my parents' victory garden. We hoarded our Kerr Wide Mouth Mason jars for canning. They, too, fell victim to the war effort.

By the time I waded through all of the gobbeldy-gook of stamps for food, stamps for gas, and made out my list, the lines were already long. I stood in line for butter, and we got plenty sick of sausages, because sausages is what the butcher had most. The Piggly Wiggly didn't have any fresh meat at all, but Spam fried in butter was a tasty substitute for ham. My sister-in-law and I pooled our rations and bought a ham once. We even had the butcher split

Rosemary Eckroat Bachle

the ham hock for us. I didn't drink coffee, but sugar was a coveted item. I made cookies packed in popcorn for my husband, Leonard, who was in the Counter Intelligence Corps at Sparrows Point in Baltimore, and my brother, Art, a paratrooper in the Japanese conflict. Hershey bars, my brother's favorite candy, were a rare treat, and there were no banana splits because, yes, there were no bananas!

Everything was rationed during the war. I went to several stores to get Kleenex. Paper commodities were scarce, and some of the grocers saved wrappers from grapefruit and oranges for customers to pick up to use for toilet paper. There was no wax paper or paper napkins. Some of this didn't bother me. I didn't have money to buy such luxuries anyway. Waste kitchen fats were saved and redeemed for ration points.

In one of my letters to my husband I told him I went to four of the biggest stores to buy crib sheets. There were none. Finally, I decided to make my own sheets, but, while shopping at the John A. Brown store for a coveted pair of hose, I spotted some sheets. The salesgirl was a friend of mine, so I asked her if she had any crib sheets. She went to the back room and came out with a sack and a charge slip to sign. When I got in the Rio Flying Cloud, I immediately looked in my sack—lo and behold there were two white crib sheets. Towels were hard to buy, and pots and pans were extinct. My mother and friends raided their cupboards and came up with towels, tea towels, handmade hot pads, pots and pans, and even a square cast-iron skillet for baking cornbread.

My parents owned a Phillips 66 station next to a feed store, and the farmers and truckers gave them their extra ration stamps. The stamps were pasted on big sheets of paper and given to the boys home on leave, and the women who followed their husbands from coast to coast were always scrounging for gas. The women who worked at the Douglas Air Craft plant near Tinker Field were issued stickers for gas for their car pools. A flat tire was a disaster. Retreads were in great demand, and sometimes we had to beg the station attendant to sell us a tire. Rubber and leather footwear were luxury items, and some of us bought cardboard shoes for our little ones. There was little hope for a new bicycle or automobile.

Some of us gals made our own clothes, and I even made hats. I still have one, It is a large black halo made in brushed fur felt. The rim is trimmed in black satin, and a large black satin bow sits jauntily on the back. One hat tilted so far over my eyebrow I couldn't see. We cinched in our waists and wore shoulder pads so thick they reached our ears. Our shoes were chunky with platform soles and ankle straps. Some of us gals painted our legs with suntan cream and used eyebrow pencil to make seams on our legs. We kept our one pair of coveted hose in a Kerr jar. Baggy slacks gained popularity for Rosie the Riveter, but unless we had to wear them, we preferred our dirndl dress and snappy military suits.

A friend, Kay Johnson, reminded me of some of the other things us gals did. Some of us had sexy photos taken for our husbands overseas, and some visited their husbands in ramshackle hotels where the walls were paper thin. Because our children who were born at this time didn't see their Dad for a year or two, it was quite traumatic when they met. Kay reminded me that housing was hard. When she moved to Kansas, babysitters went up to ten cents an hour. The B coupons allowed her to have the luxury of a thousand-year-old Packard. The silver gear shift knob usually came off in her hand, and fumes came up through the floor. The fumes made it necessary to drive with the windows down no matter the weather or distance to travel. Twas quite a time for us gals, but we survived

We were young and vulnerable, but we didn't whine. No "Poor Me" tone was heard from my group of friends. We prayed a lot, sang a lot, and were frugal in all things. We held bits and pieces of our lives in suspension waiting for our husbands, fathers, and brothers to return to us.

Who said, "Nothing that happens to us goes to waste?"

ACKNOWLEDGMENTS

I would be remiss if I did not once again thank all of the ordinary women with extraordinary spirit who brought their memories to life so that our children, grandchildren, and great-grandchildren may better understand our dreams for their future.

One of my greatest pleasures has been working with so many generous people during the writing, research, and production of this book.

Thanks to my Oklahoma City Writers and Central Oklahoma Roundtable of Authors friends for their help, support, and encouragement. Especially to Dottie Abney, Barbara Shepherd, and Judy Walker for lending me their expertise and typing and retyping when my hands failed me.

Thanks to the poets in the Oklahoma Poetry Society for their poems and support and especially to Sandra Soli for her specific notes and timely suggestions.

And special thanks to my editors: Kathryn Fanning, Managing Editor of Byline Magazine, for reminding me of the basics; to Carol Welsh for checking the historical events; to Christiane Farris, German Department of Modern Languages at Oklahoma City University; to Dea Mengers, who rescued me from total chaos with her organizational skills; and to Paul F. Lambert, Executive Director of the Oklahoma Heritage Association. And, last but not least, to my daughter, Elaine M. Dodson, for her patient corrections of mistakes.

To all the authors who wrote the stories of their mothers, grandmothers, and friends, I will be forever indebted.

Most of all, my love and sincere appreciation to my family, especially my husband, Leonard, who had to share my time with so many wonderful people during the past three and one half years

Note:

Edits for clarity and space considerations had to be made, but some of the points in the stories that may be considered as not quite true or chronological have been allowed to stand, because this is a book of memory, and memory has its own story to tell.

CONTENTS

Foreword *by Cathy Keating.*..vii

A Word of Appreciation, *by Maj. Gen. Fred A Daugherty*................ix

Introduction..xi

Acknowledgments..xvii

1 ON THE HOME FRONT

Long-Awaited Homecoming *by Dena R. Gorrell*............................3

Bring-Daddy-Back Club *from newspapers*...................................4

Serendipities From World War II *by Lillian C. Boland*....................8

Long Live Peace *by Billie Marsh*..12

One Civilian's Connection With Three Wars *by Opal Hartsell Brown*....13

Reminiscences of My Tour of Duty *by Dorothy Almen*....................20

Esperiences in the War Department *by Dorothy Almen.*..................24

Christmas Memory *by Dorothy Almen*..26

Remnants of War *by Blanche Barrymore*....................................28

Sweet Secrets *by Carol Hamilton*...35

Patterns *by Carol Hamilton.*...36

Prewar China *by Betty Butler Wiseman*......................................37

The Battle For Europe *by Betty Butler Wiseman.*..........................39

God Said It's Not Time Yet *by N.E. Chapman.*.............................43

The Military Years of Rosie E. Laird *by Dwane E. Cline*.................49

A Woman of World War II *by Flo Mason*.....................................56

A Mother's Story of Five Blue Stars *by Al Waintroob*...................57

The Wives Who Wait *by Billie Riggs*..59

The Vietnam Years *by Pollie G. Blanton.*...................................66

A Day That Made a Difference *by Marj McAlister*.........................76

Global Warfare *by Marj McAlister.*...78

My Son Grew Up in a Bunker *by Rosemary Eckroat Bachle.*...........79

Remembrance and War. *by Janiece Ritter Cramer.*.......................85

Dog Tags For Kids *by Joan Naylor*...91

It Was a Matter of Curiosity *by Mina R. Zentz*............................92

A Teacher's Story *by Doris N. Taylor*..94

Flashback *by Flo Mason*...96

Willing Followers *by Kathleen Gummer*......................................97

The Tiny Riveter *by Louise L. Miller*...101

World War II Working Mother *by Rosemary Eckroat Bachle*.........105

2 LOS ALAMOS

The Secret Place in the Sky *by Rosemary Eckroat Bachle*.............113
Witness *by Rosemary Eckroat Bachle*................................116
Los Alamos Love Story *by Rosemary Eckroat Bachle*.....................120
A WAAC in Los Alamos *by Rosemary Eckroat Bachle*..................125
The Giants on the Hill *by Rosemary Eckroat Bachle*....................128

3 PRISONERS OF WAR

Eavesdropping on Journeys into Bits of Memories,
    by Rosemary Eckroat Bachle......................................133
Four Came Home *by Rosemary Eckroat Bachle*..........................137
Colonel Rosemary Hogan *by Glenda Carlile*.........................145
Leipzig After Sixty-Two Years *by Ora Harris*....................149
At Dachau Prison When I Tried Not to See *by Betty Wedel*.........159

4 ON THE FRONT LINES

Love Affair With the Air *by Elaine M. Dodson*..................163
All Hands Hit the Deck *by Estella Knapp Kernan*...........................167
A South Pacific Scrapbook *by Virginia Ridgeway McCombs*.........177
Of Life and Land *by Hanna A. Saadah*.........................189
Requim For Joan *by Stan Cosby*..............................189
Now *by Bernardine Buyez Sydner*...............................190
In God I Trust *by Susan M. Bickford*.........................191
Be Still and Know *by Lela N. Turner*........................193
The Story of Nurse Dora J. Stohl *by Rosemary Eckroat Bachle*.......194
Parachute Silk and POW Rice *by Rosemary Eckroat Bachle*...........208
Air Raids in London *by Martha Kay*.........................213
Tea Ceremony *by Sandra Soli*...............................216
Letters Home *by Irene Sturm Lefebvre*......................218
Wars of the '40s *by Dorthy Myers*.........................228
Boot Camp: Camp Lejeune *by Mary Louise Courey Glann.*...........229
My Life in the Women's Army Corps
    by Mildred L. Brezic Setterberg.........................233
A WAC in North Africa *by Irene Isaacson Ward*...........................236
Sergeat Melba Jo Gaither *by Opal Hartsell Brown*........................242

Epigraph...247
Appendices
    A: Women's Service Organizations........................249
    B. Contributors...253
Bibliography...261
Index..262

CHAPTER ONE
ON THE HOME FRONT

War involves us in its conflicts
pulls at our emotional strings
changes us forever
even if we believe
we at home are only
        spectators.

LONG-AWAITED HOMECOMING

The U.S. Army called my brother Ray
To serve in World War II. Those years away
Creased worry lines upon my mother's brow
And dimmed the twinkle in once-smiling eyes.

Each day we watched for air mail envelopes
Of blue; and when his censored letters came
We clung to every word. In retrospect, I'm sure
That Mother must have memorized them all.

A shoe box full of letters in the hall,
With each one filed and organized by date.
When Mother took that box into her room,
We knew enough to give her privacy and space.

We listened to the radio, where news
Came crackling over wires about the war.
Dark clouds of fear would settle on our hearts;
Each day our prayers implored God's watchful care.

We lived with shadows till the day we learned
The war had ended—peace could now return.
My brother, too, at last was coming home
From half a world away. How we rejoiced!

When he came back we laughed and cried, we hugged
And kissed, we sighed with great relief. God brought
Our loved one safely home on wings of love
And proved once more the joy of answered prayer.

by Dena R. Gorrell

3

BRING-DADDY-BACK CLUB GAINS SUPPORT IN STATE

from
The Altus Times, Democrat (February 1946)

Oklahoma City, Feb. 11. (U.P.) — A new organization is working, paradoxically, toward expansion and toward ending its existence—both at the same time. It is the Bring Daddy Back club. And its members—wives of service men-fathers—insist the organization can't go out of business any too soon to suit them. But until their husbands are back at the firesides, they announce intentions to expand their organization and to do everything possible to make their influence felt in congress and governmental circles.

"If they were really needed, it would be different," said Mrs. R.C. Lette, president of the OklahomaCity Bring Daddy Back Club. "But we know that many of the fathers in the army and navy are not needed."

She cited her husband as "a perfect example." He has been in the navy two years, serving overseas 18 months on an aircraft carrier. He is now stationed in a naval office at Alameda, Calif. "He hasn't done any work since Nov. 1, but he is 'frozen,'" she said. "From his letters, all it seems he does is go to work, then go out and get coffee. Then it is lunch time." The Lettes are parents of two boys, six and eight years old.

The club president pointed out that the effect on children's whole lives had to be considered, adding that "nearly every day you read of some boy eight or 10 years old being arrested or getting into trouble. The children need their fathers," she said. "If the army and navy are not making good use of them, then they should be released to come home. I feel that one person can't be two parents."

Mrs. Lette and Mrs. L.L. Bachle, another club official, reported numerous inquiries had been received from wives and mothers of service men-fathers since start of organization last December. The club here includes more than 40 active members, including some living at El Reno and Guthrie.

Similar groups have been organized at Tulsa and Edmond, and reports have been received of activities by wives and mothers in other cities and towns of Oklahoma. All of the clubs' members are wives of service men-fathers. As soon as a member's husband is released and comes home, she drops out, so that the membership is constantly changing.

Mrs. Bachle pointed out that Gov. Robert S. Kerr and Mayor Robert A. Hefner of Oklahoma City had endorsed the purposes of the local club. The club has distributed 1,000 mimeographed letters urging support of officials and the public, besides uncounted numbers of personal letters. The group is now having printed stamps bearing the words, "Discharge Dads." The stamps will be placed on all mail sent out in the future by club members.

Mrs. Bachle reported "mixed reaction" from Oklahoma's congressional delegation. She said U.S. Sen. Elmer Thomas of Medicine Park and Rep. Monroney of Oklahoma City were opposed to the club's activities, while Sen. E.H. Moore of Tulsa had promised his help.

"A great hardship is being worked on many families," she said. "Prices have gone up so much that it is much more difficult to get by on an allotment than it was two, three or four years ago. We realize everybody can't get out of service. But they have stopped drafting fathers, and we believe fathers should be given greater consideration on discharges."

All has not been smooth sailing for the wives battling to bring their husbands back home. Club leaders have received some "crank" letters and telephone calls. One member reported a threatening call from a man who claimed to be a marine.

"On the whole, we have had a very good response," said Mrs. Lette. "We are determined to go ahead and see what we can accomplish." But, she added, the club "surely would be glad" to disband at once—if all the fathers were home.

MOTHERS WANT DADDY
HOME FOR CHILDREN

from
Oklahoma City Times (January 1946)

A child's character is formed by his home life, and believing in

Waiting for the train, boat or plane to come in, are officers, and their children, of the Bring Back Daddy club. First row, left to right, are Melba Jean Mooney, 5; Larry Lette, 8; Mrs. Leonard Bachle, reporter, holding daughter Elaine Marie, and Rosellen Bachle, 4. Back row, left to right, are Mrs. E.L. Franklin, vice-president; Mrs. A.V. Money, treasurer, and Mrs. R.C. Lette, president.

that idea, Oklahoma City women organized a local chapter of the "Bring Back Daddy" club, which has swept over the nation. The membership has grown rapidly since the local branch was organized, shortly before Christmas.

Mrs. R.C. Lette, of 1701 NE 19, the president, has two children, ages 5 and 8. Her husband, Yeoman 3/c Lette, has 39 points and 18 months overseas. He served aboard the *USS Saginaw Bay*, before being stationed at the naval air station, Alameda, Calif.

One Husband in Africa

Mrs. E.L. Franklin, of 1717 N. Highland drive, the vice-president, is the mother of an 8-year-old boy. Her husband was an assistant supervisor at Douglas Aircraft plant before entering the army. He is now at a port of embarkation for overseas assignment. Treasurer is Mrs. A.V. Money, of 1313 1/2 N. Hudson, who has a 5-year-old daughter. Her husband, overseas 12 1/2 months, is now in north Africa. He has been in service 21 months.

Mrs. Nelson Wright, of 1232 NW 43, the secretary, has two children, 4 years and 8 months. Her husband, in the army eight months, is at a port of embarkation, also "going the wrong direction."

Baby Shoes Mailed

"The St. Paul Minn. chapter tells us to get the co-operation of our newspapers and radio stations," Mrs. Wright said. "They said they have had various demonstrations. We have sent baby shoes to our congressmen. One congressman reported to the newspapers he was going to send the shoes he received to the needed children of Europe. That was pretty sarcastic, don't you think?"

The women agreed the idea of the club was to bring the fathers back to their children. Demonstrations have been confined to sending baby shoes, letters and telegrams to the congressmen, and making personal visits to the mayor, city council and governor.

Difficulties Cited

Club members think it best not to have too much personal publicity. They have received letters and calls from people unable to see their viewpoint. "We don't blame them," Mrs. Wright said. "It's just that they can't understand the difficulties which arise when one must care for young children without their fathers assistance."

The next meeting of the club will be announced. They have no regular meeting place.

SERENDIPITIES FROM WORLD WAR II

by
Lillian C. Boland

On December 7, 1941, I was 22 years old and thrilled to be an acting apprentice at the Dock Street Theatre in Charleston, South Carolina. There were four men and one girl. We typed scripts, painted scenery, directed children's plays, and acted in the plays. It was a community theatre, so members of the community played some of the roles.

The bombing of Pearl Harbor frightened me, and I thought that we might be bombed immediately in Charleston.

As usual, with theatres, the Dock Street suffered financial reversals. To finish the season, the apprentices found jobs in the area, a wide area from which to choose—the Army Port of Embarkation, the Coast Guard, and the Navy base. I was hired at the Port of Embarkation by 2nd Lieutenant John L. Boland, who later became my husband on December 30, 1942.

Our marriage was a pleasant one. Miss Estelle McBee, sister of the president of Ashley Hall, an exclusive girls' school, was most interested in the Dock Street Theatre. I had rented a room from her before our marriage, and she developed an apartment for us in her large home after our marriage. Miss Estelle's home was next door to Ashley Hall. In the summer there was no school, and we were permitted to use the indoor swimming pool and the outdoor tennis courts. We had many young married friends who were in the service. One of our forms of entertainment was preparing meals for one another. A group of us rented a home at Folly Island and we had a place to change our clothing and keep cool by playing in the ocean on weekends.

My husband John was learning about shipping supplies all over the world by ship. Later, he was placed in the Inspector General's department and inspected ships as they came into port. One most

Cheers to you

Lillian Boland

Lillian Boland (left) was one of the Red Cross ladies who worked at the Charleston Port of Embarkation. Guadalupe Duke, wife of General Duke, is at right.

interesting evening happened when he brought Field Marshal Montgomery's brother to our home for hamburgers. The brother was serving as a chaplain on a ship and had expressed the wish to come into a home for an "American supper." We asked several couples to join us, and Miss Estelle was thrilled to think that we had a celebrity in our home. Chaplain Montgomery said that he was hungry for a banana. In no time, Miss Estelle was back with a whole stalk of large bananas.

The evening was very interesting, and both chaplains were excellent conversationalists. However, later we learned that Chaplain Montgomery had managed to pinch the "fanny" of each of the female guests. Perhaps I was moving about too fast, but the hostess was missed. We laughed to think what an active chaplain he was.

Gasoline and food were rationed. We ate lots of hamburgers because it took less coupons than steak. We planted a one-tenth acre "victory Garden."

The wives of the officers worked in the Red Cross. They rolled bandages, made doughnuts, and met hospital ships that brought in the wounded. They served milk, ice cream, and doughnuts to the wounded.

The wives were in the Port of Embarkation Red Cross. We might drive out to the base at 2:00 a.m. or 3:00 a.m. to make doughnuts. We had huge bowls and mixed the dough with our arms. The general became tired of his wife smelling like a doughnut, so he bought a doughnut machine that mixed and fried them for us. It was a labor of love, but since doughnuts have little or no nutritive value, we might have been better off to serve peanut butter or pimento cheese sandwiches.

The general's wife was beautiful and a charmer. She was so gracious to all the young couples. Her name was Guadalupe Duke, but everyone called her Lupe. One day she called one of my friends and said, "This is Lupe Duke." My friend couldn't believe the General's wife was calling her and thought that someone was playing a joke on her. She replied, "Boop-boop-eedoop." Was she embarrassed when she found she really was speaking to the general's wife.

The war was good to us in many ways. A little gal from Oklahoma spent eight weeks in New York City while her husband attended an Army school in New Rochelle. We had eight weeks at Leavenworth, Kansas, while John Boland attended a streamlined Command-General Staff School. These travels broadened our horizons.

John did go to Japan, but the war was almost over so the personal tragedy of World War II did not harm us.

The benefits of the GI Bill enabled John to get his M.A. and Ph.D. from the University of Michigan. I earned my master's degree there at the same time.

We moved to Oklahoma in 1951 when John was hired by the University of Oklahoma. Later, he went into private practice and continues today.

Memories of the war years are tied with youth, hope, idealism—strong family ties. It's frightening to us today to see children having children—no family ties—no really solid role models. It's time to rally round and see how in some small way we can help remedy this situation.

LONG LIVE PEACE

Communism is dead.
The cold war is over and we won.
Maybe. Maybe not.
Mother Russia lies bleeding, dying
while her children fight
among themselves,
each wanting what the other has.

In Bosnia the body count mounts
while diplomats boast of peace.
In Guatemala a mother mourns
for her son taken away in the night.
In Colombia a drug lord lives
in splendor and fear while
in a Chicago project a mother screams
rage over the bullet riddled remains
of her child.

In Washington, D. C., lobbyists
and politicians party
across from the park where a Vietnam
vet sleeps under newspapers
and dreams of finding work to buy food.
Desert Storm has passed
but dictators and evil live on.

Man, being of a lesser order
than the angels, will always insist
on borders, Mason-Dixon lines.
There will always be wars
along the borders, only the names
of the places change,
the grieving faces of the mothers
are always the same.

by Billie Marsh

ONE CIVILIAN'S CONNECTION WITH THREE WARS

by

Opal Hartsell Brown

Three of us women were putting the finishing flavors and flairs on lunch that Sunday afternoon, December 7. 1941, in Laesione, Oklahoma, when our two guests dashed from the living room into the kitchen. "The Japanese have bombed Pearl Harbor!" one of them shouted. "It just came in on the radio," the other one broke in.

Ida Mae Lewis, her daughter Allie Mehard, and I whirled to face the young soldiers in uniform. We stared at one another in rigid shock! The war, which had been raging in Europe since September 1, 1939, had now struck us. Life and the world hung dead still.

We women had met the young men from nearby Fort Sill at church that morning and invited them to lunch. Our regular custom was to take turns hosting military personnel on Sundays. It was Ida Mae's and Allie's turn that day, and a good thing. My husband, Gorden, was in Fort Worth, Texas, where the FBI had called him to identify his taxicab and two soldiers who had beaten and robbed him on the road to Duncan a few nights before.

We women and our guests finally broke our stance to dash into the living room. The radio was spilling over with deadly news. "One hundred fifty Japanese bombers and torpedo-carrying planes launched an early morning attack on Pearl Harbor.... Battleships *Oklahoma* and *Arizona* were sunk, and many more were wrecked and burning.... The number of casualties still unknown.... (Later, it was determined to be 4,500, 2,300 of whom were fatalities.)

What would happen now to us and our loved ones in service? Douglas, Allie's husband, and Jesse Hartsell, my brother, were in the 45th Division stationed in Abilene, Texas. Jesse, however, was on TDY (temporary duty) in Oklahoma City, displaying weapons and promoting War Bonds. He was scheduled to spend January of 1942 in Tulsa. J.B. Johnson, Ida Mae's son and Allie's brother, was stationed in Florida.

Opel Hartsell Brown

It was mid-afternoon before we pulled ourselves away from the radio to reheat and eat the lunch. The conversation was gloomy and short. The last bite taken, our guests excused themselves, thanked us, and said, "We will have to get back to Sill and call our families. They'll be worried about us." They hurried out to catch a bus. Knowing that people were caring for our loved ones, we continued hosting other military men throughout the war.

With no personal transportation, I walked to our little house and turned on the radio. Despite the fact we had only two rooms on the alley, we were fortunate to have any shelter at all. Laesione was overflowing people who had nowhere to go.

The radio announced that Japan had joined the Axis, Germany and Italy, and had declared war on the United States. Its military forces had struck many places in the Pacific: Hawaii, Shanghai, Guam.... Was there anywhere else for them?

The next morning I tried to work on a writing course from the University of Oklahoma, but bad news and sad thoughts held me prisoner of the radio. Working on a master's degree, I hoped the news would soon get better. It didn't!

The voice of President Franklin D. Roosevelt broke into the room. "The United States is now at war with Japan!" he announced with condemnation of the "dastardly act. It will go down in infamy...."

Bursting into tears, I fell across the bed and shook with sobs. Sometime that day I would have to contact my parents, Aubrey and Nannie Hartsell, in Sulphur. I had no telephone, and neither did they. Telephones were scarce items those days.

I cried my soul dry and my mind empty. "God help us all," I said and went out to find a telephone. Three days later, Germany and Italy declared war on the United States, and Congress declared war on them.

Gorden returned from Fort Worth with his car. It needed repair, and he needed to recuperate. His naturally dark face and brown eyes were still bruised and swollen.

"The guys who took my car," he said, "are to be brought back to Laesione for trial. I hope they get life forever."

We had not recovered from that blow and the attack on Pearl Harbor when all the world seemed to be on fire. Our country was at the bottom of the kindling. Only worse.

In spite of bad news, Gorden got a break. The local draft board had teenagers sufficient to fill its quota of recruits and reclassified him. He had been 1-A in Seminole, our former home. Believing he would be inducted into service soon, he had come to Laesione to join his brother in the taxicab business and to learn about Army life. When school was out, I followed.

Transportation became most important in Laesione, so Gorden stayed in that business. We took up the payments of $25 monthly on the new FHA home of our friends, John and Mae Boren Axton. John was going into the Navy. Mae and the boys, Hoyt and Johnny, were going with him as far as they could.

On two occasions we rented a bedroom with kitchen privileges to Army couples. After that our home became "home away from home" for two WACs, Mable Burge from El Paso, Texas, and Dorothy Wrey from Campbell, Minnesota.

While completing my correspondence courses, I volunteered at the USO, chalking up about 150 hours. Next, I became a reporter on the *Laesione Morning Press*. My beat was the Comanche

County Courthouse, Laesione City Hall, School Superintendent John Shoemaker's Office, and just about everywhere.

My first salary was $25 a week; then I became society editor for $30 a week. My connection with the newspaper in that international city gave me considerable connections with the military: the trial of a WAC accused of murder, interviewing foreign war brides, meeting the wives of Allied officers studying at the Fort.

I kept in touch with my parents and with the war abroad. The Americans in North Africa, including Douglas, moved into Italy and France. Jesse was in England, where his squadron was bombing Europe night and day. J.B. was still in Florida. Germany's new "Buzz Bombs" were pounding the British Isles.

On the local front, Gorden and I came home from our jobs on June 5, 1944, and worked in the Victory Garden until late, snacked, and went to bed. I was so exhausted I fell asleep immediately. About midnight I awoke from a disturbing dream: I was sitting behind the wheel of a car when Jesse appeared outside the door. He gazed at me with sadness, but never spoke. "Oh, Lord," I said, "I forgot to pray." That I did, then drifted back to sleep.

Two hours later Gorden and I awoke to the wailing of sirens. Were we being bombed? He switched on the radio beside the bed. The Allies had launched the invasion of Europe! It was D-Day!

Thousands of troops, bombers, and carrier planes had hit the Normandy Coast of France, fighting and dying! So were the Nazi occupants. Was Jesse's appearance at midnight an omen? Tears flowed down my cheeks. There was no more sleep that night.

Later in the week a little news stated Allies were island-hopping on the other side of the world. By August, General Douglas MacArthur had returned to the Philippines.

When we heard from Jesse, he said the two missions his crew made on D-Day were the easiest they had had. "The Germans were so busy on the ground," he said,"they didn't send up much flak." By September of that year, Jesse had chalked up 69 missions and got to come home.

Considerably shaken, his reunion was doubly celebrated. He and his fiancee, Sue Futch, a nurse in Shreveport, Louisiana, were married. His next assignment was at Shepherd Field Air Base, Wichita Falls, Texas, as an instructor.

I left the newspaper to teach in Laesione Public School for $150 a month. That gave me weekends, some holidays, and summers to write and do some traveling—when traveling became more available and acceptable. Automobiles and their accessories were still rationed. Transports displayed signs: "Is this trip necessary?" But time was changing things.

Suddenly on April 12, 1945, a much worse news bulletin hit the press and airways: "President Franklin D. Roosevelt died today at Warm Springs, Georgia...." The world stood still again. What next!

Vice-president Harry S.Truman took the oath as president. The war roared on. In the Far East at some strange place, Iwo Jima, our beloved war correspondent, Ernie Pyle, was killed. He was buried in Honolulu's Punch Bowl, Hawaii—another grievous occasion.

Back in Europe, the Americans and Russians met in Germany, and the war in Italy ended. Mussolini and his mistress were hanged upside down by their own people. On May 1, Hitler and his woman reportedly committed suicide.

That same month, Berlin fell to the Russians. The Germans surrendered at Rheims. May 8, 1945 was declared "VE-Day." Japan battled more viciously.

That brought revenge. On August 6 the United States Air Corps hit Hiroshima with its "secret weapon," the "Atomic Bomb." That stunned the enemy. Two days later, the same type bomb fell on Nagasaki. That terrified the world! The two cities were partially cremated.

Japan surrendered on August 14. Its representatives "signed the documents" with General MacArthur aboard ship in Tokyo Bay. The Allies celebrated and wept with America. We three women, who began this war together, and our loved ones were among the celebrants. Our three men had survived.

Douglas switched to the Reserves. J.B. came home from Florida. Jesse reenlisted in the Air Force. We never heard from our guests that Sunday, December 7, 1941.

Peace did not last. War got another curtain call, this time in Korea. Strange, the slaughter was never called a "war," but a "conflict." Gorden and I were nudged into that in 1950 and into the one in Vietnam.

The director of the Army Education Center at Fort Sill, Russell

Crooch, asked me to teach Basic Education two nights a week. Always ready for a challenge, I agreed.

That fall I took a night class in Conversational English for Korean officers. My co-worker was Ruby Forbess, librarian at Laesione Junior High School. Besides regular classes, Forbess and I took the students on field trips to the Wichita Mountains Wild Life Refuge, Holy City, and to a drive-in theater. When we left the theater, Major Kim Jin Koo said, "Americans should be happiest people in world. They have everything to make happy."

During the next decade and beyond, I continued my regular schedules in Laesione Junior and Senior High Schools and taught more military men and women. Then came an additional challenge: the Laesione Women's Forum asked Gorden and me to be civilian sponsor for foreign officers training in the World's Artillery and Guided Missile Center. The Forum was cooperating with Fort Sill and Laesione officials in the project. We chose the Turks first.

I hoped to get information for a biblical novel I was writing. Furthermore, my brother Jesse was stationed in that country. One of the Turks was especially helpful. He had been stationed in Haran, the main setting of the novel, and became our guide when we visited that country in 1963.

Our next officers were Ethiopians. One of them was a guard at King Haile Selassie's palace in Addis Ababa. He said the king really had lions in his courtyard, thus the title, "Lion King." Also, he said that Selassie was a descendant of King Solomon and the Queen of Sheba.

One of my classes at Fort Sill had only two Americans. All backgrounds were unusual. For example: Wolodymire Tarnakov, a Russian, had been taken to Germany with his family as slave laborers during World War II. When the Americans freed them, Tarnakov came here and joined the Army. Henry Ufnal, a Pole, had been taken from Warsaw by the Russians and sent to Siberia as a slave laborer. He stashed away food until he got an opportunity to escape to Iran, Turkey, then Germany. There he joined the American Army of Occupation. Yugoslavian Ivan Jakovinak did somewhat the same thing, but with greater ease. A soldier in his own country, he walked across the border into Italy and joined the Army of Occupation there.

My last class at the Army Education Center began with 40 new recruits in Basic Education. The war in Vietnam had deepened the chaos in the United States: riots, fires, and near revolution. The new recruits were training for possible disaster. Every week some of them told me, "I won't be here Monday. I'm goin' t' Nom (Vietnam)."

As I looked out over those dear sons, brothers, husbands, and friends, I wondered how many would ever return. About 12 remained to complete the nine-week course.

Gorden and I were sponsoring Moroccans when he died suddenly with a heart attack in 1967. That was sundown for one of my lives. Several months passed before I reached the dawn of another. But I had stored a mental library overflowing with wonderful experiences.

REMEMBRANCES OF MY TOUR OF DUTY IN LONDON, ENGLAND, ON THE SECRETARIAL STAFF WITH THE UNITED NATIONS ORGANIZATION (UNO, now UN)

by
Dorothy Almen

NOTICE TO VISITORS TO ENGLAND DURING WWII:
There are no coaches to carry you on your sightseeing tours;
There are few guides to show you around
    places of historical interest;
There are no vans to deliver goods you buy;
No paper in which to wrap your purchases;
NOTWITHSTANDING, London, shaking the debris from her hair,
Rises to greet you, and bids you welcome!

One of the most memorable experiences of our London experience was the official welcome by London to the UNO! This took place in Royal Albert Hall, a huge, completely round building seating what looked like half of London. When I stepped into the building, I was immediately confronted with thousands of faces looking back at me, giving me almost a sensation of "stage fright." I've never been in an auditorium where it seemed everyone was seated in everyone else's lap!

For sheer pageantry, the evening had no equal. On the stage were displayed all the colorful flags of the member nations, officials resplendent in the symbols of their offices, chief among them the Mayor of London, one of the most splendid of all, wearing his heavy ornamental necklace on which dangled his huge seal of office; a famed Welsh choir was seated, and there were rows of top officials of participating nations, including the United States. I spotted Mrs. Roosevelt seated next to the Archbishop of Canterbury

Dorothy Almen with two friends from the UNO staff visiting Anne Hathaway's cottage and Shakespeare's home on a day off. Rain seemed constant in England.

just five rows ahead of me. I was able to attend only because my boss could not make it and gave his ticket to me, for which I will always be grateful.

At the start of the proceedings, we heard the powerful whine of bagpipes accompanied by a tremendous rhythmic pounding of feet which actually made the whole auditorium seem to shake. Down the long aisle came the Queen's Royal Guards, about two dozen of the largest men I've ever seen, in their plaid kilts, wheezing on their bagpipes. "Sturdy" hardly describes them. The power they exuded as they stomped along, all the way to the stage, was stunning. I noticed especially the size of their knees, which were as big around as small hams, with cheeks (expanded with the breath required for that musical exercise) a bright red color. I might have thought they were rouged if I had not seen other British men, women and children with the same ruddy cheeks. I was told it was the result of the constant damp, cold weather to which they exposed themselves, but I could not resolve this because everyone in London did not have red cheeks.

At any rate, they were the most impressive sight and sound I found in my weeks in London I know I haven't done them full credit—one had to be there. It took a while to clear our heads after their procession ceased. The speeches were all inspirational and gracious with words of hope for the future peace of the world. The chairman was Field Marshal Sir Harold Alexander, and both Mrs. Roosevelt and the Archbishop were on the program. The choir of the Welsh Temple of Peace performed magnificently, and after the last impassioned address sang, "These Things Shall Be" by John Hughes, very fitting, to close the meeting. Printed on the bottom of the program: "And God save the King."

Too many other things I could supply, but it would take a whole book. Returning to America on the *Queen Mary*, we had as fellow passengers 1,777 war brides, an experience in itself. They made light of their situation by poking fun at themselves in a program they presented.

I learned that 29 of the war brides were bound for Oklahoma, and some of them questioned me whether the Indians made life dangerous in Oklahoma. I was happy to reassure them. Many were carrying babies, and we felt great sympathy for these English girls who were leaving their homes, perhaps forever, to face unknown dangers and challenges, perhaps even hostile or unfriendly in-laws.

As the ship drew away from the Southampton docks, we were among those brides, waving our little white handkerchiefs to those remaining on the shore, my own friends among them. It was obvious there wasn't a dry eye on either side. As far as the eye could still see, we could make out the white handkerchiefs being waved by the vanishing figures.

As we approached the New York harbor, all the brides were on deck in their little neat suits (probably acquired from stockpiling "points" of many in the family) with proper makeup and hair in place, anxiously peering toward the Statue of Liberty and the crowd awaiting us. At one time, a big boat came out with a band playing "Sentimental Journey," and we saw a huge banner across a building that said, "Welcome Home!" We didn't know if they meant the delegates and us or the brides, but it warmed us all. Later, we were happy to witness the reunion of several brides being happily welcomed by their new families, and saw one man lovingly cradling his new grandchild in his arms. We hoped for all the brides such a fine greeting.

EXPERIENCES IN THE WAR DEPARTMENT DURING WORLD WAR II, 1941-46

by

Dorothy Almen

An interesting sidelight of my life in wartime Washington, D.C., concerns shortages. While having lunch with a friend in the Pentagon Cafeteria, I became increasingly aware that a nice looking young officer across the way was paying exceptional attention to me. However, my girlish excitement was quickly dashed when he approached me with, "Young lady, are those real safety pins you are wearing around your neck?"

Indeed, my necklace consisted of a large number of silver-colored safety pins arranged side-by-side and attached with cord to resemble a sort of "slave" necklace, very attractive, together with a like bracelet. I replied that they were the real thing, and that he was very perceptive to have noticed their identity. His interest stemmed from the fact that there was a new baby in his home, and they had been unable to purchase any safety pins in the shops due to the national shortage of all such metal for non-military purposes.

I truly was reluctant to sacrifice my favorite jewelry even in the face of such dire need, but, sparring for time, I did take his name and room number with the promise to contact him. In the meantime, I returned to my office and shared the young man's problem, which elicited immediate sympathy among my fellow workers. With guilt as motivation, I went home after work and searched throughout my apartment for every spare safety pin, as did my coworkers, and the next morning we were surprised to find that together we had assembled a good number of these precious items. I put them all in a paper bag and called the officer with the good news that his troubles were over as to safety pins. Needless to say, he hastened to collect his treasure from us, with sincere gratitude to all concerned, and went on his way rejoicing.

We later had a handwritten note of thanks from him and his wife. Granted, we were all gratified by this happy ending for our collective "good deed," and I personally was relieved not to be required to relinquish my favorite jewelry to the war effort. Nevertheless, I never quite felt the same enjoyment in wearing my "slave" necklace as I had before. Safety pins since then have had special significance to me, as one might well imagine.

CHRISTMAS MEMORY
by
Dorothy Almen

Memories of wartime Christmases seem to be more indelible than those of peacetime, which tend to blend together into a comfortable meld of happy family gatherings. One such holiday memory transports me back to World War II in Washington, D.C., where I worked at the Pentagon Building as Junior Administrative Assistant to John J. McCloy, Assistant Secretary of War at that time.

Wartime shortages extended to everything from soap and cooking oil to stockings and, in this particular instance, to Christmas tree decorations. A lovely seven-foot tree was brought into our office complex, and the problem of what to do with it was brought to my desk. None of us furnished-apartment dwellers, detached from home bases, could boast an attic of holiday trappings, and the stores were uniformly barren of the accustomed balls and tinsel, all such metallic fripperies being channeled somehow into the military effort.

The challenge of a perfect tree standing unadorned stimulated our creative juices. From desks in various offices came truly original suggestions—a dangling earring dripping with sparklers hanging; red and yellow pencils hung by rubber bands; red ribbon bows tacked here and there; paper clips in silver, gold, and copper colors coupled and strung across the fresh green limbs in place of tinsel. Searching for more color, we discovered that the small, bright red "Confidential" and "Top Secret" cards used daily for inter-office correspondence looked just dandy when paper-clipped to the branches. An unsuspected office genius constructed a silver star for the tip of the tree out of aluminum foil "borrowed" from a shipment of meat in the cafeteria. As a final touch, we resurrected several huge light bulbs from disposal, the type used in larger light fixtures that bear a silver coating. When stuck deep into the tree, these rewarded us with a lovely, shining glow, the mark of all-proper Christmas trees.

Its cheer not only brightened up our office, but there was prob-

26

ably never a tree that received as flattering attention as ours in Suite E-924 of the Pentagon. A steady stream of admiring visitors came to express their amazement and delight and take pictures We were "written up" in the Pentagon newspaper together with a picture and prominent headline. Naturally, we took great pride in our achievement, and I have little doubt every person involved in the creation of this artistic expression shares my remembrance of the dark cloud of war which was momentarily turned inside out by our improvised silver lining.

REMNANTS OF WAR
by
Blanche Barrymore

I awoke at 3 o'clock in the morning. I got up and walked the floor. The room was filled with a presence—Eddie's presence. "I wonder if he's dead," I said aloud to myself. I didn't have long to wait.

My phone rang at 8 a.m. It was Jim, Eddie's brother. "Blanche, Eddie's dead. Heart attack."

"No, no," I cried. It couldn't be. He was due to come back to Oklahoma from Germany in a couple of weeks after being gone this time from me, the second time, for two years.

Eddie and I had been together four years in a small rural high school. I was so young when I finished high school I didn't date much, but didn't feel the need to. Eddie was just always there, my best friend, and on some level I always knew we were in tune with each other. He was a talented musician, playing several instruments, but it was his singing that captivated ne, as well as local audiences he held spellbound. Many times we were paired as a singing duo, but I acknowledged his talent far more than mine.

Then college came, and we went to separate schools. Time was just going by, and we were meeting other people and our lives were enlarging somewhat.

But before I could get through college, war had become a reality, and my generation was hit hard. Young men, boys actually, were being called up to enlist, to fight an enemy they didn't know existed, and they were scattered far and wide, overseas and the United States. The world was thrown into a way of life that bore little semblance to my previous environment. We'd all have to adjust and learn new ways each day. Many who were not drafted or enlisted went to California to work in defense plants and earn "real" money for the first time.

It was a time when patriotism was uppermost in the minds of all Americans, and strangers from all walks became friends. It was

28

Blanche Barrymore.

also a time of great upheaval when friends and others were being killed in battle, missing in action, or scarred physically and psychologically for life. Movies fed us war propaganda, and our fears for a peaceful life ahead held us in a grip of bondage and worry.

Toward the latter part of my college I met Larry. He was three years older than I and had already graduated. But he came back to take some additional courses, and in a short while I became infatuated with him and told myself it was real love. My goal, at that time, was to get married and be a wife and mother.

But the war was affecting Larry's destiny, and it would not fit in with my plans. His time came to be drafted or enlist. He chose to enlist in the air cadets to serve his country. The training was in Texas. It was goodbye time for me, and my future simply evaporated. In desperation I went to California with a girl friend who had contacts there. Even though we were just two little naive country girls, never having been out of our native rural Oklahoma, we landed in Los Angeles unafraid. And, like everybody else, the war was changing all lives rapidly. It more or less was like "live today," as no one knew whether or not we'd see troops fighting on American soil tomorrow. No one had long-term plans. We were just living out the war.

I did contact Larry. I was in California and was holding onto a fantasy I'd perhaps marry him eventually, and my safe and happy life would be fulfilled. He was nearing graduation, so what better gift than my photograph.

It didn't take long to find a photographer in Hollywood who was a creative artist; his trademark was to glamorize the American girl. Flattered and impressed with the "new look" of me, I sent them to Larry.

Even though he loved the pictures, there was too much distance between us, and somehow we lost contact with each other. The war was in control of our lives, and I knew he'd been called for active duty. Where, I didn't know.

I felt lost, not knowing where I belonged, so I took a job in downtown Los Angeles, working for temporary Civil Service, an agency set up specifically for wartime. But before too long, I sought a new direction for my life. I married the photographer. To avoid being drafted, he enlisted in the Navy, and we were sent to Chicago, a city of soot, grime, and cold wind. I hated it there and longed for a warmer climate. Besides, I didn't know anyone in the area and was not happy in my marriage. So I made the best of it.

After a year the Navy moved us back to California, and the birth of my baby girl filled the void in my life somewhat. The war was still raging, and we wondered how much longer.

Suddenly in 1945 Japan surrendered, and the country was both happy and sad—happy it was over, but sad to learn of the horrible atrocities committed on our American prisoners of war.

I think I always felt I'd see Eddie again some day, but I wondered about Larry. I knew he was a flyer—had he survived?

The war now being over with Japan, newspapers were plastered all over with the aftermath. While reading the Los Angeles paper, something on the front page seized my attention. Was it fate? The article was about: a high ranking officer shot down over Japan during an air raid. Captured, he had been thrown into the worst prison camp, tortured, starved, and forced to walk naked through the streets. He was one of the few survivors. How could a young man's life be changed so drastically at the hands of a cruel enemy? It was only one of the many horrors of war we'd come to know about in time.

I cut the article out, kept it secret from my husband by hiding it under cover for some time. I'd take it out when alone, reread it, then hide it again someplace else. Many times I pondered how my life had changed because of the happenstances of war. Eventually I destroyed the article and filed it away in my mind as one of the many tragedies of war. The chance was gone forever now to see if we were right for each other, but that seemed trivial now after knowing how he had suffered. I had to face life as it was unfolding each day now and had no time to look back. The laughter and joy of being young and dreaming of a carefree world faded forever. It was time to grow up.

But where was Eddie? I didn't know whether he was in service or not. I often longed to see and talk with him and bring us both up to date on our lives.

A few years after the war ended with both Japan and Germany, we moved to Oklahoma where I needed to reclaim my roots. Also, to give my children (I had a son by then) the opportunity to interact with my parents, their grandparents, and to live as best we could a somewhat happier life. But my marriage soon disintegrated, and I was left with two teenagers to raise alone.

Twenty years passed without knowing anything about Eddie or what he'd been doing, where he had been—it was just a blank. But through those years I always had the comforting thought that he loved me—and perhaps was the only one who truly did. I had been 16 and he was 17 when we stood together, locked in an embrace and he said, "Marry me." Too young to think about marriage, I turned away and unknowingly hurt him deeply.

Now he was coming through loud and clear in my mind again. I do not think it coincidental that an unexpected relative ran into me, saying, "Eddie has just returned from Germany, where he has been since the war, and here is his phone number—in this city, no less."

I made haste to see him, and when I did every cell in my body cried out that this was the man I should have married. I was not mature enough when the war came to understand my emotions or to follow my heart's desire. But as Eddie walked me to the car, he said, "You and I should have gotten together. We belonged together."

"Yes, I know," I said. I felt pain, literally, for the lost years, and the companionship of this beautiful and intelligent man. An inner bomb had hit me, and I woke up to the true love I couldn't find. Now, was I being given a second chance to get my life together?

In the ensuing year I learned he had been with Intelligence during the war and afterward in Germany. It would be five years before he was allowed to break the secrecy to me about the operations, he said. I never suspected he had unfinished business in Germany until one day he called me from New York (I didn't know he was out of town). "I have to go back to Germany for awhile to straighten something out, and, when I do, I'll be back. Meantime, write."

A feeling of being alone came over me once more, but I wasn't about to break this connection, so for two years I waited and only occasionally heard from him. He indicated he was going through much stress, and something wasn't going right, but I didn't know from what.

Then the letter came that lifted my spirits. I called his brother, Jim, and it was good news. "I have been diligently working with an attorney to find the reason I was blacklisted and dismissed from my position. At long last we've found an erroneous report that was planted in my file. It's going to be straightened out now, and I'll be home in three weeks."

The long wait—finally coming to an end!

Then the call at 8 a.m. "Blanche, Eddie's dead—a heart attack."

I went into a tailspin. Numb with shock and disbelief, I waited for the return of his body from Germany. Due to red tape, it took three weeks to get his body returned. His ashes, rather—he had to be cremated.

Three weeks later I was at the airport, but it was to put my daughter on a plane to Houston. As I was leaving, the plane came taxiing in that was carrying his ashes. I'd planned to wear my prettiest dress and meet him as promised, but not this way—not this way. I hurriedly left the airport and didn't look back. His brother met the plane.

Trying to get through the funeral as best I could, I didn't expect to see the urn holding his ashes—it seemed to be too much for me to absorb. This was Eddie's unplanned homecoming, not the one he was looking forward to!

Then my mind shifted, and I suddenly recalled an experience I had when I was a freshman in college. I had the lead in a play—I was a young woman waiting for my husband to come home from the war. Eagerly expecting him to walk through the door, instead it was a messenger. He handed me an urn containing his ashes. The curtain came down as the words to the song were sung, "Going home, going home, I'm just going home." It was like a rehearsal for the real thing happening now, years later.

But the aftereffects of this performance would not end when the final curtain came down, and his ashes were laid to rest in the local cemetery.

My mind started doing tricks. After the shock came the denial. Perhaps the ashes were not Eddie's. Since he'd been in under-cover work, maybe he'd been kidnapped and was being held in East Germany and I'd see him again. For a long time I could not accept the reality of his death until I talked with a well-known seer one day, a retired colonel, who was in town. I knew he wouldn't think I was crazy when I poured out this imaginative scenario to him. He listened intently, paused, and then said, "No, dear, he's here in Spirit."

Only then did I accept the finality of never seeing him again in this life, but I couldn't get over the feeling I was inexorably bound to him. It was an invisible cord that went deeper than any words, an unending love.

A few years later a new experience emerged. I found myself sitting with a well-respected spiritualist minister and medium. I was there simply because a friend asked me to take her and had no expectations for myself. But then she asked me if I'd like to come in for a reading, and I said, "Sure, why not."

She relaxed, seemed to be in another state of mind and then, surprisingly, these first words from her, "Your soulmate has died. He had a heart attack."

Soulmate! That which we all seek and seldom find! I'd found it, then lost it, unable to fulfill the life that should have been mine. Tears rolled down my face as I recalled Eddie's last written words to me a few days before his death, "I've looked all over the world and never found anyone I love like I love you."

And I heard the words of the song again, coming back to me, "Going home, going home, I'm just going home."

It took 20 years for the war to deal its final blow.

SWEET SECRETS
by
Carol Hamilton

The tangy sweet taste of the strawberry soda foamed up the straw and over my tongue for a moment before it dissolved, leaving my tongue covered with the tiny seeds I could take one by one and flatten between the few back teeth which came together as they should. In those days I had a terrible overbite, and money for such things as orthodontists was for people several steps up the economic scale from us.

I saw my aunt, her black hair piled in a sloppy bun, leaning over the Woolworth grill frying hamburgers which sizzled and popped with the gusto of a chorus of stout-hearted men. It was her patriotic duty to work then, for the men were overseas, and her man was overseas. And since it was her patriotic duty to work there, I must surely be pretty patriotic to be her niece there watching her work and having my first strawberry soda.

My bare legs, which mortified me by being so heavily endowed with black hair, could feel the cool metal of the counter stool where I had coiled them around and crossed my brown oxford shoes behind the pole. Around me the cacophony of Saturday afternoon dime store sound swirled, and smells of chocolate, peppermint, and perfumed dusting powder joined to be the familiar odor of cheap variety and infinite interest.

Behind me children were being dragged by—whining, slapped, then screaming—miserably tired from the Saturday doings. But I was spooning out thick white ice cream and placing it on that bed of seeds I was saving on my tongue and sucking up more of the carbonated tang to wash it all away, thinking they did not know that she was my aunt, and they did not know how patriotic we both were being.

Author's note:
This was written about Carol's aunt whose husband served in North Africa.

PATTERNS

Each tokens a young man,
a white cross for a life,
a bronze plaque to replace
hopes and dreams.
Row on row
the refrain goes on:
    Pearl Harbor
    Gettysburg
    Arlington Gardens.
Tombstones, where the span
between birth and death
cries out of stone
uncommonly short,
denote families constricted
about the land.
Stark alliteration there
of signs we erect
to denote devotion,
patterns of silent pain.

by *Carol Hamilton*
Poet Laureate of Oklahoma

PREWAR CHINA
by
Betty Butler Wiseman

My earliest memories extend back to the age of about 12 months. My parents were Presbyterian missionaries assigned to northern China. In my mind's eye I am sitting in the middle of a handmade wool rug with an overall leaf design in shades of light mauve. The border of the rug is a deeper mauve with a blue Chinese border of Greek key design. On each of the four sides of the large rug are pots of lotus, a sacred flower. The rug is heavy, and the vegetable dyes used in the colors are still vibrant after more than 70 years. It is in my living room today.

At the time my early memories were formed, we were living near Peking (current Beijing). Because this period of the mid-1920s was turbulent, around 10 to 12 families, sponsored by Protestant and one Catholic denominations, lived behind the walls of a compound. Each of the Chinese warlords maintained a standing army to protect his territory. They would come raiding out of the hills at night. In the southwest was the army of Chiang Kai-shek, fighting his way to Nanking in the civil war.

Many were the nights in which I was bundled up quickly, valuables buried in the ground, furniture moved into the hallways, so that the house would look deserted, belongings packed on heavy carts that clacked over cobblestones as we hurried to the railroad station. Our escape routes were carefully planned, and we would stay away sometimes for several days until alerted that our return would be safe.

When we were able to remain at our residence, my parents attended language school from 8:00 a.m. until 4:00 p.m. My Chinese nanny was called an amah. Her method of caring for me was pragmatic: everyday we went on a long walk, usually two miles. Amah's feet were unbound, and she was therefore unmarriageable according to the customs of the times. From her I learned Mandarin Chinese. In 1929, after moving his family 12 times in five years,

37

my father decided to return to the United States. He secured a position as professor of English at East Texas State Teachers College in Commerce, Texas. What a change I felt! Here was a totally new world, and the adjustments were many.

I loved the college environment and excelled in school, competing with boys rather than bonding with girls.

As a senior in high school I formed a friendship with Jack Covington, nephew of my math teacher. Jack encouraged me to explore math and the sciences in college. Over time I decided to become a doctor. My parents forbade me to pursue this on the grounds that I would probably work very hard for 12 years, then fall in love, marry the man, and never practice. Nevertheless I majored in Chemistry and had math, biology, and English minors.

Jack fell in love with me, but World War II was starting and he joined the Air Force. After becoming an officer, he returned to propose to me. I had to turn him down since, to me, he was only a very good friend. Jack became the navigator on one of the B-29s based in Guam that bombed Tokyo in the early 1940s. His plane suffered a serious hit, and only Jack and the pilot elected to go down with it. Recently I learned that Jack's name is engraved on a monument in the Punchbowl Cemetery in Hawaii.

THE BATTLE FOR EUROPE, WORLD WAR II

by

Betty Butler Wiseman

My future husband, Earl Wiseman, spent his early years in Arkansas, moved to New York City at age 13, but then spent his senior year in high school in Oklahoma City. After two years at the University of Oklahoma, he took the tests for the ASTP (Army Specialized Training Program), passed, and found himself in a group of engineer trainees at E.T.S.T.C. in Commerce. We met at a party at my church in the fall of 1943 and started dating. Quite often I tutored him in calculus or a science. We became close in a hurry as wartime speeded everything up. When we learned Earl was going overseas, we said our goodbyes, too fearful of the ravages of war to become engaged.

Earl was assigned to the 99th Infantry Division, 393rd Regiment, Company M (mortars.) The division was rushed to Boston, then to the front lines in Belgium with such speed that it earned the nickname of the "Battles Babies." In the meantime, I had graduated from college, summa cum laude, and hired as a chemist in a research lab at Texas A. and M., where my best friend, Olive, was employed. Earl and I wrote to each other on "VE mail," a single page of writing, folded up four ways, and delivered air mail for a three-cent postage stamp. When the men would write, their letters were so censored that we could not guess where they were.

As winter approached, the casualties became heavier. When I met Earl's parents, I sensed at once that his mother was an extremely intuitive woman. For example, on the morning of the start of the Battle of the Bulge, December 16, 1944, she picked up the phone and called me at the same time I was ready to lift the receiver to call her. Rena Wiseman said, "Earl is in trouble."

I replied, "I know." For a week we worried, while nothing appeared in the newspapers. In hindsight, we did not learn of all the

Betty Butler Wiseman

terrible events until the end of January 1945.

What America knows about the Battle of the Bulge is the story of the south flank of the Bulge at Bastogne. The tremendous efforts of the men on the north flank was not told until many years later. Had the north flank not held, Hitler would have succeeded in his drive for Antwerp, and the war would have lasted much longer. As Olive worried about her pilot friend over Germany and I about Earl, I asked her "What can we do to help?" She said "Think of your background."

I replied, "Pray," and she nodded. We went to church regularly after that and found some solace.

Living in the small town of Bryan near Texas A. and M., we had to make up our own entertainment. Olive and I sometimes went to movies, concentrating on the newsreels. They reported on the winter of 1944-1945 as being the coldest in 20 years in Germany. Images of contorted bodies frozen in the snow were burned into my brain.

Reports of Earl's wounded buddies flown to English hospitals trickled in. I felt then that casualties were much greater than news-reels and radio reports indicated. Late in January I finally got VE mail from Earl with summaries of the battle. The 99th Infantry Division had been driven back west of Krinkelt, Belgium, and had dug in at Elsenborn Ridge for a month. My worst fears were real-ized when I learned Earl had been wounded and his feet frozen. However, he was the only man able to figure the angles for the mortar fire, so they carried him back to the front line. At least 50 percent of his unit was among the casualties.

In retrospect, it appeared that German intelligence was quite good. They had hit the line hard where the unseasoned troops were located. Finally, in early February, the Allied troops retook the ter-ritory withdrawn from. My spirits lifted somewhat as the letters reflected our troops on the move. After the Bulge the 99th fought battles at Remagen, Germany, in the Ruhr industrial district, and at Lohr, just across the Danube River. In Lohr VE day occurred on September 2, 1945. Though Olive's friend had been shot down over Germany, he had been nursed back to health by a surgeon from Dunkirk; therefore we both went to church and gave thanks.

Next Earl was assigned to the 95th Division and transported to England. In August of 1945 the atomic bombs were dropped over Japan and World War II ended. Time seemed to drag very slowly for me, working in College Station, Texas, waiting for Earl's last five points to accumulate to a total of 90 (needed to justify ship-ment back to the States).

Finally, in February of 1946, with Earl released from service, I was able to join him and his parents in Norman, Oklahoma. He proposed at once and gave me an engagement ring. Somehow our wedding date got moved up from June to April! Then it was back to Oklahoma University with Earl in law school, helped by the GI Bill, while I taught Chemistry labs to the most dedicated students I have ever met. Most of them were World War II veterans.

In 1991 we traveled to Europe with a battlefield tour group com-prised of 99th Division members, retracing Earl's steps through Swit-zerland, France, Germany, and Belgium. There was a celebration given for us by the German veterans at Remagen with brass bands, children's choruses, and a delicious lunch. Special German wine was served in beautiful glasses designed for the occasion. They erected a monument to the 99th Division, dedicating it to "This Time in Peace." The tour of the actual battlefield where the Bulge was fought was most important, the beauty of the Ardennes forest having been restored. Will Cavanagh, a 44-year-old Belgian expert on this battle, answered all our questions. Cavanagh had recently published a book on this subject, entitled *Dauntless*. The tour ended at Henri Chappelle cemetery, site of the burial of many or those slain in the Battle of the Bulge.

HENRI CHAPPELLE CEMETERY
Just as we arrived at the top of the mountain, the rain ended, and a beautiful rainbow appeared to illuminate the endless white cross spirals against the green grass. It was a moving experience that provided a fitting close for the tour.

GOD SAID IT'S NOT TIME YET
by
N.E. Chapman

The call came during the first week of January 1996. I heard a man's voice. "This is Mark, Doctor Dickie's assistant. He asked me to call you. Your son is in the Intensive Care Unit at Arlington Hospital here in Texas."

My heart jumped. "What's wrong? How bad is it?"

"He has a staff infection and he's critical. The doctor will explain details. Can we expect you?"

A wave of fear washed over me and my voice almost failed. "Yes. I'll be there as soon as possible."

Then with a trembling voice, I called my other son, 18 months younger, who lived in Eufaula, Oklahoma. After I told him about his brother, he said, "Mom, I'll leave right away to pick you up."

When we reached the Intensive Care Unit at Arlington, a nurse met us at the door. "Your son has developed pneumonia and could no longer breathe on his own," she said. "We had to put him on a life-support system."

After she led us to his room, I felt as if a cold hand had squeezed my heart when I saw him connected to all sorts of machines, tubes down his throat and his nose. Wires and beeping machines surrounded him. I felt dizzy and swayed a bit until my second son helped me to a chair.

"Is he in pain?" I asked.

The nurse nodded. "We're giving him morphine through a tube in his arm as often as we can."

"Oh, God!" my heart cried. Then the doctor appeared and motioned us to follow him to the hall outside the room.

"I'm Doctor Dickie, your son's principal physician. We have several specialists on his case. A staph infection spread throughout his blood system, and he's developed pneumonia. So far we haven't found the right antibiotic to combat his infection."

"What is his prognosis? Will he make it?" I asked, afraid to

43

Roy C. Borthick has his wings pinned on by his mother, Nora Chapman, at Laredo Air Force Base in 1955.

hear his answer.

The doctor's eyes reflected compassion. "We estimate a 20-percent chance of recovery and 80-percent he won't survive. All we can do is keep trying to find the right antibiotic and pray."

I returned to my son's bedside. His eyes were closed. I leaned over and kissed his forehead. He opened his eyes, and I knew the tube in his throat wouldn't allow him to speak. "Honey, your mother and brother are here with you." He nodded and closed his eyes.

I leaned my head against his bedrail, and with tears washing my face I began to pray. Then my thoughts coiled back like an unwinding tape. Each fearful occasion emerged and glowed in a blazing white light, and all time stopped for the moment while I recalled the other times when I thought I might lose my first child.

The first time was when he was born. The effects of The Great Depression made it difficult for my young husband to find work. There was no money for a hospital, so we had to find a doctor who would come to the house. After 24 hours of hard labor, the doctor said, "If I don't take the baby with instruments, we may lose it."

He turned me sideways on the bed and told my husband to hold my shoulders. Then he inserted the forceps. I could see the doctor's face. He braced his feet on the bedrail and pulled until his neck veins stood out like thick cords.

"Oh God! He's going to pull my baby's head off! God help us! Don't let my baby die," I cried. Then after one long hard contraction, he pulled the baby out. Although barely conscious, I knew something was wrong. But the doctor revived the baby, and finally I heard its weak cry.

After the baby was placed beside me, I gasped. The forceps had cut a deep gash beside his right eye and another one on the left side of his neck. I looked at the doctor. "The poor little thing. Will he be all right?"

"The wounds will heal," the doctor said. "But he'll have a scar beside his eye."

Then an angel whispered to me, "God said it's not time yet." I responded with a promise to teach my son to love God, himself, and others.

I thought about the next fearful episode. It came on his tenth birthday. Fumes from an empty gasoline can exploded in his face. When I saw huge blisters covering his face and neck, his eyebrows and hair burned off, my heart trembled. By the time the ambulance got us to the hospital, my son's nostrils and mouth had swollen so much, he was gasping for breath. The doctor inserted a tube in his mouth so he could breathe. I watched him suffer, knowing pain from burns is probably the worse kind. I prayed for my beautiful little boy.

Again, I heard the angel whisper, "God said it's not time yet." Although it took a long time for his burns to heal, my prayers were answered. He had no scars.

When my son graduated from high school at age 18, he had to register with the Selective Service System and became eligible for the draft. He'd always loved to plant and tend flowers, and his ambition was to become a horticulturist. So he enrolled at Oklahoma State University in Stillwater, Oklahoma. He became a member of the ROTC Program, and his draft status became a 2-5 deferment as a full-time college student.

After his first two years, he was required to undergo a complete physical exam to be eligible for the Advanced ROTC Program. He had a hernia, was turned down, and lost his deferment. Once more my heart trembled, but again the angel whispered, "God said it's not time yet."

I didn't want either of my sons to be foot soldiers and knew my younger son would not be drafted; he'd been seriously injured in a car wreck and was classified as 4-F.

After his hernia had been repaired, my son was accepted in the United States Air Force to train as a pilot. I forced myself to not worry too much until he finished training at Laredo, Texas, Air Force Base. I drove to the Air Force Base for the ceremony where he'd receive his wings. Each graduating airman made a solo flight for his family before the ceremony. While I watched my son take off in his plane, my heart fluttered, but once more the angel whispered, "God said it's not time yet."

I felt so proud of my son, standing tall, proud and handsome in his uniform. When I pinned his wings on his jacket, I whispered, "I love you. Always be careful."

Time passed. Newspaper and radio reports about the savage Vietnam War were frightening. I feared my son would be sent over there. One day I opened my door and saw him standing on the porch. Before I could utter a word, he took me in his arms. "Mom, I got a few days leave to come home. The Air Force is sending me to Vietnam."

My heart trembled again. I wanted to shout and scream, "No! You can't go. You might get killed or be taken as a prisoner." But I managed self-control. He told me his job would be to fly low over enemy territory and mark places for the bombers.

"Oh, Honey. That will be so dangerous. Promise you'll be careful and we'll both ask God to take care of you."

He nodded.

I was with him at the airport when he was ready to leave. Holding my tears, I gave him my love and again urged him to be careful. I stood at the window until his plane was out of sight, then I cried.

For the next 18 months I was afraid to read the newspapers, afraid to listen to the radio, afraid to answer the phone or open the door at a knock. I prayed with my every breath that my son would be safe.

One morning I felt especially worried. A close friend had just learned her son had been killed in Vietnam. I fell to my knees and prayed for her and for my son. All at once I felt a cool breeze on my face and heard the angel whisper, "God said it's not time yet."

That afternoon I received a long-distance call. "Mom, I'm on my way home."

"Thank God. I've waited so long to hear from you." After I cradled the phone, once more I fell to my knees and gave thanks to God.

When my son came home, he didn't talk much about the war, only that he held a fellow pilot in his arms while the man died and that he had once crashed a plane. But I knew from other stories I'd read what a terrible experience he'd been through. After 20 years in the Air Force, my son retired as a lieutenant colonel and began his life as a civilian.

My thoughts returned to the present. Through tear-dimmed eyes, I looked at my son, once so strong, now so helpless and so sick. My mind wandered back to three years earlier.

He called me one day. "Mom, I have to tell you something," he said with a catch in his voice. "I had a lump in my groin; it was surgically removed, and it was cancer."

For a moment, I was speechless. The word *cancer* chilled my very soul. "NO! NOT CANCER!" my mind shouted, but I knew I had to comfort him the best I could. "What did your doctor say? What will happen now?"

"I'll have to take a series of chemotherapy treatments. Mom, don't worry. I have faith that everything will be okay."

During the following three years, I often talked to my son by phone. I knew how awful the chemotherapy treatments were and how sick they made him, and that he lost all his hair. Although I was fearful, I asked God to give me the strength to comfort my son. And I urged my son to be optimistic and to have faith. "We'll ask God to reach down and touch you with His healing hand."

My son remained hopeful and had confidence in his doctors.

Once more, my thoughts returned to the present. I raised my head from his bedrail and looked at my son. His eyes were open. I leaned over him and whispered, "Honey, your brother and I are praying for you, and so are your doctors. Keep holding on." Although he couldn't speak, he nodded. For the next three days, my son hovered between life and death. I called several friends in Oklahoma City, whom I knew believed in the power of prayer, and asked them to pray for my son.

On the fourth day the doctor said he'd found the right antibiotic, and it was working. Then I heard the angel whisper, "God said it's not time yet."

Two days later, he was removed from the life-support system. His first words were, "Mom, Bro, I'm so glad you're both here."

Choking back tears, I held his hands. "Honey, an angel told me you'll be all right now."

My son made a miraculous recovery from such a critical illness. His cancer has been in remission for several months. He, his brother, and I have every hope it will stay there.

Recently, he visited me. "Mom, you told me I almost didn't make it when I was born, again when I got burned," he said. "God protected me while I was in Vietnam, and I've lived three years with lymphoma cancer. That staff infection almost killed me, but I recovered. Now I know God has something special for me to do in this life. I believe I know what that is."

"What is it? Can you share that with me?

"Yes, I will. I believe God wants me to spend more time with you and my brother. And he wants me to live my life in such a way that others can see the love of God I feel in my heart shining in my eyes. Mom, I'll do my best to follow His command."

After my son left, I thought of a promise in the Bible: "Bring up a child in the way he should go, and when he is old he will not depart from it." I have tried my best to follow that promise with both my sons and believe with all my heart, the angel was sent from God each time I heard the whisper, "God said it's not time yet."

THE MILITARY YEARS OF ROSIE E. (MARSHALL) LAIRD

by

DWANE E. CLINE

Rosie was born in 1916 on a farm, the first of eight girls. She was seasoned feeding hogs and chickens in never-ending Oklahoma winds. Summer's heat tempered her metal while working horses and mules in the field. Then she was tested for brittleness by milking cows in winter's blustery cold.

The mid-1930s were tough years. Few jobs were open to men, much less a young woman who had just graduated from high school. Rosie took whatever came available. This meant doing whatever, whenever, wherever. In 1937 she was working in Oklahoma City when Bill Laird came home from the Army. They were married in El Reno on April 29, 1937.

Bill had been in the Army since 1929, but military experience wasn't very valuable when it came to finding a job. He worked at Blackwell in the smelter while Rosie maintained a home in Oakwood. Later they moved to a school lease where she brought twin boys into the world. A twin delivery wasn't that unusual, but both babies alive was.

When the cry of "WAR" blared across the country, Bill and a couple of friends joined the Army Reserves. In February 1941 Sergeant Laird rejoined his old company at Fort Sam Houston in San Antonio, Texas. Late in the spring Rosie followed with the twins in tow. They had a short stay in the busy city before moving on to the country.

Large tracts of farm and ranch land around Fort Bullis had been purchased by the Army for maneuvers training. Civilians were sneaking onto the ranges and causing problems, so military range riders were dispatched throughout the area to keep them out. When one of the jobs came available, Rosie insisted Bill take it.

Rosie's persistence and the added $30 a month led the Laird family to a desolate farmhouse several miles out in the country.

Rosie and Bill Laird with their twin boys, ages two and a half.

Nobody except Rosie thought it would be a workable situation. No electricity, no running water, cooking was done on a wood-burning stove, this was not the Ritz.

However, it was a quiet paradise with no busy streets. The twins could watch deer and wild turkey water at the stock tank where a windmill pumped water for the household and the overflow provided for the wildlife. Fresh country air kept the twins healthy. Freedom to enjoy it kept them busy while Bill rode horseback patrolling his area.

Town was a long way off, but with training companies coming and going, there was little need for town. When a group would leave the bivouac area, they would tell Sergeant Laird to be at some location at a certain time. Extra supplies from the training groups were left to supply the Range Rider and his family.

The good duty ended in March when Bill was replaced. Bill was physically combat capable, but his replacement was not because he had no teeth. When given the reason for Bill's replacement, Rosie said to the ranking sergeant, "Why didn't you tell me that two weeks ago. Between you and me, we could have knocked Bill's teeth out."

Rosie and the twins moved in with a family in San Antonio. It was back to the busy streets and people everywhere. Orders followed sending Bill to Camp Shelby at Hattiesburg, Mississippi, where his outfit was to train recruits for combat duty. A few weeks after Bill left, one of the non-coms that had been out to the farmhouse to visit stopped and told Rosie he was going to Pensacola, Florida. Then he asked, "Where is your husband now?"

"He's at Hattiesburg, Mississippi," Rosie answered.

"Is there anybody there you can stay with? My wife and little girl and a lady that has never been out of San Antonio are all that are going to Florida so there will be plenty of room for you, the boys and your things." Rosie's things amounted to two small suitcases when packed.

Rosie had an uncle in Mobile, Alabama. What she didn't have was money. Not even a penny. She called Bill in Hattiesburg by phone. He wired back to go to the golf course and see Doctor Pockavich about borrowing money for the trip. The landlady drove Rosie to the golf course, where she found the doctor sitting at a desk. When he asked if he could help her she answered. "I have kind of a problem. I'm William H. Laird's wife of Company H, and I need some money?"

"What are you going to do," he asked?

"My husband has been sent to Camp Shelby, Mississippi. I have a ride from San Antonio to Mobile, Alabama." A little quaver slipped into her voice, "But I can not go with no money!"

"Well, how much do you need?"

"Ten dollars will be plenty."

Dr. Pockavich, eyed her closely, "Ma'am, you can't get anywhere on ten dollars."

"With the price of food, it will more than feed us, and it's not going to cost me anything else."

Pockavich handed Rosie the money, and she said, "When we get some money, we will send you yours." And that is how it was repaid.

Neither the sergeant's wife nor the lady from San Antonio drove, and Rosie had never driven an "up town car" like the sergeant's. He told her she could drive it, but it took some convincing. Finally he got her behind the wheel, and he got in the back seat with the three kids. His instructions were, "Stop and wake me before going into Beaumont, Texas.

Rosie found the car drove fine, and when a sign came up saying Beaumont, Rosie asked the other two ladies, "Shall I stop and wake him?"

"You're doing fine," they agreed. "No need to stop."

Traffic wasn't bad, and all was going great until at a stop sign the car locked in gear. There was no getting out of it; the sergeant had to be roused. Rosie was sure he would be upset, but his wife said, "Don't worry; he won't blame you." She was right; he wasn't peeved at all. There was a service station nearby, and they were soon back on the road. They crossed the Mississippi River late in the night, and after driving around Mobile for sometime Rosie located her Uncle Hal.

The next three weeks Rosie and the twins stayed with her uncle. When Bill found a place, he called and said to catch a bus. It wasn't quite that simple. Servicemen had top priority to ride, then servicemen's wives. The first morning at 5:00 a.m. Rosie and the twins watched the bus fill and leave with servicemen and some of their women. The second morning was the same thing with a "Sorry, ma'am, it's full," from the driver.

On the way back to Hal's, Rosie declared she and the boys would be on the bus the next morning. "I've been observing, and a lot of those women are not servicemen's wives. I WILL get on that bus in the morning. All I've got to do is make that driver realize that I know all those women are not soldiers wives."

When Rosie and the boys reached the bus door the third morning, the driver said, "Ma'am, you'll have to step aside. There are only a few seats left, and there are that many servicemen behind you."

Anger lit her eyes and determination steeled her voice as she turned to the driver. "SIR! I have observed for two mornings. And, I know what's going on."

"Well, servicemen first," the driver shot back.

"But, those women that got on this bus were not those men's wives. You need to ask for some identification."

"Get on the bus," the driver growled.

With a boy on each side and hiding a smile of triumph, she did. It was a short-lived victory. A few miles out of Mobile, the driver stopped at a crossroads. "Gather your boys up; you'll have to get off and catch another bus!"

Everyone on the bus knew there was not a good reason for Rosie and the boys to be put off. Rosie turned to the rider in the nearest seat, "I'm not getting off, and I don't think he can make me get off." Then she added, "I'll get off, but these boys are staying in this seat."

The driver squared off by the luggage rack, legs spread and a dark scowl wrinkling his brow. "Ma'am I told you to get off and bring those boys."

Rosie faced him, head up, back stiff, and hands on her hips. "I'm not taking those boys off, and you're not puttin' my luggage off. You're taking me on to Hattiesburg. I can't help it because my husband is in the service, and I have to follow him. Besides, you've got our ticket money!"

Every eye and ear was locked on Rosie and the driver, and he knew it. Red ran up the drivers' neck, and his ears flushed scarlet as he muttered, "Get on the bus!"

Bill had an apartment waiting when they reached Hattiesburg. It sat across the street from a cemetery so it wasn't a very busy street, which allowed the twins to run pretty much at large. One day they didn't come back when Rosie thought they should have so she went to find them. It didn't take long. The twins were across the street hanging on the fence watching a funeral in progress.

Six months later, Bill received orders for La Count, Louisiana. Bill's first sergeant lived off-post on an old plantation owned by the Neelys, a 67-year-old bachelor and his 73-year-old sister. Between the first sergeant and Rosie, they convinced the Neelys the twin boys would not be any problem. The Neelys had never rented to anyone with kids, and they were not sure.

The three-story house sat half a mile out from town. It had a cypress porch that went all around the house overlooking the plantation. The Lairds only rented them one upstairs room, but it provided all their needs. There was a bed and cooking facilities. A coal oil stove furnished heat, and coal oil lamps furnished light. An old ice box on the back porch was shared by First Sergeant Mullins and the Lairds.

Ice was rationed, and demand already exceeded supply. Mr. Neely had considerable pull in the town and talked the ice houses into letting the Lairds have some ice every other day. This posed another problem because the Lairds no longer had a running car. Again, Mr. Neely's kind nature came through by letting Rosie use the car to get ice and groceries. There was one restriction: "You non-coms, do not go over to the officers' quarters."

But it happened anyway. Sergeant Mullin's wife and Rosie went shopping, then started over to a captain's wife's house to visit and on the way blew out a tire. Mrs. Mullins asked, "What are you going to do?"

There was no hesitation. Rosie said, "Well, I'll have to change it. Maybe not really. Because the first farmer that comes along will recognize the car and stop to help." With that, said she went to work, and everything was going fine until she started jacking up the car. The jack broke and flew to pieces! Nothing then but wait for help.

A farmer did come by shortly and did change the tire, then Rosie took the tire to the service station to be repaired. The trip to the captain's wife's house was canceled, but they were still late getting home. Mr. Neely was pacing the yard worried because of their lateness. Mrs. Mullins saw him and asked, "Oh my, Rosie, what are you going to do? He's mad!"

"Just tell him the truth, tell what happened. I'm not going to tell him where we were headed for, though." Mr. Neely was relieved, the broken jack was in the car, the blown tire being repaired, and the two ladies were safe.

Between trips to the grocery store and ice house, laundry had to be done. A scrub board and Sad Iron served the purpose to clean and press the clothes, but nothing to replenish those outgrown by the twins. Rosie's Mother sent feed sacks when she could, and sometimes remnants could be bought for 10 cents each.

Between duty stations, the Lairds usually returned to Oakwood where they kept a house. On December 17, 1943, Rosie gave birth to a baby girl there. Bill had used up all his leave and had to ship out the following morning. There were several duty stations that followed, and each had its own story. Bill could have gotten out of the Army in July of 1945, but chose to stay. Rosie and family were with him at every station on American soil.

In 1950 the Lairds left the converted hospital living quarters at Camp Stoneman, California. Rosie and the three kids returned to Oakwood. Bill shipped out for Eniwetok in the Marshall Islands to help in testing atomic and hydrogen bombs.

In December 1951 Bill was stationed at Fort Bliss, Texas. The quarters were the best of all their years, but there Bill ended his military career. On October 24, 1953, cancer caused by exposure to radiation took Bill Laird's life.

On October 25, 1953, Rosie cleared quarters for the final time. Life's trials certainly were not over, and many stories have come from Rosie since then, but none bring the sparkle to her eyes like those times spent following her husband from one Army post to another.

A WOMAN OF WORLD WAR II

Aunt Etta laid iron to cloth
   pressed love with each hand slide—
      as if a perfect uniform
         would protect her youngest son.

We were there to visit
   before he crossed half a continent.
      Apprehension turned silence into sound.
      We shared unspoken dread.

We were there when Cast Guard Envoys
   brought news of his death.
      Aunt Etta pressed lips together
      to ensure silence
As if acknowledgement would verify her forewarned fear.

Aunt Etta never wore
   our country's uniform.
      Her generation lived out Milton's lines
      They also serve who only stand and wait.
      Her participation was by bond.

We were there when
   Aunt Etta joined husband and son
   in adjoining graves

      and BEYOND.

by *Flo Mason*

Placed First in "Women's War Memoirs" Category at the
POETRY SOCIETY of OKLAHOMA Awards March 8, 1997

A MOTHER'S STORY
OF THE FIVE BLUE STARS
by
Al Waintroob

In the middle of the depression years, Anna Bermant, widowed, struggled to keep her family together. In those days families with lots of kids were often the norm. Anna had one daughter, the oldest, and four sons, and she was quietly proud of her kids.

When the war news from Europe foreshadowed the future, Anna was inwardly apprehensive, and sometimes almost terrified. There were relatives in Europe, and the memory of World War I was ever present. In the first war she had lost a brother and an uncle.

Today there were four sons to worry about.

April 1941 came, and number three son received his Greetings from the president. He was to serve for one year only, and his friends, fellow workers, and family members threw him a fancy going away party. Parties like this were almost a normal event. Anna hid her tears.

Pearl Harbor exploded on the world, and with it the world changed forever for everyone alive. It was only a short time later that son number one was drafted. This time there was no party.

Like countless other families, a blue star on a white satin background was hung in the front window for each person serving his country. Son number two was married and a father. His deferment lasted longer, but soon another blue star joined the first two. The only thing keeping number four son at home was his age. He was still in high school.

Anna, who had never worked outside the home, was among those who served. She wasn't a nurse. She didn't fly airplanes, and she was no Rosie the Riveter. She went to work in a small grocery store near her home. The Grocer's two sons had gone to war.

A telephone call came one day. Her daughter's husband, a pharmacist, had been called up. She moved back to her mother's place, and another blue star was added. Her daughter worked for a steel processing plant.

And to those whose loved ones had gone to war and were serving in every Godforsaken place in this world, they cried unseen tears, straightened their backs, and did their duty.

The war continued, and son number four graduated from high school on February 1, 1944. In March he was in infantry training, and in August he was in France as a replacement. Another shining blue star on a white satin background.

The tempo of the war increased, and the headlines and radio screamed the hated news. Anna and her daughter often refused to read or listen.

Despite the victories that came, the inevitable costs were there. The horrible waiting was always there, and one day the dreaded news came by telegram: "The President regrets to inform you............."

The third blue star had to be changed to gold. Anna cried for her only grandson, who would never know his father.

More time passed, and soldiers that were young kids a short time earlier became heroic victors, and with it the slow return to normalcy from a world that had tolerated madness for altogether too long. Anna welcomed the return of her family, but she, too, had changed. The war had taken much from her health. She had become a casualty of the war as much as any one who served in uniform.

For those that lived through those times, we know there were many like Anna. And they deservedly have all our heartfelt thanks.

THE WIVES WHO WAIT

by

Billie Riggs

My husband-to-be returned from Europe in the spring of 1946 and was discharged from the Army. We were married in August 1946 at Olivet Baptist church in Oklahoma City by a missionary to China. My husband was in the reserves and worked for Frisco Railroad but returned to Oklahoma University to work on his degree. I worked as a secretary for the Oklahoma Education Association.

In the spring of 1948 I began my big adventure in life as a military wife. My husband returned to the Army, was reduced one grade to return to military service, and had orders to Germany. The Department of the Army told us I could join him in approximately one year. Our many moves had begun.

We stored our furniture at his mother's house and my clothes and personals at my parents'. We took off from work to go with him to Fort Dix, New Jersey, until he sailed. But we were asked if I'd like to go with him as a member of the first group of wives to accompany their husbands. Naturally we jumped for joy. But I had no papers with me to apply for a passport. Since I was born at home, I contacted my grandmother for an affidavit as proof of birth. She didn't know what that was, so she wrote a letter—not acceptable. What I had always used as a birth certificate was a paper stating that a living female child was born that date to my parents.

We sailed with two changes of clothing for me and no passport. Upon our arrival at Bremerhaven, we watched them off-load our car and took off in a 12-car convoy for Bad Mergentheim, where I was in an a barracks for women, and my husband reported for assignment to the 18th 1st Infantry Division in Manheim. We were assigned an apartment in Howscht. The other 12 wives had a house in a guarded compound. We had no children, so I had an apartment above a department store with one other military couple (Air Force)

59

and four American civilians working for the U.S. government and Armed Forces Network. I didn't know how to drive, had no clothes, and spoke no German.

The apartment was furnished, but we had no linens, curtains, pots, pans, dishes, silverware, or light bulbs. After two days to settle me in, my husband went on maneuvers for six months at Graffenwohr. I threw myself on the mercy of the Quartermaster (supply) and got one light bulb which I moved from room to room. I found a coffee can, rusty fork, and pie pan in the garden, cleaned them, cooked in the coffee can, and ate out of the pie pan with the fork.

The commissary was just beginning, but had few groceries since nearly everything had to be shipped from the USA and distributed. Food and personal hygiene items were very sparse. I was allowed one gallon of reconstituted milk per month, one orange plus bread, and very limited staples. My parents shipped canned goods to me.

After eight months our household goods arrived!! With the exception of linens and clothing, everything was damaged—a total loss of all our wedding china, crystal, and furniture. In 1949 we moved into government quarters in Aschaffenberg. It was great. We were a family again. We took several trips to Paris, Austria, Berlin, Holland, and Switzerland. In Holland the restaurant would try to guess at your nationality and put the appropriate flag on your table. However, they thought I was German since no American wives were in Germany, and I was refused service until I produced my passport. The French Riviera was wonderful—figs the color and size of egg plant and fresh olives. We often drove to Strasburg, France, to eat and shop.

Our son was born in December 1950 at the 97th General Hospital in Frankfurt, Germany. As per our country agreement with Germany, he had a dual citizenship until the age of 21. He was a German citizen at birth, and we had 10 days to apply for his American citizenship. This is called *Jus soli* (Latin for "right of the land") and *Jus Sanguinis* (Latin for "right of the blood").

The Berlin Airlift had begun, and all wives with infants were sent home. Our son and I landed in New York City and spent the night in a large hotel. The chef and I were trying to make formula at midnight in huge kettles, substituting sugar for Karo and condensed milk for regular milk. We spent several months with my parents in Oklahoma City then flew back to Germany. Almost a year later we came home to go to Pueblo, Colorado, where my husband was Professor of Military Science for two high schools. It was fun to be back in a civilian community and particularly to find our neighbor's brother had been with us in Germany. I repeat. We learned it's a small world. Our daughter was born at Fort Carson, Colorado, in 1952—again a lengthy drive to the hospital.

From Colorado we went to Fort Banning, Georgia, which proved to be our "Home Away From Home." I believe we lived in every type quarters that Fort Banning has. Again we were with many friends from Germany. After the Advanced Course and Jump School, we went to Fort Bragg, North Carolina.

The children and I went to the beach at Carmel almost daily to watch the sea lions and to build sand castles. This was my first experience with ice plant and sand fleas. With two fair-skinned children, the sand fleas had a feast. Ice plant covered our area and leaves brown stains (not removable) from clothes and skin. Again I worked with the Red Cross volunteer program and the Officers Wives' Club. A fashion show seems to be a favorite activity to raise money for many charities. I was to model a red evening gown, and they wanted to tint my hair red to blend with the dress—however, a mistake was made and henna was used. My hair became redder by the day until I was a red fire truck. Another learning experience.

After a year or so, my husband left for Korea, and the kids and I returned to Oklahoma City and rented a house. But our furniture, which left California the day we did, simply disappeared. Three months went by with us in our empty house. The moving van was finally found. The driver had decided to quit—and took the truck onto a dirt road in Arizona and abandoned it. The truck was finally found, and our furniture arrived. It seems whenever your husband leaves the country, every appliance breaks down, the children catch all communicable diseases, the furniture disappears, and I break or sprain an ankle. I firmly believe each of our 26 moves was the equivalent of a train wreck.

We remained in Oklahoma City about two years, then were off to Fort Bragg, North Carolina. There I worked as a Red Cross volunteer, home room mother, and Den Scout Mom. Naturally when my Cub Scouts wanted to jump from the parachute "jump tower," I had to lead the way. I have always had a fear of heights, but with the "help" of a sergeant and a push from the rear from him, we all sailed out without incident. A static line is attached to a cable, and you slide 50 feet or so down it. I'm still afraid of heights.

Next came Fort Leavenworth, Kansas, for Command and General Staff College—and back to small quarters. We were so close together, my neighbor and I could have coffee together through our bedroom windows when we made our beds. Again I worked with the Red Cross and had many interesting experiences, and renewed old friendships as well as made many new ones.

Off we went to Tokyo, Japan, where my husband was Airborne Advisor to the Japanese Self Defense Forces and attached to the U.S. Embassy. All branches of the services were in the group, and all wore civilian clothes. Again I worked as a Red Cross volunteer at Grant Heights and was on the Teen Club board. I helped with volunteer staffing of American school nurses and our Wives' Club. We had wonderful bazaars to raise money for Japanese orphanages. This gave us contact with many fantastic business people. I worked with the field director of the Red Cross and attended meetings all across that area. Our son went to St Mary's school with children from the 30 embassies and countries. This afforded all of us an opportunity to learn all cultures and customs.

We both went to Japanese language school beginning two days after our arrival in Japan. We went to class eight hours a day and studied many hours at night. It was one of the most difficult courses we ever undertook. However, we were taught "court" Japanese, and this was almost useless with the average person and our household help. But it certainly was a necessity for the functions at the American Embassy. While driving on the Embassy grounds, you drove on the right side of the road again. That was a treat.

While in our area of Tokyo, we had about 40 or 50 families and only 12 or so of us drove. Our husbands were not allowed to drive. They were taken to work by bus or staff cars. There were no street numbers and few street names in Tokyo and surrounding areas. You had to go to advertising signs or buildings to know where to turn and approximately where you were. I assisted the Red Cross Field Director in delivering emergency messages to the military personnel. This was my first encounter with typhoons, and if a sign had blown down I would still probably be driving in circles in Tokyo.

While in Japan we took a 30-day trip—space available to go where ever the Air Force plane was going. We got visas for nearly every country since we did not know just where we would be going. The visas were no problem, but the government felt we should appoint or give temporary guardianship to someone there to take our children and see that they would be sent or taken back to Oklahoma to their grandparents in the event our plane should crash and we would both be aboard. That certainly does give you pause for thought. We went to Okinawa, Philippines, Thailand, Hong Kong, and New Deli, India. All are interesting countries, each in its own way. India was beautiful in some parts. The poverty in some areas was unbelievable, and in others the riches were. The Taj Mahal was beautiful. To think only manual labor and few tools were available to build a structure of that magnitude is incomprehensible.

We also flew into Vietnam so I was able to see the country where my husband would later be stationed. So many of these countries have such beautiful women and children. It was a delight to see them in native dress. Our Embassies around the world are magnificent, and we should have great pride in them and the many countries we have helped.

As we prepared to leave Japan, all packed and luggage stacked in our quarters, we were robbed. Our passports were taken and all our money. We offered a reward and said that upon the return or our passports no charges would be made. The next morning all was returned and left on our front porch. Upon our arrival at the terminal to leave, the Japanese Airborne group presented us with a stone lantern. Luckily the Air Force let us bring it aboard.

We returned to Fort Benning where my husband was an instructor at the Infantry School. The move went smoothly and furniture arrived in great shape. The Vietnam War began, and the mass exodus of troops and planes began from Benning. My husband went to Vietnam on temporary duty for a few weeks so we did not have to move off-post. However, a few months later he left again, this time on a permanent assignment, and we moved again. Before he left, I was privileged to escort Mrs. Eleanor Roosevelt to a luncheon where she was guest speaker. This was truly a lovely lady in every sense of the word. Her memory for names was phenomenal. There were approximately 400 women in the receiving line, and she could recall almost all of them upon her departure. What a gift.

With so many husbands gone and so many families living all around the surrounding area, we formed a group called "The Wives Who Wait." I was co-chairperson and later chairperson of this large group. We met for luncheons, to play cards, to support each other, and spend time together as best we could. I rented a house from a couple who helped find the extras for the movie John Wayne was making called "The Green Berets." Because of this, I had occasion to meet John Wayne and nearly all the others in the movie. They were a very interesting and amusing bunch of people.

The casualties were very large in Vietnam, and I began to get calls from wives who found telegrams from the War Department stuck in their mailboxes or on their doors during the night. Most had no families nearby, some had no families, and many were from other countries. I was so upset that I called the White House and asked to speak to the president. I spoke first with his aide and then to Mr. Johnson and told him that I felt he was unaware that this was happening and could something be done about it. He asked for my phone number and stated he would call me back in 15 minutes. This he did. He told me that he had checked and that this was happening as I had stated and that he had put out a directive countrywide that all death or missing-in-action notices were to be delivered by a chaplain and would I accompany them if possible. I did this and attended most of the funerals of those persons returned to Fort Benning for burial. Many were close friends of ours and it was a mentally stressful time.

It was amazing that the president could be reached so easily. Later he came to Fort Benning and asked that I come on base to review the troops. He asked if there was anything he could do to help us, and I asked if Air Force 1 could be opened so that our kids could tour it. This he did. He was a kind and soft-hearted person, at least to me, and greatly disturbed by all the Vietnam casualties. He looked very tired and old beyond his years.

We left Fort Benning for my husband to go to the University of Nebraska at Omaha to complete his degree. We rented a house, and our kids left to return to Oklahoma University to school. After three months I came to Oklahoma City, to be close to the children, and he remained in Omaha until completion of his schooling. We bought our home in the city, and the cat and I moved in—again to await our furniture which was in storage. The cat and I lived with a mattress on the floor, the television, some pots and pans, and a couple lounge chairs. But the household goods did arrive, and the long, slow process of unpacking and putting up was done—lots of sore muscles and frustration over trying to hang curtains and drapes myself.

My husband had orders to Thailand, so I remained in Oklahoma City and went to work at Mercy Hospital in the Cancer Registry. It was interesting and rewarding to learn from a fantastic pathologist. Later I changed to secretarial work in Nursing Administration. I was recommended to Mercy Hospital by the Red Cross.

Two years later my husband returned, and we moved to Scranton, Pennsylvania, where he was National Guard Advisor. A few months after our arrival, the big flood hit Wilkes-Barre and Scranton, Pennsylvania. I volunteered to help with those persons flooded out of their homes. They were housed in the Armory on cots. It was necessary to secure safe drinking water, and Seagram Distillery bottled water for us; Northern Toilet Tissue shipped loads of tissue. Many inoculations had to be given since most had been exposed to all types of infectious materials. Language was a problem since that section of Pennsylvania was a composite group of nationalities, so I devised a method of colors to put on their arms for each type of shot given. Some had taken the shots several times because of the language barrier. I called the governor for assistance to locate displaced families and got it.

We returned to Oklahoma City, and my husband retired. Our moving days are over!!! In looking back over all our years in the military. I must admit I enjoyed every one of them—good experiences and bad. It was a privilege to meet so many world leaders and wonderful people in the military and in various foreign countries. The experience for our children was priceless. It gave them understanding and tolerance. Also a sense of independence and self-worth, as it did each of us. There is so much I have skipped over or left out, but writing my story has been an opportunity for me to remember so many incidents in our full and wondrous lives. I would do it again in a minute.

THE VIETNAM YEARS
by
Pollie G. Blanton

"Is Daddy a baby killer, Mom? Mom? Mom?" Cindi yelled as she came home from second grade. "The kids at school say he's a baby killer, just like that lady on the phone! Well is he? Is he?" she persisted!

What happened to the years when military men who fought for their country were admired, even respected? How had things gotten so bad in America that children were told their soldier fathers were killing babies! I held the memory close to my heart of the Vietnamese officer who said that his wife and baby were in hiding away from Saigon, and without American help they would all be killed. There was a certain urgency, coupled with sadness in his voice.

The captain was at Fort Bragg, North Carolina, for specialized training and would soon return to his wartorn country. Duane was on orders to go as well. Both were at the Special Forces training center, Duane for training in many things, including psychological operations.

Aside from the fear of his going was the added concern of caring for our four small children alone. A trip to Washington, D.C., had alerted us to problems that we had not faced before. When we stopped for lunch at a restaurant in Virginia with the three girls (adopted from our previous assignments: seven-year-old Cindi, Chinese from Taiwan, four-year-old Becky, Aztec Indian and Spanish, and 3 year old Kari, Korean), we were refused entrance. The waitress fumed, "We don't serve Orientals here!"

My mouth dropped opened! The children looked horrified and began asking almost in unison, "What did we do, Mamma, what did we do?" It was a question I was to hear often in the years to come. I was livid with anger and saddened that the children were exposed to such idiocy.

Duane arrived at the door—he'd been parking the car—and

Pollie Blanton, holding baby Derrick; Jeffrey, Duane, and Kari; back row: Cindi and Becky. On the floor is the family dog, Foo-Foo.

asked what was going on. The waitress was only too happy to expound upon her statement. While he handled the waitress, I tried to explain to the children that they hadn't done anything; this woman had a problem. The waitress was obviously startled to see that Duane was white. His no-nonsense attitude and military bearing made the waitress step aside. We went in for lunch, but it was most unpleasant and an experience we vowed would never be repeated. From then on, one of us went inside before we got the children out of the car to be sure we would be welcome.

We purchased a small legal encyclopedia that became a constant companion. Old laws reflected the attitudes of people and gave us a better perspective as to how things should be handled. The 60s were hectic times. It seemed to be a world gone mad! President Kennedy ended segregation, he legislated the end in law, but that did not legislate changes in hearts and minds. There were to be hard times yet to come. Kennedy was assassinated. Lyndon Johnson became President. The war in Vietnam escalated. There were constant riots and demonstrations everywhere.

Television covered every demonstration with glee, showing only slovenly, unshaven young men returning from the war with the young "hippies" of the time denouncing the war, the system, and shouting insulting epitaphs. It was selective broadcasting at its worst.

We were not prepared for the problems that resulted after we adopted 25-month-old Jeff, our Cherokee Indian son. He had been badly mistreated in his short lifetime. The first 20 minutes he was in the house he gave Becky a split lip and Kari a bloody nose. Cindi escaped his blows only because she was taller. Jeff didn't laugh, cry, or talk, but he could fight! The girls suggested that we give him back to the Indians! There was a lot of work to be done with this child! A woman had mistreated him, so he ignored me and clung to his new dad. He needed his dad at home.

Aside from Jeff's problems, there were many unpleasant phone calls, some downright nasty, including the call from the minister of the small Baptist Church we attended. It seemed that members of the church had become "insulted" by the colors of our children. We were asked to take our family elsewhere!

"Don't you people sing, 'Jesus Loves the Little Children'—you know, that part, 'red and yellow, black and white?'" I asked astonished.

"Yes, yes" he interrupted, "and we believe that, but there are so many complaints, that until we have more Indians and Negroes in the church, you'll just have to go somewhere else!"

"Just how," I asked trying to hide my fury, "are you going to have Negro and Indian members if you don't let them in the building?" The pitch of my voice raised against my will. It was not the first discussion of this type; other phone calls had prepared me for some of this, but it was unexpected from a minister!

It was useless to argue, like the woman who tried to explain to me that the Ku Klux Klan was just a social organization and nothing more. It was best to hang up the phone.

We lived on an integrated military reservation and had no problems at all with our family there. Our neighbors were both black, white, and Oriental. Life seemed good; we expected the same from the civilian community. This was not to be. When we found a small Methodist church that welcomed us with open arms, we became Methodists.

With Duane going to Vietnam, it meant that we would have to move off the military base and the children would go to school in

Fayetteville. Another surprise came when we visited some preschools. Jeff and Kari (three and four years old at the time) were about the same size and were often mistaken for twins. However, I was informed that Indian children could not go to school with whites; they had to go to school with "their kind!" The woman had to ask which child was Indian and which was Korean, but she was certain that one of them was "uneducable!" We were told that Becky could attend a white school as she could "pass," but she must never tell anyone she was Indian.

"We wouldn't do that," I informed the woman in very measured tones. "We are proud of her heritage." We then were told that if anything happened to Duane while he was in Vietnam, that part of his estate which would go to the two Indian children would revert to the state of North Carolina! We couldn't believe it!

Duane had been considering South Texas as a retirement possibility, and we headed to McAllen, Texas. Texas had no laws opposed to the nationalities of our children. However, we drove through Mississippi and Louisiana without stopping. We were barely settled into the house at McAllen when Duane flew to Vietnam. The children and I were alone in a strange city at what seemed to be the very end of the world, an eternity away from either of our families.

Our children always attracted attention, so it wasn't long until a reporter wanted to do an article on the family. The kids thought it would be fun so I agreed. That article was how the community at large knew our name and the fact that Duane was in Vietnam. Psychological Warfare and 5th Special Forces had an ominous ring for many people. The community support that had been given in past wars to wives of soldiers was not available for wives of men in Vietnam. We were treated as the "enemy" ourselves. I hated to answer the phone. Aside from the possibility that it would be bad news about Duane, there was the added irritant of "citizens" who felt their need to vent their hostilities. It wasn't safe to let the children near the phone—no telling who was on the other end spewing filth into their ears.

We became members of the St. Mark United Methodist Church where we made many friends and were happily received. Some members became sources of great strength for me. Always there were differing opinions on the makeup of our family. It amazed me that people could feel so righteous about their questions, yet so angry when they didn't get the answer they wanted. I learned that to make it through this life without loosing my own equilibrium, I would have to come up with some "quick answers," answers that I could fire back at people without pausing to think—not letting their questions reach my inner core of anger.

To those little old ladies who would smile at the children and say sweetly, "Are they illegitimate?" I would reply, "Heavens no, Duane and I have been married for years!" To those younger couples who would ask the same insensitive question, I would simply raise my eyebrows and say, "Are any of yours?" Without fail, they would become highly indignant. It never seemed to dawn on them that they had just asked me the same question! In my heart I said small (sometimes large) prayers that I would not loose my composure and embarrass the children or myself. I longed to tell people how stupid, thoughtless, and unkind they were, but other responses were the best approach for me. It tore at my heart to hear that question, "What did we do, Mamma, what did we do"? Children see prejudice as somehow caused by their own behavior, not by the idiocies and shortcomings of adults.

We had long talks about the inhumanity of men, women, and children. Inadvertently I was learning a new coping technique, "the family conference." In years to come those family conferences were proven to be invaluable.

The hot Texas sun had turned all the children into various shades of brown. Brochures that claimed, "average temperature 80 degrees," failed to mention the many days of 103- and 105-degree heat. Jeff became the color of deep mahogany. There were many questions about his color. Many times I was asked why he was black. I learned to say, "Part of the packaged deal," and just move on. He would squeal with the joy of a three year old. I loved the varied colors of the children, and made no bones about it to them or anyone else.

The war was on everyone's mind, the injustice and the horror of it all. Cameras right on the front lines showed the gore and mayhem which kept military families in a state of dread. The possibility of seeing our husbands wounded or killed on the evening news was real. The military stopped making notifications of missing and dead by telegram. A Survival Assistance Officer was sent to each respective home to deliver the news.

At Christmas the mail became so heavy that Army National Guard Jeeps were used to help deliver the backlog. When I saw a Jeep in front of the house, I began to tremble. By the time I opened the door, I was in tears. When I saw the mailman, I just blurted out, "Why don't you have a U.S. Mail sign on that Jeep!" The poor man realized what had happened. There was a sign, but it was on the opposite side of the Jeep. He apologized over and over. From then on, the mail Jeeps were marked on both sides.

My reaction was a surprise. I thought I could handle things so well. The Special Forces Group Commander had informed the men going to Vietnam that statistics indicated there would be 20 percent casualties. Then he instructed the men to "prepare your families so they will not be a drain on the military!" Duane had prepared me. I hated the thought, but there was the three-ring notebook filled with instructions of what to do, by the numbers, should he be killed, wounded, or missing. Every eventuality had been covered. I prayed that it would remain unused.

Christmas was celebrated with the usual church programs and a Mexican piñata. Toys that said "Some assembly required" were avoided. Daddy was sorely missed. I missed the intimacy of morning coffee and late night conversations. I also missed the ability to discuss small problems with another caring adult, which kept some issues from becoming magnified.

Then there was the car. Why did the brakes fail when they got the least bit wet? What were those strange noises under the hood? There was the necessity to find good mechanics, good doctors, someone to fix the furnace, the plumbing. Was it something I could do, or should I call professional help!

Our Maltese dog, Foo Foo, brought in a tick which laid eggs which hatched in my bedroom! The ceiling and wall were covered with moving specks! The house had to be fumigated. A scary lizard lived in the tree in the back yard.

Those were some of the things I yearned to share. The yard was taken care of by a kindly Mexican man whose son was also in Vietnam. The gardener patiently tolerated Jeffrey's trailing after him when he came to work. One neighbor told me that she had been so curious to see what a "Green Beret" looked like that she was pleased when she saw my husband out cutting the grass! We had a good laugh.

There is a very complicated yet important aspect of being a military wife. It deals with independence and responsibilities. The men want their wives to be competent, in charge, and never ruffled when they are gone. But the minute they are back, they expect their wives to assume second place while they are the ones who are in charge. Sometimes it was like walking a tightrope. Duplicity? Maybe, but a way of life! If a woman couldn't assume the responsibilities of family and home when her man was gone, it placed a terrible stress on him when he needed his attention to be most focused upon the job at hand. Sometimes the adjustment took a little time.

The children had a thousand questions as to where Daddy was, so I bought a world map. We hung it low in the family room. We drew lines from McAllen, Texas, to the Mekong Delta. They felt better, and so did I. At Duane's request, I sent a book of bedtime stories. He began taping stories to the kids. He would get down inside his bedroll with a flashlight and recorder and read to the children. On those nights he was more worried about his contemporaries finding him than the Viet Cong. The children loved hearing Daddy tell them stories.

Duane's letters were full of the valor and determination of the Vietnamese troops he worked with. He admired them greatly. I noticed in the few photographs he sent that he never wore a helmet, when I wrote him about it, he said it was enough to be taller than the Vietnamese without intensifying that height by wearing a helmet! The Viet Cong just picked off the tallest man; that way they shot the American advisors.

Many of our friends were killed. His letters were somber; one from Tan Sun Nut said that the smell of death was everywhere; the heat and the necessity to clean bags had kept the putrid smell hanging in the air.

I bought some cheap perfume. I wanted him to think of me part of the time anyway. I sprayed the inside of the envelopes until they were soaked. Then I'd slip in the daily typewritten letter, all the while chuckling to myself. Duane never mentioned the arrival of a perfumed letter.

It was nearly impossible to find time for myself. I didn't like leaving the children. A maid came in once a week so shopping could be done when she was there. Going to old Mexico was a particular joy. It was, however, complicated taking the children as Kari was not yet a citizen; we had to use her Korean passport. It made things very confusing at the border.

Even though I was surrounded by small people, I felt terribly alone. Baths were taken with children outside the door. A sense of apprehension often hung over the house. I could keep the TV off and the newspaper out of their sight, but their friends at school asked questions and telephone calls were overheard. I developed the habit of asking, when I was bathing or dressing, "Is any one bleeding?"

"No," would be the response of all four small people.

"Is the house on fire?" I'd ask again.

"No," came the same response.

"Then I'll be out in a minute," I'd reply. Years later Cindi told me that she had an unusual fear of the house catching fire as a result of that childhood game.

Packages were always fun to get from Daddy. There were silk "pajamas" and plastic dolls—those same plastic dolls that were filled with explosives then given to U.S. soldiers in Vietnam. They caused many casualties and even deaths. The dolls arrived about the same time as the news report of the "doll bombs." We were a little shook at the stories, even more so when those dolls manifested themselves at our house. I thought it best to call the local police. When I asked the policeman if he had seen the newscast, he said he had, but there were none of those dolls in McAllen. I said. "Oh, yes, there are; we got three today!"

"Okay, lady," he said, "throw them out into the backyard, and if they blow up, call us back!" Shaking my head, I did what he asked. We hid behind the inside wall while the dolls flew through the air and plummeted onto the rich Texas earth. No explosion. "Okay, kids," I said, "you can play with them now!" Jeff received a pair of pint-sized camouflaged Army fatigues. He was ecstatic to look like Daddy.

As Duane's 12-month tour wound itself down and we could look forward to his return, we made a paper chain of the remaining days until he arrived. We used colored paper and glue, and the children took turns removing one "sticky" chain for each day left in Vietnam. It gave them a "visual" on Daddy's time left overseas. We were all anxious for his return, but at the same time we were apprehensive. The children had not been around a booming male voice for a long time, and they were a bit leery of his presence in the house. I vividly remember how unsettling it was to have my father back from World War II. Would he be strange, angry, shell shocked? Would he be the same man who left?

The day finally came. Joy was mixed with concern. Duane was jumpy! We learned very fast not to approach him from behind or touch him without his knowing we were there. Cindi was the first to find out how fast Daddy could move when she came from behind and slipped her hand in his. His reaction scared us all! We learned quickly. He tried to be careful; we tried to be noisy calling, "Hey, Dad," often. I didn't dare brush against him in the night. I'd slip out of bed and sleep on the couch. He never talked about the war.

Kari became a naturalized U.S. Citizen. It was an exciting day—we were fortunate to have witnesses who knew her long enough to fulfill the law. She was four. I held her up in my arms and took the oath for her in Spanish! She loved the entire day; her small American flag waved all through the subsequent party. For Kari it was a good world.

Things settled into some sort of routine with Duane on leave as we packed for the our next assignment. The war was far from over; the country was still in great distress. Our orders were for Fort Worth, Texas, where Duane would be working with the Texas National Guard. We moved into our house, and life took on some normalcy. Duane was soon sent to Texas Christian University to complete his degree. For him it was like going from the frying pan into the fire! Peace demonstrations on campus made it necessary for him to wear civilian clothes. It became a time factor. If he wanted to get across campus to a class, he had better not attract attention to himself by wearing a uniform.

The immediacy of the war was over for us for the time being.

The United States would be involved there for some time to come. When the end came, it was as tragic as the war itself. There were acts of kindness we would remember forever. We never did get accustomed to that question, "How many babies did he kill"? But we could say "None dear, none!"

A DAY THAT MADE A DIFFERENCE
by
Marj McAlister

April 19, 1943. This "I regret to inform you..." date, though long ago, is more vivid than yesterday. My mother's only son and brother to three sisters was killed on this date on Guadalcanal. Russell piloted a B-17 Flying Fortress which went down on takeoff in a fiery crash with full bomb load. It also carried a crew of 10.

We wondered at the newscast word, "Guadalcanal." Its location and significance were foreign to us. Later, this dot in the Solomons became unthinkable. So it remains today.

Mother did not try to deter her son from enlisting in the Air Corps. However, she harbored a premonition which tragically came true. For us he will remain forever 25. He loved flying and hoped to became a commercial pilot. If he were living, he would have been retired over 10 years ago. This I cannot comprehend.

Russell Ray Dougherty was born on a farm west of Edmond, Oklahoma, on August 7, 1918. His life began in WWl and was snuffed out in WWII. It was incongruous for an Oklahoma farm boy to be stationed in the jungles of the South Pacific, serving on island-dots with unpronounceable names. The battle plan was to start from Hickham Field, Hawaii, then island-hop down the South Pacific chain. Russell made it halfway to Guadalcanal in the Solomons.

We were proud of our brother and his uniform. The Air Corps was the elite branch of the service. Russell passed the three phases of training with honors.

But we still thought of him as a blonde, curly-haired cherub with a winsome smile. However, he loved to tease and play practical jokes. Between an older and a younger sister, he held his own and more.

We could not picture his flying a huge plane. Rather, we remembered him with his dogs, pet pig, and pet goat. We recalled his days as high school wrestling champion and his winning the Citizenship medal and the Danforth award. To us he was a dear brother rather than an airman.

To Mother, Russell was her pet and favorite. We girls resented this, but not too much. His charm won our hearts also. This affection extended to neighbors, who had but to call and he came to fix whatever they needed to have repaired. His mechanical ability extended to fixing ailing Harley-Davidson motorcycles. We complained but not too loudly at the side porch strewn with parts and containers of oil and grease.

High school girls found Russell charming. He gracefully fended their attentions. But one who did not seek his favors was Winifred Hoffman. They were married the day he received his wings at Lubbock Air Force Base.

They were stationed at Eprhata, Washington. After a few months, Russell was sent to Hickham Field, Hawaii.

Russell's son, Russell Chris was born three months after he was killed. Chris is married and has twin grown sons. He served in Army Intelligence until retirement. He is now a minister and hospice care-giver.

Russell was the first young man from Edmond to be killed overseas. A grade school was built on North Boulevard in Edmond in 1947. It was named by the school board Russell Dougherty School. His family is proud of this and feels it to be among the highest of honors. Many young people have attended the school. The teachers have taught them about the school's namesake. The building was remodeled two years ago. All the Dougherty relatives attended the dedication. Russell's son Chris addressed the attendees.

At the 1947 dedication, the president of the school board stated, "In honoring the name of Russell Dougherty, we also honor the names of all the fine young men from Edmond who gave their lives for their country."

Honors are commendable. But their price can be beyond measure. The "I regret to inform you..." day passes, but it does not go away.

GLOBAL WARFARE

A globe stands on my desk.
I cannot conceive the distances
and differences colored areas depict.
I overlook squiggle-dotted islands.

That is, before April 19, 1943.
The island landscape suddenly changed:
Barracks, makeshift runways, bombers.
A Flying Fortress with full bomb load
faulty takeoff, blinding flash.

Incongruous: An Oklahoma farm boy
on faraway Solomon Islands.
Guadalcanal strangely appears in the news.
Mind and heart reject
official explanations and military logic.
How justify eleven fine young men obliterated?

Through the years the globe remains on my desk
I find Guadalcanal promptly.
Over it I see my brother's face.

by *Marj McAlister*

MY SON GREW UP IN A BUNKER

as told to

Rosemary Eckroat Bachle

Irmgard Marchant met me on her spotless porch. The sun cast a hazy glaze over perky flowers in clay pots. She didn't seem nervous, but as she greeted me with both hands and ushered me into her charming home I could tell she was anxious to tell me a story she had never told before.

Irmgard was born the oldest of six children in 1920 in Hattenheim, Germany, near the Rhine river, population 1200. As every child in her age group did, she had to join the Hitler youth and became a member of the B.M. (Organization of German Girls).

"I never liked living in that small town with all the gossips," she explained, "so in 1939 when World War II started I saw my chance to get out of my hometown."

She volunteered as an Air Force aid in Frankfurt where she received eight weeks of specialized training as a telephone operator who would decode signals and identify bomber planes.

"I was very good at identifying the bomber planes by sound and could tell what the plane was and where it was from. The Spitfire from England was the fastest plane at that time. I was the first woman to do that job," she exclaimed proudly in her thick German accent. "Usually the men did this." Irmgard's decoding work was a part of the German air raid warning system. Her messages were translated and turned into air raid alarms. "There was constant bombing," she recalls. "My most vivid memory was of the 'Christmas Lights'—enemy flares used nightly to light up bombing locations." Irmgard worked underground in the palace of Leopold and Astrid in 8- to 14-hour shifts.

As a very qualified operator, she was sent to Brussels, Belgium. She lived in the Cloisters at first, then, in recognition of her excellent work, she got her own apartment in a high-rise about a half hour from work. The German military workers had a special streetcar to ride, and sometimes the ride was scary. She worked with a team of seven men at an underground center in the Royal Belgium Theatre.

"We were supposed to wear arm bands, you know, showing we were German, but I never did wear one. My father never liked Hitler.

"Then I was transferred to France where I met and married a German military man. Oh, it has been so long ago, over 54 years, you know. My first husband was so funny. I remember one night a beautiful girl friend and I were in a theatre, and he was sitting behind us. I never thought he would want a plain, tall German country girl like me, but a few weeks later we were at a party and he came up and pushed everybody away and he said, 'Nobody touch—she belongs to me.'"

The telephone jangled Irmgard's memories as she tried to put her thoughts together. "Oh," she said, "let the darn thing ring."

She continued, "When I was six months pregnant, I got sent back home to Regensburg to await my release from the Air Force and the birth of my son. Then my husband was transferred to Lillie, France. I still wasn't out of the Air Force. I went with him to France, but not for long. I was so young. I just couldn't handle it. So my wonderful husband sent me back to my grandmother and the kids in Regensburg. I went to talk to my overseer, and she said, 'You know you two cannot live together in one town. You are still in the service.' I begged her to give me six months, and I really surprised my husband when I returned to France I worked underground there, but there was no way I could stay in France so I went home."

Irmgard met her husband only once after that; he was sent to the front and did not return. She heard from a friend later that he had starved to death in a Yugoslavian prison camp.

Irmgard married again and had a second son who died after just two weeks. Again, living near Hademar, Germany, she delivered the child during an air raid.

Irmgard's vacant eyes were glued to the tea cup on the table. When she lifted her eyes, her story got more intense, and the words poured out of her. I strained to catch the meaning behind her heavily accented words in a jumble of part German and part English.

"I've never told this story before. The bombing was terrible.

Every night we had alerts at three o'clock, six o'clock, and 12 o'clock. We usually sat in the bunkers. Many sleepless nights were spent in the bunkers with our frightened children. My son was born in the bunkers. Oh, it is so difficult, so difficult. Shrapnel hit the headboard when my child was born. They were shooting up the whole street. My baby was born at two o'clock, and by 2.30 I was in the cellar. It was across from the police station. They said, 'What are you carrying?'

I said, 'My baby. My baby!' So they got me into the bunker and put me on a bed.

"The people were burned from phosphorescent bombs in the fields and underground in the cellars. They were dead. The babies and the kids. With blown away faces. Some burning people jumped in the Rhine River. They all were dead. They wanted us to help get the people out. I couldn't. I couldn't. I told the wardens, 'I don't care if you kill me; I can't do it.' It was very bad to see something like this. Even people walking down the street with skin peeling off."

A daughter was born in 1943 under constant worries. Medical conditions were desperate in those days; few medications were available, and medical personnel were sparse. It seemed like there were constant air raids. Once she was out with her girlfriends in the middle of the day when a British Spitfire came right at them. Scared, they hid in a shallow ditch, talking of boys, to get their minds off the danger, and praying. Her sister recited the Lord's Prayer, Irmgard recalls, and got stuck right in the middle of the familiar words. "How does it go; how does it go? I've forgotten the words," she screamed, and that little scene made everybody in the ditch laugh and forget their anxiety.

The telephone in the other room exploded into sound again, but Irmgard pushed the blondish gray hair from her perspiring forehead and with a wave of her hand continued her story. "I have to tell you this. The Hademar came in closed trucks and rounded up the crazy people. I had a 15-year-old girl friend that was not quite right. She was supposed to be burned. She escaped and ran 25 miles home."

Hademar was an institution with a notorious reputation; it was run by Nazi government agencies for the disposal of the mentally insane. Irmgard recalls that people would be loaded on trucks and driven through the town. If the winds were right, they could smell the odor from the deadly furnaces.

When Irmgard turned toward me, her face remained impassive, despite the intensity and sadness of the experience, as she related the horror stories of the crazy people. She recalled her little sister's phrase on such an occasion. Too young to grasp the horror of the conditions, the little girl would say "They are being dyed again." (*Die werden wieder gestorben.*)

The front door bell rang, and we both heaved a sigh of relief as Irmgard got up to pay the paperboy and make us another cup of tea.

She continued with stories of the conditions they had to live in. "One Sunday afternoon right after my baby died, my father said to me, 'You need to get out of town and try to forget.' So my sister and I and some relatives went to the movie in Hadamar, which was just over the hill. We were all tall, over six feet tall. All of a sudden seven Spitfires started shooting at us. So we jumped in trenches full of water. We were all lying down on our stomachs. My sister had a brown coat and a hat on, and she was lying like this watching the airplanes and we were all praying for different things. I said 'Dear God, let me come home. I just lost a baby.' And my sister was praying for something else. Then people got us in the house and cleaned us up. 'What next?' we thought."

When we lived in Hattenheim on my little boy's first birthday, we were sitting outside at my friend's house and opened the cellar door so we could run down. We had a cake on the table. That cake was shot up, and all the shrapnel from the table flew all over and around us. This went on constantly, you know."

The end of the war saw enemy trucks loaded with bombs come into town. All the town's people hurried home to get off the streets. Josef, a Swiss translator, interpreted for them so they would know what to do and how to observe curfew. In those early days of the armistice, conditions were even worse than during the war. Rape and looting were the order of the day. They stole watches and clocks and everything else they could.

"I hate to say this," Irmgard related, "but they raped a girl friend of mine. She was only 23 years old. He tied her skirt over her arms and head and choked her to death. I had to walk 15 miles to Weisbaden to tell her parents that she was dead. They even raped an old lady. They threw her things out of the upstairs window. The Negro GI's helped us gather them up. They were the most decent. I was tall and strong," she laughingly said. "They never bothered me." She remembers that the GIs (she called them Sheeies; I finally understood she meant GIs) had to dig emergency graves by the Rhine to cover the dead.

"They came in across the Rhine River, 16,000 strong I am told. My sister was in a Russian camp, and the Americans freed her, and we were all together again."

The hours ticked away, and we still talked. We discussed the Holocaust and Hitler's role in German history. Then I asked, "Irmgard, tell me how you met Irby." Irby is the GI she married who brought her to the USA and to Midwest City, Oklahoma.

"I had a Russian girl friend who got a job on the base for the Americans. She could speak pretty good English. She asked me if I would like to meet this colonel she worked for. We were supposed to meet at this elegant restaurant, but she didn't show up. Then this GI came up to me and asked who I was and told me my girl friend couldn't come because she had to work. Now this restaurant wouldn't let the GIs sit with the Germans, so he and his friend sat across from me and we talked. I knew a little bit of English."

Irmgard showed me a picture of Irby and continued her story. "The next day I got a telephone call. I had been thinking of him all day. He picked me up, and we went to the pavilion house. Then he brought me to the train. He told me he was to be transferred to the south, but he changed with a guy and stayed in Frankfurt so he could see me. He wrote on the top of a letter that song, 'Don't Sit Under the Apple Tree With Anyone Else But Me.' Even to this day I cry when I hear that song.

"Nobody knew that I was going with a GI. He picked me up every Sunday. Then one day he came with a car to my house. I said, 'Oh my gosh. If my dad sees this, he will throw me out of the house.' Irby didn't even know I had kids. Then he was transferred to Turesier, France. He came to see me every four weeks. When he walked in the door, my father walked out. One day I had a ring

"Don't Sit Under the Apple Tree...." Drawn by Dorothy Ivens.

on and we were sitting in the living room, and he came and said in Dutch to my dad that he wanted to marry me. Irby was 10 years younger than I, but he didn't know that. I said 'So What.' So we got married, and I moved to France. We could not be married in Germany. After three years in France, he was transferred to Germany for seven years. He was still in the service stationed in Midwest City, Oklahoma. He was a master sergeant. After the seven years we moved here and bought this home, over 30-somewhat years ago. We had a good life. Now that Irby is dead and my daughter is dead, I will be moving to Montana to be with my son.

"I'm glad I told my story. It was painful, but it gives me a great deal of relief and satisfaction. I feel much better now."

REMEMBRANCE AND WAR
by
Janiece Ritter Cramer

Young women had few options during the 1930s and 1940s. They either got married and had a family, trained to be nurses, or, if their families could afford it, they went to college.

I was one of the lucky ones. My father was postmaster, and he hired me. We were sorting and "putting up" mail on Monday morning when President Franklin D. Roosevelt's voice boomed across the airwaves, interrupting our radio program. On Sunday, December 7, 1941, the Japanese made a sneak attack at Pearl Harbor in Hawaii, he said. Most of the United States fleet was left burning in the harbor. My life and thousands of others changed forever with that outrageous event. Many of us in the heartland had never heard of Pearl Harbor, but we were fighting mad and ready for action.

I was one of 28 graduating seniors at Wyandotte High School in May 1941. Many of the senior boys had already joined the Army, Navy, or Marine Corps. Those who chose to join the armed forces at mid-term were given their diplomas if they had passing grades. Pre-empting the draft gave men their choice of the branch of service in which they served. Enlisting was motivated by two things: basic pay for privates of $21 dollars per month, and a sense of duty to their country.

Men were drafted, and women were pulled into the vacuum as defense plants tooled up for war. Early in 1942, I trained as a teletype operator in the Western Union office at Miami, Oklahoma. After I worked three months, our district superintendent asked my boss if I were sufficiently trained to replace the manager at the Seagraves, Texas, office. He had been called up for active duty. My boss assured him I was ready, and that very day we started a crash course on bookkeeping duties required of a manager. Less than a week later, I boarded the train at Miami for Seagraves, Texas, with a "pass" provided by Western Union. I spent the first night in Amarillo because the train to Lubbock didn't leave until morning. I

*Janiece and Bill Cramer
on their wedding day,
September 10, 1944, in front
of the Presidio Methodist
Church, San Francisco,
California.*

was 18 and had never spent a night in a hotel before in my life. I wasn't sure if I should leave the key at the desk when I went out to eat, so I asked. The young man behind the counter snickered as he said, "Yes." I hid my embarrassment with a haughty air.

The next morning I arrived in Lubbock where I waited for my train to Seagraves. Early in the afternoon, the "Tri-Weekly-Maybe" was ready for boarding. It was really a freight train with one very small passenger car attached to it. When I stepped into the passenger car, five black men were there already. A railroad official came right behind me and moved all the black men out. I don't know where they rode. I was the only passenger in the car.

Life in Seagraves, Texas, was dull, and my work was boring. Exciting things were happening in California, and that's where I wanted to be. The district superintendent denied my request for a transfer to San Francisco, but I was determined to get there. I asked my cousin in San Francisco to speak personally with the manager of the Western Union office and ask if he would hire me. He said he would. With a job assured, I left Seagraves by bus September 27th. Eighty-five cents an hour as a clerk in the Treasure Island office sounded a lot better than 32 cents an hour as a manager at Seagraves.

The Communications Section in the Navy Purchasing Office at San Francisco had an opening. I applied for the Civil Service position and was given the appointment. The office was within walking distance of my apartment, and the salary was higher. When purchases were made for supplies or repairs for battle-scarred ships, I not only knew the extent of the damage, but also the location of the ships. Such information was important to our enemies, and we did not discuss it with anyone in or out of the office.

I had left Texas with the idea of going into defense work, so I resigned and went to the hiring hall in the shipyards. I wanted a job as steel checker. To qualify, I had to join the Shipfitters' Union. At the union office in San Francisco, I paid the $15 dollar initiation fee and left with a Shipfitters' Union card. When I reported to the Quarterman, he said, "How in the hell did you get into the Shipfitters' Union?" I couldn't answer that question because I didn't know it was supposed to be difficult. He just smiled, shook his head, and told me where to pick up my hard hat. I started work immediately on the swing shift, 3:00 to 11:00 p.m., six days a week.

The men working on the various assemblies tried to send me for "striped paint," but I wasn't taken in by that. When I received an order for fifteen "dogs," I ignored it, and it took the word of the Quarterman to convince me that it was a legitimate order. Once a teamster brought an order to one of the ways (a structure on which a ship is built). He jumped out of the truck and said, "Back this in for me." He thought I couldn't find reverse, but my father had taught me to drive a truck when I was 10. I slipped in behind the wheel, shifted into reverse, and backed the truck to the proper place for unloading. The men working there never let him forget the joke that backfired. As I learned about the steel in one storage section, I was transferred to another until I knew all the steel components in the Liberty ships we were building. Delivering orders promptly earned me a promotion to Steel Expediter. I was Steel Coordinator at Permanente Metals Corporation for the three Kaiser shipyards when I resigned to be married.

I married William L. Cramer on September 10, 1944, at the Park

Presidio Methodist Church in San Francisco. Bill and I met at the home of his father and stepmother, my cousin. Bill had survived the bombing at Pearl Harbor, the Guadalcanal campaign, and the landing at Milne Bay at Papua, New Guinea, and had been granted a brief leave before resuming duties at the Brooklyn Navy Yard. We left by train for New York City the day after the wedding, mistakenly believing we would have six months together while Bill attended a special school.

When we got to New York, we found out the school had been canceled. Housing in New York City during the war was almost impossible to get. We were there two weeks and moved three times. We lived in the Latham Hotel the first three days, but rules prohibited our becoming permanent residents in a transient hotel.

We moved from the hotel to a second-floor room in a sleazy rooming house where we shared the first-floor bath with several other people. While Bill spent his days in Brooklyn on shore patrol duty, I spent mine looking for better living quarters. The last place we lived, an apartment hotel near Riverside Drive, was small, in our price range, and very nice. We had maid service daily and an eccentric elevator operator who had a stack of hats in the corner of his elevator...hats he changed frequently during the day.

Bill was assigned to the *Shangri-La*, an aircraft carrier being prepared for its shakedown cruise in the Portsmouth, Virginia, shipyards. I didn't hear from him for a week after he left, so I went to Virginia. On the overcrowded ferry to Norfolk, a sailor offered me his seat. I told him I had come to Norfolk to find my husband. When we docked in Norfolk, he asked the USO to help me find a room and advised me to call the chaplain at the Navy Yard who could help me contact my husband. The chaplain asked me where I was staying and promised to do what he could. Early that afternoon, Bill knocked on my door. The crew had been restricted to the ship since his arrival, and he couldn't contact me.

My first room in Norfolk was the music room of a private residence. Another new bride in an adjoining room, separated from mine by French doors covered with gauzy curtains, asked if she could leave the doors between our rooms open. She had never been away from home before.

I later moved to a house on Raleigh Street in Norfolk. My landlady rented rooms in her three-story brick home, her contribution to the war effort. Though I was just renting a room, the landlady insisted that I eat with the family because she thought it was unsafe for me to go out alone in the evening. When I tried to pay for board as well as room, she wouldn't hear of it.

I was ill one day, so I asked Commander Bill *Ham*, a resident at the house also, to call my office when he went to work. I worked for Mr. *Steaks* at the Naval Air Station. Bill Ham refused to give his name when he made that call.

When the *Shangri-La* returned from its shakedown cruise, my husband got a short leave, and we went by train to Oklahoma where he met my parents for the first time. During the war, trains were very crowded. Many times I sat on my suitcase or stood for hours on a train. Freight trains had priority while passenger trains sat on a siding.

The *Shangri-La* sailed from Norfolk to Long Beach, California, shortly after we returned from leave. When the *Shangri-La* went to Long Beach, I returned to Oklahoma and lived with my parents. Our first child was born there while Bill was off the coast of Japan. He saw her for the first time when she was three and a half months old. The war was over, and he still had a year of his enlistment to complete.

We bought a used Plymouth coupe to drive to San Francisco where the *Shangri-La* was supposed to be. Bill and I and the baby, with all that's required to travel with a small baby, headed for San Francisco. Each night we unloaded the baby buggy from the trunk and used it as her bed. Bottles had to be sterilized, formula had to be prepared, and not one person in any restaurant ever refused to help us. Once we stopped at a farm house in a desolate area of West Texas and asked a lady to warm a bottle for us. She fired up her wood stove and warmed the bottle as we visited.

When we arrived in San Francisco, the *Shangri-La* had gone to San Diego. Bill's leave expired the next day, so Bill, his dad, and brother took our car and drove all night to get Bill to San Diego on time.

A short time later I drove to San Diego with the baby. While searching for housing, I lived in a motel. The manager inspected the rooms daily to see that no cooking or washing was being done in the room. I washed diapers and hung them around the room to dry, and when the manager came for inspection, I hid the wet clothes in a suitcase under the bed.

The rules denying permanent residence in transient motels made my situation desperate. My brother suggested I contact one of his former shipmates who lived in San Diego. We went to see my brother's friend, who had retired when the war ended. They moved their young son out of his room and let me stay there with my baby.

The *Shangri-La* was sent to the Bikini Atolls for further testing of the atomic bomb to see what damage might occur if our ships were in range. I returned to Oklahoma.

Bill was discharged from the United States Navy on December 16, 1946. The next few years were difficult as Bill and I struggled to support a family and help him get a college education. He received his engineering degree from Oklahoma A. & M. in 1953.

When my children were in school and we lived in Norman, I enrolled as a freshman at the University of Oklahoma. I was graduated with a Bachelor of Arts (With Distinction) on May 31, 1964.

As I look back at all that happened during the years covered by "Remembrance and War," I believe that I was one of the luckiest people in the world to have lived during that exciting period which changed the world and had such a dramatic effect on my life.

DOG TAGS FOR KIDS?

by
Joan Naylor

I was almost nine years old when Pearl Harbor was attacked. Old enough to understand what happened but not how it would affect me. At that age you know you will always be taken care of. You know your parents will never let anything happen to you.

The realization of war became clearer as the war progressed. One day my teacher told us we were going on a field trip. We all loved field trips; after all that meant no school work. However, this trip turned out to be different. We were taken to a local police station and fingerprinted. They gave us a small, round, plastic disc with a chain through the hole at the top. It looked just like the dog tags the military men wore. It was our dog tag with our name, birth date, and a number. We were told to wear it every day. In case New York was bombed and we were killed, they could identify our bodies. I wore my tag every day, but I never worried about getting killed.

On the lighter side, I remember standing in line. If you saw a line, you got in it. That meant the store had received a shipment of either butter or sugar. You never passed up a line. Sometimes the lines would be two city blocks long. It was a great day when the store was a shoe shop. A line in front of a shoe shop meant they had stockings. Stockings were silk then; nylon came later. War with Japan cut off the silk supply, and stockings were almost impossible to get.

This all seems trivial to me now, but what else did I have to worry about? Didn't I say I knew I'd always be taken care of? Didn't we have the bravest, most honorable fighting men in the world? Didn't I know, my father, who was drafted at the age of 35, was going to lick the enemy, come home, and everything would be okay?

I did know it, and I was right.

IT WAS A MATTER OF CURIOSITY

IN AN OLD ABANDONED TRUNK
I FOUND A PACK OF LETTERS:
THE RETURN ADDRESS WAS LONDON.
MY CONSCIENCE SAYS LEAVE THEM ALONE,
BUT MY CURIOSITY GOT THE BETTER.

I PLACED THEM FIRST IN ORDER
OF THE DATES THAT THEY WERE MAILED:
TWO YEARS WAS THE SPAN OF TIME.
MY CONSCIENCE STILL IS SPEAKING
BUT MY CURIOSITY PREVAILED.

I OPENED UP THE FIRST ONE;
IT'S FULL OF MEMORIES. I SIGH
AS SHE RECALLS THIS LOVE AFFAIR,
THIS ENGLISH GIRL FROM LONDON TOWN
AND HER AMERICAN GI.

EACH LETTER TELLS THE STORY,
IT UNFOLDS AS IN A PLAY.
HER HOPES AND DREAMS ARE PLAIN TO SEE,
YET DOUBTS APPEAR BETWEEN THE LINES,
AS SHE WRITES OF HIS RETURN ONE DAY.

THE LETTERS STOPPED ABRUPTLY,
LEFT ME HANGING IN MID AIR.
I WONDERED HOW I'D EVER KNOW
WHAT KIND OF ENDING DID IT HAVE
THIS SIMPLE WARTIME LOVE AFFAIR.

I ASK AROUND FOR NEWS OF HIM;
OUR TOWN WAS RATHER SMALL.
I FINALLY FOUND SOMEONE WHO KNEW
THAT THOSE LETTERS HAD STOPPED COMING
BECAUSE HE RETURNED TO HER THAT FALL.

A STORY WITH A HAPPY END,
FOR AWHILE I THOUGHT IT SO.
NEVER MENTIONED IN HER LETTERS,
NOW PERHAPS SHE NEVER KNEW;
I LATER LEARNED A WIFE AND CHILD
WERE SAD TO SEE HIM GO.

A STRANGER'S THOUGHTS THAT I ONCE READ,
WHY REMEMBER IT SO LONG?
PERHAPS IT'S JUST A LESSON LEARNED
TO LISTEN TO YOUR CONSCIENCE
ALTHOUGH, CURIOSITY'S AWFULLY STRONG.

By *Mina R. Zentz*

A TEACHER'S STORY: WWII USO VOLUNTEER

by

Doris N. Taylor

In the summer of 1939, my friend Hazel and I sat on the beach at Waikiki, Honolulu, Hawaii, and saw a shipload of scrap metal from the United States going to Japan. Of course, we did not then know that it was to be shot back at us later.

In August 1941 my friend Harriet and I were on a ship returning from Alaska. At night the ship was blacked out except for a spotlight on the American flag. I asked a young soldier why all the precautions in American waters. He said, "Japan."

I said, "Surely they wouldn't be so stupid?" He shrugged, but apparently realized—yes they would.

On December 7, 1941, when my mother and I got home from church, it was announced on the radio about the bombing of Pearl Harbor. My first thought was, "Oh, my beautiful Hawaii!" but of course, I later realized WAR.

On December 8, 1941, several classes of our students at Taft Junior High School in Oklahoma City met in one room where we heard on the radio the speech made by President Franklin D. Roosevelt about the "day that will live in infamy."

My father was a captain in the Medical Corps in World War I stationed in Louisiana. A flu epidemic killed many of the soldiers stationed there, as there was no flu shot at that time. My brother was a captain in the Medical Corps in World War II stationed in the South Pacific.

During World War II, I was a volunteer with the USO. We worked in various locations. One was a small building just north of the Skirvin Hotel on Broadway in Oklahoma City. We furnished coffee and cookies, and sometimes we took members of the Armed Forces to our homes for dinner.

Members of the USO also worked at the bus station. We gave

94

out information about the city to members of the Armed Forces who were "stranded" in the city, and we always supplied change for people needing to use a pay phone.

I served most often at the Rock Island Depot, north of Main Street. There, from 6:00 to 9:00 p.m., I gave information about the city, including a list of possible rooms for travelers if hotels were full. One evening I had trouble telling one man that his wife should not go to a certain hotel we knew was not acceptable for women alone.

The most memorable experience I had as a volunteer for USO during World War II occurred in the basement of the Hightower Building on Main Street. At the counter the volunteers made malts or milk shakes or fixed sandwiches. The men who came in were asked to pay 15 cents per serving so they would feel they were paying for their food. One evening a disgruntled soldier asked me, "Where do you get off naming your airport for Will Rogers. You have your nerve!"

I answered, "We wanted to honor our native son."

"Why, he was not a native of Oklahoma. He was from California."

I explained "Will Rogers was born in Oolagah, Oklahoma, near Claremore, and he always bragged about it. He is buried in the Will Rogers Memorial near Claremore, Oklahoma." The young man was flabbergasted and wanted to doubt my word, but decided not to. I wondered how many other visitors in our state knew so little about us that they begrudged us the name of our Will Rogers World Airport.

Author's note.

Doris N. Taylor is a legend in Oklahoma City. Many of us owe her a great deal for lessons we learned in her classrooms. Doris taught at Taft in 1933, at Classen, at Northwest Classen, and from 1945 to 1959 at Central High School (now known as "One Bell Central"), where her biographical information is in the Central High School Museum. For ten years, 1974 to 1984, Doris volunteered for Oklahoma Library for the Blind and Physically Handicapped and for Baptist Medical Center, and she taught adult education at St. Luke's Methodist Church.

Doris Taylor died on May 13, 1997.

FLASHBACK

Television featured our soldiers off to a faraway land.
These young warriors were dressed to fight
in suits camouflaged like Arabian sand
when they solemnly boarded their transport flight.
Forty-nine years then came hurling back in a flash
and sharp dread recurred like a terrible whip-lash.

Immediately I was back in World War II
seeing my husband as he boarded the plane
with his Air Force crew.
I waved with Lee's wife
not knowing if ever we would see them again.
My husband returned, but Darrel Lee lost his life.

Again my heart was torn apart as I saw the tears
of families bidding their loved ones good-bye.
I remembered deep fears when my husband left,
not knowing whether he would live or die.
Some families will smile again
but for those who will have empty arms—I wept.

by *Flo Mason*
as told to me by my friend Freda

WILLING FOLLOWERS:
LEE GUMMER MCDONALD'S STORY
by
Kathleen Gummer

Lee Gummer McDonald was one of many young women who followed her husband from one military base to another, endlessly searching for a place to call home for whatever time they would be there. They willingly endured hardships unimaginable to their granddaughters who live decades later in times of opulence and prosperity.

Housing was scarce for enlisted men and their wives at every base in the country. This Lee discovered shortly after she married Technical Sergeant Donald F. "Stub" Gummer on October 31, 1942. In a period of five years Lee moved more times than she can remember, sometimes taking any place available while looking for something better. One time three couples shared one motel room, not for the sake of economy, but because of shortage of rooms. Every third night one couple would get the room while two couples slept in the car.

She recalls living in Hondo, Texas, in an apartment which featured a makeshift kitchen with no running water. At Travis Air Force Base in California, limited housing forced them to live in a trailer with no tub or shower. They used an outside community shower, available for all residents of the trailer park.

Memories of Malden, Missouri, bring a smile to Lee's face as she tells her account of being there. "Maiden was a very small town with only one restaurant and one shabby old hotel. The food was so bad we couldn't eat it, and the hotel room was infested with bugs. In the middle of the night we discovered bed bugs, and we got up and out in a hurry!

"Luckily," she recalled, "it wasn't long until I found another room. An older couple rented three bedrooms in their home to military couples. The other wives and I used the bathtub to do our

Lee Kestler McDonald

laundry. We stirred clothes with a plunger I found, hung them on a clothesline in the yard, and rinsed them with a garden hose. In those years improvisation was the key to survival!

"The Service Club on the base was the only place we had to eat and spend time. We could get short orders, sandwiches, and steaks, and, best of all, it was cheap! There was a place to sit and write letters, or we could play ping pong and pool. On Saturday nights at midnight we all lined up to see the weekly movie."

In Santa Ana, California, Lee found a room with meals provided in exchange for caring for the child in the home, but this nice arrangement lasted only one week. The landlady's sister came to live with her, and she let Lee go.

A vivid memory is of the landlady from North Platte, Nebraska, the town where Lee graduated from high school. The woman took care of her as she would have her own daughter, serving her toast and coffee every morning and even doing laundry for her. When Lee was sick, the woman called her son, a doctor, who made housecalls to see about her.

When Lee's mother had a heart attack, she went home to help. That's when Stub wrote saying he was being transferred to North

Carolina on his way to China, Burma, and India. Actually, he got only as far as Panama. He was there a little over a year before the war ended.

During these war years Lee found paying jobs to keep her busy and to provide extra income. She worked in a fish cannery, she was a silk presser at a dry cleaner, and she made gasoline tanks at a Firestone plant. After she became experienced working in banks and telephone offices, those were places she applied when they moved to a new town.

Lee and Stub thought they would like being civilians again, but soon discovered that employment opportunities were dismal. After a few unsuccessful jobs, Stub met a recruiting officer who offered him his rank back, so he reenlisted. Lee recalls living in a nice apartment in Texas when their first child, Kathleen, was born in May 1947. Stub was sent to Germany in August 1949, and he was gone when their second daughter, Kay, was born in November 1949.

Stub was transferred to Hickam AFB in Hawaii in 1951. It took six days by ship to get to their new post, but it seemed even longer because of the rainy, cold weather and inevitable seasickness.

"The children loved the beach and being outside all the time. The longer we were there, the smaller the island seemed to become for this farm girl from Nebraska," Lee recalled.

After three years they left Hawaii for Travis Air Force Base in California. Before long they were able to buy a tract home. They lived happily near many friends they had known during the war until the summer of 1957. Flight crews were on alert that entire summer as trouble between Russia and Germany erupted, and tragedy hit their home. Stub's plane was lost from radar going into Yokota Air Base in Japan. It disappeared, and after a long, five-day search they were presumed dead.

"Our girls were eight and ten," Lee said. "It was so hard on us because we couldn't give up, but finally, after six months, we did.

"The greatest help came from our friends. We had been together so many years we were like a family, and Stub's buddies were like brothers. Everyone called or wrote. I will never find words to express what this support meant to me.

"One of Stub's friends was William E. McDonald. He was a

flight engineer in the Air Force flying the same planes Stub flew. He came to help me paint the house and make other repairs that needed to be done."

Later Lee married Bill McDonald, and the family continued its military life with memories of Stub intact. They moved to Oklahoma when Bill became advisor to the Oklahoma City Air National Guard unit at Will Rogers World Airport. He spent his last two years in the Air Force before retiring at Tinker AFB.

Lee has lived through many conflicts, including World War II, the Berlin Airlift, the Korean War, the Vietnam War, Desert Shield, and Desert Storm. She watched as her grandson, Steven Grant Denman, Jr., was shipped to Saudi Arabia and Kuwait during all actions of Desert Shield, Desert Storm, and Desert Watch. She prays daily that none of her family will ever have to go to war again.

THE TINY RIVETER

by

Louise L. (Lord) Miller

When the war started, I always wondered how a female could contribute to the war effort. Remember, in those times women were not considered to be first-class citizens, much less capable of defending their country. I was employed in a restaurant and was saving all my tips so I would be able to continue my education. A short time later I heard about a school to train women to work on aircraft. I had to pass a test to see if I qualified to enter the school and was really pleased to have passed the first time I tried.

What an awakening those classes were. We had to do everything required to repair an airplane and be able to install any modification. We were even required to read blueprints. Of course, I did not think I could ever do that.

The first plane I worked on was a Navy "Hellcat." I was so shocked to discover that the wings were made of cloth. I just could not believe a plane could fly with cloth wings. I quickly found out what they did to the cloth was the reason the plane was able to use that kind of material. It was sprayed with a liquid called dope that dried clear and looked like varnish. We were required to apply three coats, let it dry, then spray paint the color that was called for. This was the most foul-smelling place to work and the hottest, as the heat dried the dope as quickly as possible. This was the least desirable part of my training. Thank goodness, shortly after I started my training, we switched to different types of aircraft.

I was a terrific riveter, so I believed I would be doing that because I was small then and could get into the smaller places where riveting was used. I graduated in the top 10 percent of the class. We were guaranteed a job when we were qualified.

I was sent to Birmingham, Alabama, to work on B-24s. The planes started at the beginning station (first installation). When the required installation for that station was completed, the plane was moved to the second station, and so on, until the plane was com-

Rosie The Riveter said, "Give me the right tools and I will hand you an airplane." Drawn by Dorothy Ivens.

pleted. Then it was flown overseas. The very first thing we were required to do was to go through a security check. That kept me on pins and needles because my mother and father had come from Germany. This was considered to be not the best recommendation for a worker in a high security area. After two weeks I was called in and questioned again. I was beginning to think I had spent my time and money for naught. Then came the long-awaited call to tell me to report to a certain hangar for my briefing before going to work. As I had expected, I was to be a riveter.

As I continued to work, my lead man (the boss) found out I could read a blueprint and give correct directions to install the job requirements, so I became his runner to acquire the proper kits and instruct others where and how to do the installations. We worked nine-hour days and changed shifts every week. When you did that, you hardly knew when to sleep and eat. It was not the greatest way to work, but I was young and I did enjoy the work. It made me feel like I was doing a necessary job.

Lots of things occurred while I was doing this work. For a time, we were having our planes fly out of the last bay, or station, and they would just get airborne and then crash. Of course, an investigation was started at once. In testing the wreckage, according to the grapevine, it was discovered that someone was sabotaging the hydraulic lines. I was called back to security to be grilled again about my German heritage. I passed again; however, another person in our hangar did not fare as well. He left to go to security, and nothing was ever heard from him again.

Sometime later I was told to report to security again. By this time I was tired and was even thinking of doing something else. I think the man in security realized this because he said I would not have to go through another big security check. However, he did want to give me more instructions on security and tell me where I was to report to work on Monday. I was told not to tell anyone what my job was to be or anything about why I no longer worked at my former position.

I knew the building I was to report to was a new installation and that it was a huge building like nothing that had ever been built before. When I walked into that building, I saw the largest airplane that one could ever imagine, the B-25. After being introduced to my new supervisor, I was told to come with him. He then took me up into the cockpit where they had a kit I was to learn to install. I was again instructed to never tell anyone what I was doing on the installation nor that it was the Nordon Bomb Sight. The first plane to have the bomb sight was the English Air Force, as the Germans were bombing London and almost anywhere else they wished. I was having a perfectly horrible time trying to install the bomb sight.

The English wanted a steel plate installed under the pilot and co-pilot, which was easier said than done. We had drill bits that were to be used only on aluminum. We were trying to use oil to drill through the steel, but that just burned up the drills. I was swearing about the English having to have the steel plate when I saw brown shoes appear. An English voice said, "I say, are you having a spot of trouble?" I explained my problem. Then the general kindly explained that this plane was going to be flying long distances and flying over German cities. They would be receiving lots of gunfire, and, in order to save the pilot and co-pilot's lives, the steel plate was a requirement. He was so very nice to explain this to an up-tight girl, but it made me feel like a nitwit. I continued to burn up the drill bits until that plate was finally completed. Before the next plane moved up to our bay, we were equipped with the proper bits.

I did many more of the planes. However, when winter came, I was on the sick list with either flu, pneumonia, or bronchitis from too much cold coming into the hangar. I was transferred to Macon, Georgia, where I worked inside in instrument testing and repair. I held this position until I got married. That was a hoot, also, when I was informed that I could get married. However, I could not go to San Francisco with my husband. My reply was for them to be down at the train station and watch me wave goodbye. The reason they told me I could not leave was that I was an essential worker for the war, and we were required to continue to work for as long as the government wanted us.

My husband was in the U.S. Navy and his ship, the *U.S.S. Indianapolis*, was in dry dock for repair. When the ship was repaired, he would have to go back to sea, so we were trying to spend as much time as we could together. I had to report to the labor board as soon as I had a permanent abode. In one week after arriving in San Francisco, I was called to report to the labor board. They told me I had to join the union, report to the ship yard, and report to welding school.

I was petrified because I knew that I would be required to do lots of climbing. It was likely that I would have to climb up high, which would be bad for me because I want to jump when I get up into a high place. I would not let anyone know that I had this phobia. When they made us practice climbing up and down on a ladder, I gritted my teeth and never looked down.

I certainly did not like welding, and what a laugh that was. I was small, so guess who got the job of working in the double bottom of the ship? Thank goodness, I didn't have to go into high places. However, it was close, hot, and filthy in the double bottom of the ship with little or no fresh air down there. As if that wasn't enough, my husband's ship was repaired, and he departed for parts unknown. I was prepared for a long time working at a job I really did dislike. Imagine my great surprise to get a letter from my husband. He was not on the ship after all. He was to be shipped to Washington, D.C., to attend a school. I was delighted to be able to be with my husband, and I got the added benefit of quitting the job at the shipyard. When I got to Washington, I got the very calm and normal woman-type job of telephone operator. Thus was the end of my effort for the war.

I did not finish high school, but later in life I did pass the G.E.D. test.

WWII WORKING MOTHER

as told to
Rosemary Eckroat Bachle

Madalynne Norick remembers World War II well. She worked at several jobs during the war years, cared for her young son, Ron, and followed her husband, Jimmy, from base to base when he was stateside.

While sitting at the Norman naval base, Jimmy Norick and a friend decided to volunteer in the U.S. Navy. They had children the same age; Ron was only one year old at the time. The men's wives moved in together to manage food and rent because the take-home pay was not very much. Madalynne's mother worried that they might be hungry, so she kept bringing over food, especially ham. "I don't know how much ham she thought we could eat, but we ate a lot of ham," Madalynne says. "We certainly didn't miss any meals."

Jimmy worked on the base without a uniform for 30 days and never did go to boot camp. A graduate of Oklahoma Military Academy, he was offered a commission in the mechanized cavalry, which he decided to turn down in order to join the ship's company at Norman, Oklahoma. He worked in the pay office as a storekeeper for 14 months until the WAVES were sent in to take all of the office jobs. Once a month Ron and Madalynne would go down to Fourth and Harvey, next to the Oklahoma Gas & Electric building in Oklahoma City, and watch Jimmy and the pay officer come in to pick up the payroll for the base, a payroll that was usually well over $1 million in cash. Madalynne always knew when they were coming and was pleased to see Jimmy, at least from a distance.

One Christmas, Jimmy was in sick bay, recovering from a case of three-day measles. Navy regulations required that he spend 10 days in the hospital, and that would include Christmas Day. Madalynne was upset because Jimmy was to ship out right after Christmas to go overseas. She called the base commander who quoted her the rules and regulations about the quarantine ward and

Madalynne Norick and Ronald James Norick on his third birthday, August 5, 1944.

would not bend the rules. Madalynne remembers she could not quell her tears.

She also remembers happier times, especially the many weekends spent on the base where she danced with the Navy men while Jimmy played in the Tex Beneke Band. The band recorded a few masters as they played for the dances in Building 92. When Jimmy went into the service, Madalynne also decided to join in the country's defense. She applied for work at the Douglas Aircraft Factory in Oklahoma City.

With their schooling and background, Madalynne and her roommate were hired as artists. They both had visions of a studio and lots of artistic work, but they were in for a surprise. A train track ran through the west side of the plant where heavy equipment, including drop hammers and everything it took to build the C-47 airplane, was unloaded. After men unloaded the heavy equipment, they would hammer in the U.S. Air Force number on each piece. Then the "artists," with a bucket of yellow paint and a wide paintbrush, would rub the paint into the numbers and wipe it off with a cloth.

Some artist job! However, because of the nature of their work, they were given a bicycle, a perk normally reserved only for supervisors. The women also had badges that would allow access to any department; everyone else worked exclusively within his or her own department and had no other access. At that time the plant was only half completed with the number one airplane all boarded up inside the plant. The women got in to see it and crawled all over it—for no apparent reason except they had the right badges to do so.

Madalynne reluctantly gave up her bicycle and good badge when she landed a job in the executive lobby where she dispatched for a courier service. She dispatched eight women who would drive cars to the airport and pick up people who came in to buy the airplanes manufactured at the factory. She vividly remembers seeing the Russians and the Russian planes out on the runway with a big red star emblazoned on the planes. No women were flying planes, not even to ferry or courier them out, but women did transport many people, which made for an interesting job, one that Madalynne thoroughly enjoyed.

When the orders came in for assignments overseas, James Norick's name was listed. Most of the men were assigned to tankers and aircraft carriers, but Jimmy was assigned to a fleet tug. When landing crafts would go in to let the troops off, a fleet tug would go in and pull the landing crafts off the beaches. They were under fire most of the time.

Madalynne gave up her job in the executive lobby and, with Ron, followed Jimmy by car to Charleston, South Carolina, the ship building and dry dock for commissioning of the only fleet tug painted South Pacific Blue. She was pleased that he was going to Charleston because she thought the war was almost over in Europe and believed maybe Jimmy would be no more than 50 miles off the East Coast. But when Madalynne and Ron arrived in Charleston and saw the only ship in that fleet painted South Pacific Blue was Jimmy's ship, they knew James Norick was going to the South Pacific. The ship was the *U.S.S. Chowanic 100*, which went through the Panama Canal towing a dry dock, then was taken to Guam after landing first in Hawaii.

While Jimmy waited for his ship to be commissioned in Charleston, Madalynne and Ron went to New York City to be with Jimmy's sister. They stayed in an apartment house on Staten Island where the heat was turned off in the daytime. While the sister worked, Madalynne and Ron had to do something during the day in order to keep warm, so they went to Manhattan every day, riding the ferry each way. Madalynne had nightmares of getting separated from her child in a subway, on the ferry, or on a dock, so she kept a little harness on Ron, wearing out two harnesses in the month they stayed in New York. One day in Macy's, Madalynne took her eyes off Ron for only a minute, then turned around and found he was gone. Fortunately, a nurse came down the escalator, with Ron and his little harness, looking for somebody that owned him.

After waiting in New York City a month, Madalynne was contacted by Jimmy to come to Norfolk, Virginia. She and Ron drove there and stayed a short while with Jimmy. From there, he shipped out, thinking he was going back to Charleston. Madalynne and Ron went by car to Charleston and waited until they finally received a call one night from Jimmy who was in Jacksonville, Florida. He had a three-day pass for the Easter weekend, so Madalynne and Ron drove to Jacksonville. From there, Jimmy shipped out for overseas, picking up a dry dock that was supposed to be a big secret. Only officers and their wives were allowed in the dock area, so the commanding officer was not very happy when Madalynne drove right up to the dock and saw everything.

Although gas was rationed, Madalynne only ran out of gas one time while following her husband around on the East Coast. Gas rationing was set up in zones with Madalynne living less than a block inside her zone, which allowed her to have plenty of gas. And by working in a defense plant, she was granted more gasoline than the average person.

She had saved up many extra stamps, or coupons. When she ran out of gas in Norfolk, she went down to apply for gas to go on to Florida. The station attendant assumed she was planning a trip to Florida just to spend the winter. But after two days, he finally gave her enough gas to get to Florida. When leaving Florida, Madalynne was able to drive back to Oklahoma because, when your husband went overseas, you were always given enough gas to get home. Everyone drove on retreads so it was no surprise when Madalynne had a flat near Dallas, Texas. She had to spend an extra day there to apply for a retread, a replacement retread permitting her safe return to Oklahoma City.

"When I returned from the East Coast, I decided to change my life. I worked again at Douglas in the executive lobby, but applied for something on the swing shift rather than a job on the regular day shift in order to spend more time with my son. My assignment was on trouble phones where I dispatched emergency vehicles. Calls came in to report anything from an air crash to a water leak, anything that occurred at Douglas or in the plant. One night I was working with eight supervisors and one secretary. My phones were quiet so I was studying, as was my supervisor," Madalynne recalls. "We were talking when, all of a sudden, I fainted in Salinger's lap. When I awakened, I was lying on the conference table with eight supervisors staring at me. I started crying because I just knew something had happened to Jimmy. Sure enough, sometime later I got a V-Mail the censor had let go through and learned Jimmy had shot down one of the larger Japanese planes." A Kamikaze had dived onto Jimmy's ship during a battle near the Philippine Islands. It was the first time Madalynne was aware of Jimmy operating the guns on ship. After receiving the V-Mail, Madalynne calculated the date and time of the Kamikaze event and realized it coincided with her fainting spell, almost to the exact moment.

Jimmy's ship was too small to have an escort, so it shifted between three fleets. It made seven invasions in two years, starting with Guam, Saipan, the Philippines, and several more. Madalynne received V-Mail from Jimmy during this time and, most of the time, knew where he was. They had worked out a code. However, when he coded her he was at Enewetock, she could not always locate his position on the map because many places had never been put on a map. And by switching between the Third, Fifth, and Seventh Fleets, he was difficult to keep up with.

They wrote to each other every day, numbering their letters. Not all letters came in sequence, and one time Madalynne waited 30 days without mail. She always waited on the front porch for the postman but finally gave up after 30 days. That same day the doorbell rang, and the postman handed her 30 V-Mails. The postman was as excited as she was.

Of the many things rationed, butter was one item difficult to obtain on the homefront. As a storekeeper aboard ship, Jimmy and the captain would go into port to order stores, the food for the ship. They had so many units of butter they traded some of the excess to the Australians for cheese and mutton. They even threw butter overboard because it would get rancid before they could use it all. Madalynne remembers, "They just got oodles of butter, and back here we couldn't get *any* butter."

One day Madalynne and her roommate decided it would be fun to send something more than just regular letters to their husbands. The young women set up the dining room for a photo shoot and entertained themselves for an entire afternoon taking sexy-looking pictures to send overseas. When the husbands wrote home, the girls were surprised that only Jimmy got a big kick out of the photos, and the other girl's husband was pretty upset over them.

When a voice on the loud speaker at Douglas announced the war was over and everyone could leave early, most people left to go downtown in Oklahoma City to celebrate. But the announcement affected Madalynne quite differently. She cried and stayed until the end of her shift, feeling very sad and not wanting to celebrate. She picked up Ron at the sitter's house about midnight and went home to await word of Jimmy's return. Because he was the only storekeeper on board and could not leave until a replacement was found, Jimmy had to stay three more months. Expecting him to be home immediately, Madalynne and Ron went to meet all of the transport ships in San Francisco, California. When Jimmy finally arrived three months later, Madalynne missed his ship, and he went on to Shumaker in Oakland, California.

When word came that Madalynne could visit him, there was a three-day waiting period before he could get his discharge papers. Madalynne remembers, "Ron was two-and-a-half then and he didn't know his father. I was telling him to be sure and hug him, so when we met just outside the gate, Ron was squeezing his father's legs for all he was worth."

The family of three took about a week to return to Oklahoma City where they settled down to a wonderful family homecoming and Christmas. Their daughter, Vicky, was born nine-and-a-half months later.

CHAPTER TWO
LOS ALAMOS

In memory of
each life
forever changed.

LOS ALAMOS:
THE SECRET PLACE IN THE SKY

by

Rosemary Eckroat Bachle

Los Alamos, New Mexico
Large lava beds are visible
then salmon-colored cliffs,
clean and high, tower to the
secret place in the sky.

In 1943 when the wives of the Los Alamos physicists and the women in the Armed Services were bound for an unknown and secret place in New Mexico, I was a blissful housewife and mother, totally unaware of the horrific atomic age about to be thrust upon us. My only worry was when or if my husband, a precision inspector for Douglas Aircraft near Tinker Field, Midwest City, Oklahoma, would no longer be classified as essential to the war effort and exempt from the draft and called to serve our country.

The Manhattan Project's atomic weapons laboratory in Los Alamos, New Mexico, was a well-kept secret. We wouldn't know this secret until before dawn on August 6, 1945, a single B-29 named Enola Gay rumbled into the air from a runway at Tinian Island, about 1,500 miles south of Japan. At precisely 8:15 A.M., the B-29 dropped its bomb. Seven hundred yards above Hiroshima, the bomb exploded like a huge flashbulb. The work of the Manhattan Project was complete. But the world was never to be the same again.

On an island in the sky, the women of Los Alamos were isolated atop a mesa 35 miles from Santa Fe. They lived with the oldest peoples in America, the Indians and Spanish Americans who were conservative, unchanged, barely touched by our industrial civilization. Meanwhile, their husbands worked on a project with an object so radical that it would be hailed as initiating a new age. Unaware that now they were a part of the top secret of the war,

On July 16, 1945, a mushroom cloud marked the birth of the Atomic Age.

the women stood by and made do. One wife wrote that the Tech Area was a great pit which swallowed their scientist husbands out of sight, almost out of their lives.

Most of the great men of physics and chemistry were there at one time or another, assembled by scientist J. Robert Oppenheimer. Los Alamos was an interesting experience partly because of the personalities involved. So many of its citizens were brilliant men and women—many with the peculiarities attendant with brilliance.

The women had babies and aged from day to day, living under conditions of uncertain electric power, water supplies that ran out, mud everywhere, no mailman, no milkman, no laundryman, and no paper boy knocking at their doors. But they realized they were part of something much bigger than themselves—a secret project, probably the most secret project that ever existed in the United States. That one fact dominated their existence.

One woman who watched the first test of "Fat Man," the atomic bomb's nickname, from her home in Los Alamos, more than one hundred and fifty miles north of the desert proving grounds, said, "At no other time and at no other place than Los Alamos has such a community mushroomed in secrecy, so apart from the world, yet with a purpose so significant that the world itself would be irrevocably changed by the product of its labor." The success of the test meant that the United States had created the most powerful weapon ever devised by humankind. The bomb's destructive power stunned even its creators.

Along with the stories of wives of the scientists are the stories of the women in the armed services. One WAC (Women's Army Corps) said they had not been told what was going to happen to them. They were alerted for overseas duty and not allowed to mention to their families they were going overseas. The truth was even more frightening. Whisked out of bed, they were sent silently on their way. When the train ran west and stopped at Lamy, just a few miles from Los Alamos, one WAC said she thought it was all a big mistake since the terrain did not look like any ocean she had ever seen. Many WACs were tearful in their early days, but they were good soldiers and now say they wouldn't trade that experience for anything. Some of them still live in Los Alamos and it is their stories are among those that follow.

WITNESS

July 16, 1945

Four o'clock a.m.
Maybe it failed.
At least our husbands
are alive.

Four thirty, cold
grey dawn rises in the east.
Nothing
Should we go to bed?

Five o'clock. Five fifteen.
Then it comes
Startling intense light
Illuminated trees
leap out at us.

It blasts; it pounces
It bores its way right through us.
A vision to last forever.
Oh God! Please make it stop.

Mountains flash into life
Golden, purple, violet
Grey and blue.
Strong, sustained awesome roar.

An enormous ball of fire
grows and grows
It rolls as it grows
Yellow flashes
into scarlet, menacing green.

The tremendous ball
reaches its zenith

and diminishes.
A double domed cloud
rises from the desert floor.
A new dangerous desert flower?

Oh, Something happened!

Something wonderful?
Something terrible?

We are a part of it.
How dare we tamper with the forces
reserved for the Almighty!

by *Rosemary Eckroat Bachle*

A Great and Terrible Day

THE world changed 50 years ago today.

On Aug. 6, 1945, a silver B-29 bearing the name of its pilot's mother, Enola Gay, dropped a cylindrical atomic bomb called "Little Boy" on Hiroshima, Japan. Capt. Charles W. Sweeney was there, piloting a plane that measured the blast. Three days later he flew to Nagasaki to drop a second bomb.

Writing in The Wall Street Journal recently, Sweeney recalled Hiroshima: "The sky was bleached a bright white, brighter than the sun. It was a sight that no human being had ever seen before."

More than 78,000 Japanese were instantly killed. Total casualties topped 150,000. Hiroshima proper was left a scorched, flattened rubble field. On Aug. 14, five days after Nagasaki, Japan gave up.

The advent of the atomic age was tragic for Imperial Japan. In the dawn of the age the United States ascended to the superpower status it has enjoyed — and wrestled with — for five decades. The bomb was a terrible weapon, but war, as Gen. William Tecumseh Sherman growled, "is all hell."

President Harry Truman and his generation knew this well. Considering the bomb's power to force Japan's surrender, Truman was right to use it. He never apologized for it, but today some think he should have. The revisionists, many of them self-absorbed in doubt spawned by Vietnam, judge their forebears outside their historical context.

They question the bomb's morality — as if any weapon is moral — and see the Japanese as victims instead of aggressors.

Revisionism fails in two key areas, says syndicated columnist Charles Krauthammer. First, today's taboos on using nuclear weapons did not exist in 1945. Those bombs were much smaller; Truman had no sense of causing the globe's utter destruction.

Second, Hiroshima critics try to distinguish between death caused by a nuclear blast and U.S. firebombings that in March of 1945 turned 16 square miles of Tokyo into charcoal with losses of up to 120,000. It's a distinction without a difference.

The lasting legacy of Aug. 6, 1945, surely should not be shame. A just war needed ending. The bomb did that. We should respect what those Americans went through. Time prevents us from complete empathy. Sweeney, a retired Air Force general, bristles when questioned by people who know little about the war.

"I believed then and continue to believe today that President Truman made the right decision to drop the bomb," he wrote. "As the father of 10 children and the grandfather of 21, I am certainly grateful that the war ended when it did. And it is my fervent hope that there will never be another atomic mission. Ever."

Amen.

The editorial at left, "A Great and Terrible Day," appeared in The Sunday Oklahoman on August 6, 1945. The cartoon above, "We Made the Right Decision," accompanied this editorial.

LOS ALAMOS LOVE STORY

as told to

Rosemary Eckroat Bachle

Jean Waiter Dabney was 22 and working for Zenith Radio in Chicago when she decided to join the WAACs. The Women's Auxiliary Army Corps started in 1942. Jean was called to active duty on September 24, 1942, and assigned to the first company of enlisted personnel. She spent six months as a first sergeant stationed at Fort Oglethorpe, Ga. When the WAACs arrived at Fort Oglethorpe, Mrs. Dabney said, "We weren't made to feel welcome at all, especially by the local women.

"Fort Oglethorpe had been a Japanese Prisoner of War Camp. It was filthy. There wasn't a cabinet or even a nail to hang things on. We were issued blankets that smelled like they just came off the horses. We had to air things out and scrub and clean the very first day. I was there for six months."

A telegram informed the commanding officer at Fort Oglethorpe to select 12 enlisted personnel to be screened by a board of officers. Of those 12, six women would be selected for special duty to be sent to a remote area for special training. All of the candidates were asked some unusual questions. She was asked how important social activity was to her and how important her religion was to her because they might not be able to go to the church of their choice. She was asked if she would resent working for civilians. Only later did she come to understand the significance of the questions she was asked.

"We were screened by three different boards. We were so excited. We thought we were going overseas, and some of us got shots for overseas. That's what I wanted to do. I was very patriotic. I had friends and a brother in the service. I had to be in there to do my bit."

The six were selected, and when they arrived in Ft. Sill nobody knew they were coming, and they didn't know what to do with them. So they sat around for a week until the commanding officer re-

Jean Waiter

ceived orders, and they proceeded to Albuquerque, New Mexico.

"I don't know why the six of us arrived in Albuquerque," Jean said. "The other Los Alamos WAC arrivees had arrived in Lamy. It probably really would have shaken us up to have gone to Lamy—Albuquerque was a big enough shock.

"I was given a phone number to call for further instructions. When I made the call, I was told we were to take a bus to Santa Fe and report to 109 East Palace Ave.

"The fun part was that we had four hours before the bus was to leave, so we decided to break up in groups and explore Albuquerque. As you might know, one girl didn't appear in time to make the bus. Since I was the ranking non-commissioned officer, I stayed behind and sent the other four on. When she finally arrived, we took the next bus to Santa Fe and were so late that every thing was closed. We finally ended up in the El Fidel Hotel.

"The next day we arrived on 'THE HILL,' and everybody ridiculed me for losing the private first class. Everybody else had ranks.

She was the lowest-ranking one, so we lost her. The dumb WACs couldn't get there on time. I remember that so vividly."

Los Alamos, or "The Hill," in May of 1943 was small and compact. A main road connected East Gate at one end with West Gate at the other. A number of secondary streets wound around in a residential area near Fuller Lodge, a log structure that had been the headquarters of the displaced Los Alamos Ranch School, a private school for boys. For Jean Waiter, life on "THE HILL" began with a meeting with Col. Ashbridge.

"The next day Colonel Ashbridge called all the WAC personnel together for a meeting and informed us we were here for the duration of the war. We could not be transferred anywhere. The only good news was that we would be doing very significant work that would contribute to the war effort, and, if it worked, it would shorten the war.

"I was so disappointed, because I had planned on going overseas, that I asked for a transfer every month for several months, and always got turned down. I thought I had come to the end of the world.

"I went to work in the electronics group for Dr. Darol Froman, a civilian from Canada, and for Dr. Alvin Graves, his assistant. Dr. Graves was one of the first persons here to receive an excessive dose of radiation and live. It was frightening and yet very interesting to monitor the changing body effects occurring almost daily to his person. The positive, cheerful spirit and thoughtfulness he expressed is something I shall never forget.

"For two years everybody worked hard, and the days were long. When Dr. Darol Froman moved to the 'Gadget Group' in mid 1944, I went with him. We did velocity testing at the Alpha and Beta sites. We worked until the bomb was tested.

"There was a social life after all. On Sundays we went on picnics. Santa Clara was great. Smoky and Julius, the mess sergeants, fixed us picnic baskets.

"As far as selections went, the odds for women were great. There were 20 men to every woman. I met the man I married on 'The Hill'. Winston Dabney was the master sergeant of the Special Engineering Detachment—best known as SEDs. I didn't want to be a war bride, so we got married in Santa Fe four days after the war ended.

"The reception was held at the La Fonda, a hotel in Santa Fe. One of the WACs was a former caterer, and she took over the kitchen. Practically everyone contributed. La Fonda's staff said they would be willing to let us use the hotel and kitchen, but they couldn't provide any food.

"Everything was brought from Los Alamos by the WACs and SEDs, including the ice. The mess Sergeant made a three-tier, pure butter pound cake. We were probably the only ones in the world who had butter up here. The liquor was obtained from the Officer's Club by Captain Baker."

Getting married did NOT mean the Dabneys could live together. If a soldier married a civilian resident, they could live in her dorm as long as he fulfilled his Army duties. If a WAC married a civilian, she stayed in the WAC barracks. If a WAC married a soldier, each remained with his own outfit. If a WAC became pregnant, she was discharged and shipped out.

"There was no housing available for the military other than for officers in Los Alamos. We went on a three-day honeymoon to Red River and fished. Then we came back, and I went to the WAC barracks and Winston went back to the SED barracks.

"I was lucky because I had some civilian acquaintances, and whenever they would leave on a short trip they would let us use their homes so we could be together. On our first Christmas we were staying in a friend's home and decided to invite 25 friends from the Army for Christmas dinner. Unfortunately, that was the year of the "Great Water Pipe Line Freeze," and there was no water in Los Alamos except what was brought up to 'The Hill' in big tanker trucks.

"Water was rationed, and there we were with lots of dirty dishes. We stashed all the dirty dishes in the bath tub and washed a few at a time as water was available. It took us over a week to clean up our mess. We were worried that our friends would return before we had the dishes washed up."

The Dabneys fell in love with their work, with each other, and with the area. Now after over 50 years they still live in Los Alamos.

"We've really seen so much in all these years," she said. "To participate in a town's development, to witness the great change in history with the coming of the atomic age. It was a once-in-a-lifetime experience to be a part of a great, caring group of people who had only one goal in mind. We all worked together to produce a weapon that would end the war. Nothing else was more important to us than to end the war, thereby saving many lives.

"What memories I have—meeting and working with all the great scientists and the other colorful people who lived in Los Alamos. This project changed our entire way of life. It was a special time in my life, and I'm grateful I was here. Also, this beautiful area and the pleasures it has afforded me make me so very aware of our environment and to preserve it. It was an experience I would repeat anytime."

Author's Note:

Mrs. Dabney became interested in Los Alamos county politics in the 1960s and was elected and served for county clerk from 1962 to 1964. It was a busy time. The town was being sold, the hospital built, and utilities put in. She didn't run for reelection. The lab called and asked her to go to work on the Vela Satellite Program, commonly known as the "Watchdogs in the Sky."

The '90s found her doing volunteer work. She was on the founding board of Sombrillo Intermediate Care Facility before it was built. She is a volunteer at the Los Alamos Medical Center lobby.

The Dabneys raised their family, two daughters, Darlene and Nancy, and a son, Jimmy, in Los Alamos. At the time of this writing they had 10 grandchildren and still live in Los Alamos.

A WAAC IN LOS ALAMOS

as told to
Rosemary Eckroat Bachle

Pat Krikorian was born in Oxford, Mississippi, into a seventh-generation American family. She was the fourth in a family of six children. Her mother and five siblings became involved in World War II efforts.

Pat's mother worked in an ammunition plant outside Memphis, Tennessee, "packing bullets," she always said. One brother was in the European theater, one in the South Pacific, one with occupation forces in Japan. A sister was a nurse at an Air Force Base, and Pat was a WAAC (Women's Auxiliary Army Corps) stationed at Los Alamos, New Mexico.

After high school graduation at age 15, she completed a secretarial course at a business college. After working at a law firm for awhile, she received a Civil Service appointment during the FDR administration and worked as a court reporter with the Farm Security Administration.

In November 1942 Pat joined the WAAC. She went to Daytona Beach, Florida, for basic training and became an instructor for the Army Specialized Training Program (ASTP). Shortly after her appointment, ASTP was transferred to various colleges and universities. Pat was given a choice of either going with ASTP to Officers' Training or overseas. She chose the latter and began instruction in life preservation procedures, including judo and learning to float using a duffle bag. She was then assigned with a group of ten women to await future assignment.

In the pre-dawn hours of a July morning in 1943, Pat was awakened and told to pack up her duffle bag and equipment and depart her quarters. She learned at a later date that her nine tentmates had been assigned to North Africa and Europe.

Seven WAACs assembled at the railway station to depart for an unknown destination. Approximately three weeks later, having traveled by train, bus, and a 1936 station wagon, the group arrived at a remote section of New Mexico.

125

Major General Leslie R. Groves had decided the Manhattan Project needed a new, isolated site where scientists could all come together. During the summer of 1942 the newly appointed head of the project, California physicist J. Robert Oppenheimer, selected this region he had known and loved for years. His family had owned a ranch in the nearby Pecos Mountains. Here he was able to combine his two great loves—physics and New Mexico.

Moving swiftly, the Army commandeered the Los Alamos School, an exclusive boys' preparatory school, the Anchor Ranch, and the small native ranches on all the Pajarito Plateau. Much was already government-owned, and soon a total of about 9,000 acres was acquired for the war effort.

When one considers how many people worked at Los Alamos itself, let alone the Manhattan Project in general, the success in concealing its purpose was phenomenal. It became the best-kept secret of the war. Neither the companies which built most of the town of Los Alamos nor the company which built the Trinity Site knew what their projects were for.

Pat said that, for a Southern girl, this was a foreign country inhabited by indians and Hispanics. For the first few days she endured an unsettled stomach and throbbing headaches until she became acclimated to the 7,500-foot altitude.

Housing was minimal, and construction of everything was either not started or incomplete. Snow came early in September. The WAACs were still wearing their khakis until they were issued a raincoat, overshoes, and a Red Cross-knitted sweater.

They soon settled in their barrack and were instructed about security, where they could go, and what they couldn't write home about. They could not write about their work nor their location, nor the weather, nor their recreation. Mail would be unsealed and censored, and no names of scientists could be revealed.

They were there for the duration. There would be no transfers. They were ordered to keep their commander informed as to where they were at all times. Passes would be limited.

After her first assignment with the fiscal section, Pat became Administrative Assistant to the Contracting Officer for the University of California. Their job was to approve everything related to the laboratory operations, including salaries, equipment purchases,

One woman at Los Alamos later wrote about her first impression, "The rickety houses looked like the tenement s of a metropolitan slum area; washing hung everywhere; and the garbage cans were overflowing."

and building contracts.

Pat's personal observations of that time were that the scientists were working on something "very special" that would end the war. She remembers the colonel she worked for as being especially tolerant of her limited scientific knowledge. When she asked, she was given a "need-to-know" answer. She arrived in Los Alamos in August 1943 and was discharged in January 1946.

In 1948 Pat married a scientist, Nerses H. Krikorian, a Fellow (a title equivalent to Professor Emeritus). She has traveled with him to China and Russia to visit laboratories. They have one daughter who also is a scientist.

Pat retired at age 55 after working for the government for 38 years. Her comment concerning her wartime experiences is, "I would not exchange it for anything I can think of doing at that time. I believe that nuclear research is our future. It can and will affect all aspects of our American way of life. It is here to stay throughout the world. We cannot put the genie back in the bottle so it behooves every American to recognize and learn and to understand the pros and cons of America's involvement in nuclear research and what it means."

THE GIANTS ON THE HILL

as told to

Rosemary Eckroat Bachle

"Los Alamos was a growing experience for me. I believe Los Alamos was the best time of my life. The stature of the people on the Hill was incomparable. The scientists there were, in my eyes, giants. I had never before been exposed to such brain power. I could never go back from whence I came."

Ida Green, R100O153, was sworn into the WAAC in Portland, Maine, on February, 3, 1943. Her basic training took place at the Second WAAC Training Center in Daytona Beach, Florida. She attended Army Administrative School and went through Commando Training. On the 14th of May, 1944, she was sworn into the Women's Army Corp, along with the other women in the Corps, serving as mail clerk, company clerk, and drill sergeant. "I loved being a drill sergeant. Judo was also a part of our training."

In early February she was ordered to leave Daytona Beach and travel with ten other enlisted women and one officer on secret orders to an undisclosed destination. The officer would be allowed to open the sealed orders when they reached a certain point. "We finally knew we would be at 109 E. Palace, Santa Fe, New Mexico."

Earlier, Ida had a lengthy interview with regard to this transfer, but all she was told was the assignment was to be in an isolated place, and there would be no transfers once the destination was reached. She was told that those chosen were the "cream of the crop."

"I took this with a grain of salt. However, she may have been quite serious. Some of the women at Los Alamos were far from run-of-the-mill." Ida's first impression of Los Alamos was that it was cold, dark, and deserted except for a lot of heavy earth-moving equipment and Jeeps careening around. Soldiers guarded the entire area. Some Santa Feans called it a submarine base for the Russians, others a whiskey mill, or a camp for pregnant WACs. Finally, the rumor was spread that Los Alamos was really making an "electric rocket." That became the semi-official response for many.

Ida's first assignment was to the Fiscal Office on the Post as opposed to the Tech Area where, she said, "the real stuff was taking place. Four months later I was transferred to the Navy Office in the Tech Area. (Navy office in Los Alamos? Oh, Yes!) Eventually there were about 13 Ensigns or Lieutenants, Junior Grade and one WAVE. I was assigned to the office of Capt. William S. Parsons, Associate Director of the Project, next in line to Dr. J.R. Oppenheimer.

"My chief function was to maintain security. Doesn't that sound important? Loosely translated, it meant that when Captain Parsons' secretary left the office, she didn't have to lock the safe with me there. I spent a lot of time delivering classified documents to the various scientists, then tracking them down when they were overdue for return."

Ida scheduled travel for nearby group leaders and remembers with embarrassment inadvertently leaving two of them stranded in Albuquerque at three o'clock in the morning. All phone calls were monitored for Washington. She transcribed long distance calls using a Soundscriber, a 7-inch record that made it sound like "the machine from Hell!"

Ida didn't feel that imposed restrictions were unfair or difficult to abide by when they were legitimate military or security restrictions; however, the arbitrary and capricious orders and decisions that came from some first sergeants and commanding officers often were unfair and arduous.

She did not find it difficult to explain or embarrassing to answer when asked where she was stationed when she was off the Hill. Locals were led to believe she was assigned to Brun Hospital just outside of Santa Fe.

In her leisure time Ida hung out at the Enlisted Men's Club, took long walks, wrote letters, developed an interest in baseball, played poker, and was invited to civilian parties. She also took tickets at the GI Theatre and got off the Hill fairly often because "a friend of a friend had a car."

New Year's Day of 1945 held no hint of the coming atomic era. When summer came it was dry and hot. There was tension and accelerated activity on the Hill with the men going south to the Alamogordo site. Explosions on the Plateau seemed to increase and then to cease.

"Since I had no technical background, I hadn't a clue as to what was going on in the Lab until Commander Bradbury (Navy) announced that one of our units was successfully dropped on Japan. I understood that the war would be ending soon, and that seemed like a good thing."

About six months after her discharge, Ida returned to Los Alamos and stayed for seven more years. During that time she married Ernest Ritchie, a post-war civilian employee. In 1953 they left for Denver and other moves which included places in Kansas, Oklahoma, and Washington.

Ida Green (Skip) Ritchie and Ernest now live in California.

CHAPTER THREE
PRISONERS OF WAR

Lead Kindly Light
Lead, kindly Light, amid the encircling gloom,
Lead thou me on;
The night is dark, and I am far from home,
Lead thou me on.
Keep thou my feet; I do not ask to see
The distant scene; one step enough for me.

by *John Henry Newman*

EAVESDROPPING ON JOURNEYS INTO BITS OF MEMORIES
by
Rosemary Eckroat Bachle

Maria and Lucy stood arm in arm on a sun-drenched porch on a ranch owned by Maria on the outskirts of Oklahoma City, Oklahoma, and watched the setting sun line the clouds in deepest shades of lavender, pink and green. They were the best of friends, but it hadn't always been that way. Every conversation started with "Remember when" and ended with, "Where were you when?" or "Yes, I know. I know. I did too."

Maria and Lucy are typical of what young women were required to do in World War II in Europe, France, Italy, Belgium, Austria, and the islands of the Pacific. In the United States of America young women were entering the services by the thousands, driving trucks, working in defense plants or taking jobs in other fields where women had never worked before, in order to release our men to fight.

Overseas, three men were plotting to change the world: Joseph, Stalin in Russia. Hitler in Germany, and Mao Zedong in China.

Maria and Lucy were 10 years old when the war began in Europe. Italy was fighting in Africa when Hitler began to form his deadly alliances. The partnership between Mussolini and Hitler was sealed.

Lucy was in Naples at the time of Hitler's parade into her home town. She remembers the people huddled around the corners of shops, and store owners locked their doors. She clung to her mother and father not knowing why she felt afraid.

Maria lived with her father, mother and two brothers in the northeastern part of Paris, France. It was a beautiful summer vacation until on September 1, 1939, Germany invaded Poland, and the terrible war, which would change her life and the life of so many others, had begun. Two days later, September 3, France and Great Britain declared war on Germany.

Lucy's father, knew the bombing would start immediately and felt that Italy was doomed. When the United States got into the war," he warned, "Fighting the United States is a terrible thing; they will kill us all." Lucy's father packed them off to the countryside, hoping it would be a safe haven. "He was drafted into the military and I never saw him again," she told Maria.

"Oh Lucy, "Maria cried, "My Papa and two of my brothers served in the military. My Papa was killed too."

Maria continues her story. "In late September I was taken out of school so I could go with Maman to see Papa board the train for his life in the army. I new what the army was. My papa was going off to fight the Germans so he could save maman and me and my brothers. I clung to him so hard that I tore his collar on his flimsy shirt. Maman cried and clung to the boys, papa and me all at the same time. I felt deserted. Papa was my life, my love, my rock. Now he was gone. " I prayed all night to God and the Virgin Mary to bring him back, right now. I hated Adolf Hitler and Germany for separating my family, for taking him into the army and leaving us alone. Little did I know this was to be the last time I would see Papa."

"What did you and your family do, Lucy?"

"We could not return to our villa in Naples. The bombing had become too intense. Mussolini surrendered to the United States. He realized Hitler had lied to him. We fought the Germans with anything we could to ensure safe passage for the Americans, " Lucy declared. "We didn't know what was happening to the Jews, but we all knew that Hitler was crazy. We also knew that the Germans would load trains with prisoners and then blow up the trains. When the Germans took us prisoner, we were dumped in a courtyard filled with hay with nothing but the clothes on our backs," Lucy said as she wiped tears from her eyes.

The past becomes a mosaic blur of feelings and apparitions as they share their stories about their families.

It was dark and cold on the porch, so Maria and Lucy went inside and poured a glass of wine. "What happened to you, Maria?" Lucy asked.

"Oh, Lucy, the next six years are such a blur now. My beloved France was a very divided country. It was all so sad. My Papa was a physician, but now, with Papa in the army we had less money to buy food. We had a ration card issued by the government. Maman stood in food lines for hours to obtain enough food for the family. We went to bed hungry many times, and we had no hot water. I was a very fastidious person, and the feeling of being dirty depressed me.

"The Germans used the coal and fuel, and left very little for us. We used to go to church or public buildings and sit by the hot air registers. But the authorities would send us home.

"Later," Maria continued, "I volunteered at a hospital. It was dreadful, but I felt like I was helping Papa, wherever he was, and I was finally warm. Families disappeared ever now and then all around us. Their homes were boarded up and we never saw them again. Later, we would sneak into the houses and take whatever food was left. Maman scolded us, but she ate the food along with the rest of us. I would go to confession and the priest would say, 'Bless you child. You are forgiven'"

" Oh, Maria," Lucy cried, "look at the time. We must go or we will be late for our meeting with Father at the church. I don't want to miss our bereavement group. Let's hurry. We'll talk about this some other time. Come on. I'll drive."

Author's Note:

When Hitler's Third Reich was at an end, Maria married an American soldier of German descent and moved to Oklahoma City to live on her husband's parent's farm. Marie's husband died in January 1997 of prostate cancer.

Lucy also met and married an American, a pilot of Italian descent. She had a hard time getting to America, but after a long struggle she finally arrived in Oklahoma and moved with her husband to a small town. Lucy's husband died in a fiery plane crash, along with their son, in February of 1997. Maria and Lucy met at a bereavement group meeting at a Catholic church in Oklahoma City, Oklahoma. They became fast friends and discovered they shared a great determination for survival. While starting their new lives in Oklahoma, Maria and Lucy never forgot what the Nazis did to their families and friends.

Names and dates have been changed so Maria and Lucy can tell their stories to their families before publication.
And so, we will have to wait for the "REST OF THE STORY."

FOUR CAME HOME
THE STORY
OF PATTY CROFT STEVENS
JAPANESE PRISONER
OF WORLD WAR II

as told to
Rosemary Eckroat Bachle

Patty Croft Stevens tells her story with pride in freedom.

"We lost everything," Stevens says of her life in the Philippines as a Japanese prisoner of war in World War II. "You learn material things aren't all that important. When the Allied Troops liberated our camp, all we cared about was that we were alive and free. Free to walk in and out of a door.

"On Pearl Harbor day, I was still in a Manila high school and tall for my age," Stevens says. "I thought I had the world on a string when I left for school that bright December morning in 1941. We were scared, but we weren't sure why. The school allowed us to go home to our families."

Little did she know that by the end of the day Manila would be under attack by the Japanese, and she and her family were just days away from imprisonment. The Japanese bombed Manila in a surprise attack right after Pearl Harbor except, because of the time change in Manilla, it was December 8, 1941, in Manila.

"We lost sixty planes on the ground because of a lack of communication," Patty says. "It was rumored that the pilots were not allowed to take off because of the officers' long party weekend; so, consequently, there was a lot of damage and many causalities. The Japanese were pretty smart to plan it on the Monday after the long weekend and on the same day as Pearl Harbor, December 7, 1941, weren't they? After that, the city was bombed constantly, forcing military personnel to move out. We were told the military used this tactic to protect civilians and keep the city from being

137

destroyed." Stevens says, "The American troops went to Bataan and Corregidor."

Patty's father had been sent to the Philippines in 1918 with Curtis Airplane Company, and her mother, a registered nurse, moved there in 1919. They met and married, then moved to China where her father taught flying for Sun Yat Sen. For a brief time, they lived in Hawaii where she was born, then they returned to the Philippines where Patty grew up.

Sighing, Patty says, "I spent 19 years there among the palm trees, and now my life as I knew it was destroyed," Patty continued. "At that time, we decided to buy a yawl to try and escape to Australia. The yacht club was selling them at reasonable prices to keep the Japanese from using them to get to Corregidor. Since my father was the commodore of the Yacht Club, we thought it would be a good deal to buy a larger yawl that would get us to Australia. It was planned that three of the yawls would follow one another. One couple finally ended up in Sandakan, Northern Borneo, and were taken prisoners; the other, a group of men, were caught off of Leyte, and beheaded."

Patty's brown eyes brim with tears as she resumed her story. "On Christmas Eve 1941, the ten on board our yawl, including my father, mother, and 13-year-old brother, decided to stay in Manila. Since the military had gone to Bataan and Corregidor, we stayed there by ourselves. Eventually the Japanese moved into Manila and took over. They rounded up the Americans, British, French, and anybody on our side."

On January 6, 1942, Japanese soldiers armed with bayonets came to our house and ordered my mother, father, younger brother, and me into the bed of a truck. My older brother was in college in the United States. Our captors said to take enough food and clothing for three days. Those three days ended up being three years and two months. They took us to the University of Santa Tomas, a large, walled compound with 7,000 prisoners, and separated the men and women. The small children stayed with their mothers in one building, and I went to another building with my mother.

"The camp was very crowded. We lived together at the beginning. The first two weeks we slept on the floor without bedding or mosquito nets, but eventually the guards put me on the third floor.

The Japanese held my father and brother in another building with about 600 other males. Later the men and young boys were moved to Los Baños (The Baths) Camp, about 40 miles outside the city on the Pasig River. They planned to build this camp using about 2,100 men.

"My mother and I were there for a year by ourselves. Many times I didn't see her for days. Prison life was difficult from the beginning, but it got progressively worse," she explained. "The first two weeks we slept on the floor without bedding or mosquito nets. Many of the captives contracted an infectious fever from mosquitoes which in a number of cases resulted in death."

Patty worked in the kitchen and in the garden where they grew their own vegetables. The main dish was a mush made with cracked wheat full of weevils. They had horse meat and water buffalo when they could get it.

Patty's mother, a nurse, managed the clinic in the main building. She had access to medications, and occasionally she'd slip her a B-1 shot. Patty says, "Though I wanted to help too, I was afraid to slip anybody extra food. We had two meals a day. At the end, we consumed between 600 to 700 calories a day, so we lost weight in a hurry. Now I have the problem of how I'm going to get it off. Everything tastes so good."

Patty continues, "We had access to some education. I went to an American school, most of the time with other Caucasians. The Japanese allowed us to finish, and I graduated from high school. They did offer special courses. We had to keep our minds active, or else we'd go crazy.

"Shoes and clothes were hard to come by. I had a khaki skirt, seersucker tops, and a pair of shorts. Our shoes were wooden slippers called *bakias*. We got one Red Cross package from my aunt, and in it was a pair of shoes. I was the only one they would fit. I was in heaven! We used rags with our name on them for Kotex—unpleasant to think of now, but we had to make do as best we could. We had no salt or toothpaste.

"My mother lost a front tooth. The dentist didn't have anything to repair it with. He put a shingle nail in to allow her to bite. One of the most humiliating incidents was the lack of privacy. Our open stall showers were right next to the toilets. Imagine what it was like for a teenage female to have the guards watching us bathe in the nude.

"Once while working in the food line, I met a handsome man who looked like Sterling Hayden, the movie star, and I told my friends that this was the guy for me, saying to them, 'You'd better keep your hands off.' Well, he came through my food line for two weeks, and I slipped him an extra ladle of rice right under the noses of the guards. Then one Sunday a friend came up and said, 'Oh, Patty, you won't believe who said Mass this morning.' I said, 'Who'? She responded, 'Your Sterling Hayden. That's who.'

"That was the end of that. Oh well, you never know unless you try."

Patty's brown eyes narrowed as she recalled the cruelty of the Japanese guards. "The Japanese started putting guards on us, watching to make sure we didn't give anybody extra food. We had roll call each morning and evening and had to bow to our captors. During that time we got only one American Red Cross kit, half a British, and half a Canadian kit. Most of the kits had corned beef, toothpaste, tea bags, powdered milk, and vitamins.

"In the last two and a half months in camp, we had a chance to move to another camp where my father, mother, brother, and I could all be together. My mother was a psychic person. Her ESP told her that, if we didn't move to the other camp, something would happen to one of us. We moved into the Las Baños camp after a long, hard trip in a sweltering boxcar. It took a whole day to go 40 miles. We were mostly women, about 50 of us. The Santo Thomas camp we had just left had about 7,000 people in it. When the Japanese came into Manila, they machine-gunned the camp, and the woman who took my mother's place was killed. So, my mother was right."

Their new camp, located approximately 40 miles southeast of Manila, had about 2,000 people, mostly American, British, and French. Conditions were bad in the camp. Medicine ran out, and Stevens said there were not sufficient sheets to wrap the dead for burial. But, at least, the family was all together again.

In this new camp Patty says she lost respect for the missionaries. They had stayed out of the camp for two years, and when they came in they received food from their missions but would not share it. "I'm talking about every religion, mind you," she says. "Episcopalian, and I used to type the sermons for a minister. I didn't get any food from him or from the Catholic nuns with whom I lived in the barracks. They sat there and ate that food in front of me, and I was so hungry. I had beri-beri. When I got up I fell over. Now that is how weak I was, and they wouldn't share. When the Japanese troops came in, they set the barracks on fire, and all the food burned up. Unfortunately, since I couldn't take anything with me, six sterling silver spoons an aunt had given me burned as well."

In December 1944 they were among the last prisoners of war at Los Baños in captivity. Their previous camp at St. Tomas was liberated February 6, 1945.

"The Japanese became extremely cruel to us," Patty continues. "Every time the U.S. forces took another island in the South Pacific, they clamped down more and more. Our captors fed us Palay, which was rice with the husk on it. They gave us three grams a day and told us to get the husks off. We did this with two pieces of wood rubbed together. Finally, we gathered firewood, which wasn't easy to find in a small area, and cooked weeds. At this point we were close to death.

"I used to dream about food. Some of the prisoners stood in line for the Japanese garbage, but I never did."

One day Patty learned from Filipino guerrillas that MacArthur knew the Japanese planned to machine-gun all 2,100 of them at roll call the next morning. At 7 a.m. on February 23, 1945, on the way to roll call, she did not know then that she might have 10 or at the most 15 minutes to live. Then she heard the familiar sound of airplanes. First a deep hum. Then the planes themselves flying with steady precision to the tune of deep-throated, powerful motors. There were nine of them, nine heavy, ugly, determined-looking transports flying by low and close. Patty realized she was being rescued when there suddenly blossomed from beneath the planes a myriad of parachutes like huge poppies against the red sky. They were "angels from heaven," the Eleventh Airborne Paratroopers.

Meanwhile, at the precise moment that all this happened, a large force of amphibious tanks came up from the river roaring into camp with guns blazing, adding to the noise of rifles and shouts of the Philippine guerillas. They all hit the camp at 7 a.m. on the dot.

Patty Croft Stevens proudly shows a United States flag with 48 stars which flew over the Los Baños Prison Camp in the Philippines after it was liberated.

One of the fellows on the amphibious tanks, who now lives in Oklahoma City, told her he actually saw the trenches the Japanese intended to put them in. "Our rescuers told us we had five minutes to get in their tanks," Patty continued excitedly. "The soldiers set fire to the barracks to get the Japanese out. We looked back to see the whole camp in a seething, crackling mass of flame mounted by huge billows of smoke. Thus went our home the past two and a half years. There were no regrets and no wailing. We were machine-gunned all the way down the river. Later we were taken to a Filipino prison full of bugs, but we were free and that's all we cared about.

"The experience changed me. We lost everything we had out there, but we did get out alive, and we learned a lot. We learned how wonderful it is to walk in and out of our front door whenever we want to, and to be thankful for what we have."

Author's note:

After this interview Patty, brought out the treasures of her life—a clump of melted spoons and a United States flag with 48 stars.

Her mother had returned to the burned-out camp about one year later and in the ashes stumbled upon the six silver spoons that her aunt had given her. They had melted together, and this piece of art illustrates her story.

Patty's father rescued The U.S. flag with the 48 stars in the early 1920s from a carnival fire in Manila. General Woods later presented the flag to her father.

Patty's mother hid the flag under mattresses and in other hiding places during their days as prisoners of war. When the family was reunited, the Japanese guards left the Los Baños, and the flag was briefly flown until the Japanese returned for a surprise visit and the flag disappeared again. Later it was returned to Patty and her brother by an American soldier. Since then the flag has been used at a few family funerals. Patty has the flag now and keeps this treasure in a safe place in her home. She proudly displays it when asked.

Love Story:

Patty Croft met First Lieutenant Paul J. Kelly in a Filipino prison south of Manila. Paul's outfit, the First Cavalry, fought the battle of Manila and liberated the Santo Thomas camp where Patty and her mother had been prisoners of war.

After Patty was taken by truck to a Filipino prison— Muntilupa Camp—about ten miles south of Manila, Paul's unit was sent close by for rest and recreation (R and R).

Paul played in a band. A group came over to ask if any of the girls wanted to come to a dance. Patty played the accordion, so she impressed him with her music. She was so skinny there wasn't much else to impress him with. But Paul saw the beauty in this slim brunette girl and started pursuing her.

One evening he baked her a chocolate cake, stole a car, and hunted all over the camp for her. She borrowed a dress from one of the other girls for their first date.

After the war Patty arrived in Oakland, California, wearing a WAC uniform and a WAVE overcoat. First Lieutenant Paul Kelly followed her there. "I was so embarrassed when Paul drove down Main street, playing loud cowboy music on the radio."

But Paul's indomitable spirit won her over. They married in Paul's home town, Oklahoma City, in 1946. Paul and Patty raised two children, Paul Jr., and Carolyn.

Paul died in 1971 and Patty moved on with her life, enjoying her children and grandchildren. With her great sense of humor, she is passing on to them her story and the lessons she learned.

Patty is now married to a fun-loving man, Q.0. Stevens. They reside in Oklahoma City.

COLONEL ROSEMARY HOGAN:
"THE ANGEL OF BATAAN"
by
Glenda Carlile

One of the first woman heroes of World War II and one of the first nurses to be awarded a purple heart was Colonel Rosemary Hogan of Chattanooga, Oklahoma. She was known as the " Angel of Bataan" for her acts of courage and service to others while being held a prisoner of war by the Japanese.

Landing on the Philippine Islands in December of 1941, Rosemary Hogan smiled, "I think I could like this place." Little did she know that what should have been a routine pleasant duty in a beautiful tropical setting would instead turn into a nightmare.

For a small town Oklahoma girl, who had never been out of Oklahoma before becoming an Army nurse, the whole world was an exciting new adventure. Now as she watched the waving palm trees, smelled the aroma of the tropical flowers, and walked on the sandy beaches she thought the Philippine Islands must surely be the loveliest, most peaceful place in the world.

Certainly it was quite different than Ahpeatone, Oklahoma where she was born on March 13, 1912. Ahpeatone, in Southwestern Oklahoma, was so small that she attended school in nearby Chattanooga, a big town of four hundred people, 25 miles southwest of Lawton. She was valedictorian of her class at Chattanooga and received a nursing scholarship given by local Doctor George E. Kerr.

It was an exciting day for Rosemary when she arrived at Scott and White Hospital in Temple, Texas, to begin nurse's training. From the beginning she knew that nursing was her calling, and she excelled in her training. In 1936 Rosemary entered the Army Nurse Corps at Fort Sill and served at the post hospital before being sent to the Philippines in 1940.

She did not have long to enjoy her tropical holiday when the Japanese bombing of Pearl Harbor on December 7, 1941, shocked

Rosemary Hogan

the world. Heavy fighting also broke out in the Philippines as World War II was declared. As disaster after disaster befell the American and Filipino forces, Nurse Hogan was sent to Bataan Peninsula to set up a 1,000-bed hospital.

As chief Army nurse, on December 24, 1941, she took 25 U.S. Army nurses and 25 Filipino nurses on their new assignment. What had before been beautiful scenery now became a frightening maze of jungle ready for an instant ambush. Rosemary wondered if the old Filipino busses camouflaged in brush would ever make it to Bataan. After a hard day of traveling, the group of tired, hungry nurses finally arrived at the site of Hospital No. 1 at Limay.

The nurses were quite dismayed to find that the hospital was a hospital in name only. It was actually only a huge warehouse with all the hospital equipment packed for overseas shipment. Rosemary quickly organized her group to unpack, inventory the supplies, and set up medical stations. In short order, to the disbelief of all involved, a functioning hospital was established. Needless to say,

Christmas Day was not a day of merriment and cheer but one of total exhaustion.

Within a short time the hospital was ordered to move closer to the fighting, a little farther down the peninsula to what was called "Little Baguio." Colonel Hogan served as the Assistant Chief of Nurses until she was wounded in April of 1942. Rosemary and another nurse were assisting an Army surgeon in the operating room with bombs falling all around them. They stayed on duty as long as they could and finally took refuge in foxholes. She was badly injured, the hospital at Bataan was destroyed, and Nurse Hogan and the other injured were taken to Corregidor to recover.

Colonel Hogan was one of the first nurses in the Pacific Theater to be awarded the Purple Heart. Proud folks back home read the following newspaper article:

The little southwestern Oklahoma village of Chattanooga, 326 residents strong, is thrilled to the account of Rosemary Hogan's fortitude on Bataan where, injured severely by shrapnel splinters, she lay uncomplaining so that dying soldiers would have access to the doctors.

Relatives and friends here are still anxiously awaiting word that she is on the big island fortress of Corregidor. Miss Hogan was reported to have been removed from Bataan with several other nurses after Japanese destroyed the Army hospital where she was serving.

But tragedy was still to come, for, as the nurses were being evacuated, their plane was forced to land on Mindanao Island and they were captured by the Japanese. Nurse Hogan was imprisoned at Santo Tomas prison in Manila until the liberation by American forces in 1945.

Perhaps it was her strong Oklahoma heritage that sustained Rosemary during those three years of internment after the fall of the Philippines. She didn't take time to feel sorry for herself but plunged into caring for the wounded prisoners.

A letter written by a fellow officer said,

During her internment, Col. Hogan performed nursing duties, helping to take care of the many U.S. and Allied prisoners held captive then. She displayed her usual courage in the face of adversity, helped cheer the discouraged, provided the nursing care possible with available supplies and equipment, and did everything necessary to alleviate the distress of fellow prisoners without regard to her personal comforts.

Liberation Day, February 4, 1945, was a great day for the prisoners. At first the prisoners thought it was the Japanese coming for them, so they feared the worst. When they realized it was the American Army, which meant freedom, their cheers and shouting rang through the camp.

Rosemary was surprised to find that one of her liberators was an old friend, Theo Tanner of Hollister. Theo and Rosemary had been acquainted during their teenage years. Imagine someone from home coming to the rescue! Rosemary did not take much time to celebrate but continued at her job of mercy, tending to the sick and wounded.

After the war, a woman of lesser tenacity would have retired from the Army and gone home to a more normal way of life. But the Air Force Nurse Corps was a new service, and Rosemary was excited by the challenge of helping to establish it as a viable service. She served in many assignments, including Chief Nurse, Boling AF Hospital; Chief Nurse, Technical Training AF at Biloxi, Mississippi; and Chief Nurse of the Tactical Command, Langley Af Base, Virginia, from which position she retired.

A major breakthrough for women in the Army Air Force was when Rosemary Hogan was given the rank of full colonel. She was among the first four women officers to hold that rank.

Colonel Hogan married Major Arnold Luciano, USAF, and after retirement they made their home in San Antonio, Texas. Upon her death on June 24, 1964, Colonel Rosemary Hogan was buried at Arlington National Cemetery. In 1977 a new dormitory at Sheppard Air Force Base at Wichita Falls was named in her honor.

Long after the war ended, many American Veterans with misty eyes still talk of the "Angels of Bataan," the heroic Army nurses who gave them the courage to withstand the horrors of the prison camp. And foremost among the names recounted is the name of Rosemary Hogan, Oklahoma's own "Angel of Bataan."

Reprinted by permission from *Petticoats, Politics, and Pirouettes: Oklahoma Women from 1900 to 1950*, by Glenda Carlile (Oklahoma City: Southern Hills Publishing Company, 1996).

LEIPZIG AFTER SIXTY-TWO YEARS
by
Ora Harris

I left Leipzig in December 1934. I was 16 years old and one of the first to leave. I left for Palestine with a group of 27 other young people. Henrietta Sold arranged and paid for our departure. She was a woman living in England who worked with a Zionist organization supported by Jews in other European countries. A goal of this organization was to get as many of the Jewish youth as possible out of Germany and into Palestine. At the time, Palestine was under British mandate, and only a few visas were given by the British to enter Palestine through legal channels. I found out later that Jews from Amsterdam sponsored my group. My middle sister traveled the same route two years later. My mother, father, and youngest sister were deported from Leipzig to Riga, Letland (Latvia) in 1942.

My departure took place in the early afternoon. At the Leipzig, Germany, train station, I boarded the train, found my seat, and proceeded to return for last good-byes. A Nazi prevented me from leaving the train, so my good-bye was in the form of a wild hand wave. I never saw my parents and youngest sister again.

After two years in Palestine, I was reunited with my sister, Vera. Later she moved to Tel-Aviv, Israel, and I joined the British Army. I was stationed at the Suez Canal as an orderly. I hoped to take care of the wounded soldiers who came in from North Africa. In 1941 I was transferred to Cairo, Egypt, where I met and married Bud Harris, my Okie husband. I came to Oklahoma on February 5, 1946.

On Thursday, November 4, 1993, I returned to Leipzig after 62 years. I arrived at 9:00 p.m. The plane in Frankfurt, Germany, could not get off the ground because of heavy fog, so our group had to come by train, a ride that took five and one-half hours.

It was cold and raining when we arrived at the station in Leipzig. I could see only the outline of the train station, which was once—

Ora Harris with her sister Vera on furlough in Tel Aviv. Both were stationed in Egypt.

and still is—the biggest railroad station in Europe. It was restored after the reunification of Germany. I was told the station had never been touched during the Communist regime, and it looked as if it had been bombed the day before the two Germanies reunited.

Waiting for us were the president of the Jewish Federation, a Protestant pastor, and several town employees. Each had been assigned a certain task, such as being our guides.

There were seven people in our group, including my cousin and her daughter. After each of us received a pretty rose, a taxi took us to our lodging called a Guesthaus—a bed and breakfast arrangement. The building was three stories high and very large. It had once been a private mansion and later the Polish consulate.

Friday, November 5, 1993

The cold weather, rain, and fog made the town look dreary. A large number of buildings were in the process of reconstruction since the Communists never did any repairs during their reign of 42 years. Many areas and streets looked like they had been bombed yesterday. The first stop was at the Karlebach Jewish School on Gustaf Adolf Street. Dr. Karlebach, once chief rabbi of Leipzig, founded the school. It had been rebuilt and is now an institute for the blind.

After lunch, my friend Lillian and I went with a small group to the Gustaf Adolf Street to find house Number 38—my house. Lillian, too, had lived in this house. I lived on the first floor; she had lived in the flat above me. Standing at the locked entrance door, I remembered the house well; it looked exactly as it did when we lived there. Now one has to call the tenant whom one is visiting, and the tenant will open the door for you. This was not so in our time.

We walked around the house and entered the backyard. A large tenant house in back was separated from the front house by a small yard. The house now is a wreck. It has no windows, and it leans to one side so much that steel beams support it to keep it from falling.

Lillian pointed out to me a cellar roof and asked me if I remembered what that was. I did not. That was the washhouse that each tenant rented every six weeks for one week. Mother used to hire a washwoman who, together with our live-in maid, did this one-week-long procedure. First the laundry was soaked and then rubbed on a washboard. After being boiled in a big kettle, it was rinsed three times and dried on the roof if the weather permitted. If not, the laundry was hung in the washhouse. After it was dried, the laundry was neatly folded, taken to be mangled (ironed), neatly folded again, and separated into bundles of towels, sheets, etc. A ribbon was tied around each bundle and put away.

As we were standing there, a man who appeared to be in his late 30s came down the steps carrying a pail of what looked like garbage. He started speaking to us. When we told him who we were and why we were there, I could see a sigh of relief on his face; he had thought that we were possible future renters or buyers of the house. He and his wife and two teenage sons had lived there 15 years. He had installed a bathroom and shower, painted, and made other improvements, all at his own expense. They lived on the fourth floor on the same side where Lillian and I had lived.

He feared they would be evicted. In the reunification of Germany, landlords were modernizing and redecorating the apartments and either selling the whole house or renting it for a price much higher than was affordable to most people. He stated that this could never have happened during the Communist regime since, once a person had a home or a job, it was almost guaranteed for life.

We accepted the young man's offer to take us up to his apartment. The entrance hall, the steps, the banister, the floor, the ceiling—all looked as I remembered. As we passed the first floor, I stopped at the door, and again I felt a lump in my throat and a queasy stomach. I wondered how many times I had gone in and out of this door. Many memories came flooding back as we toured the building.

As I left the building, I looked for the switch that turned on the light when we entered the building after dark. One evening, on Jom Kipur (Yom Kippur), we were coming home from the synagogue, and I pushed this button for the light. The next thing I remember was receiving a stinging blow on my cheek. It came from my father. Turning on the light was not permissible on this high holiday. I was about 10 or 11 years old, and what stunned me more than anything was that my father hardly ever spanked us. It was our mother who disciplined us.

As we were leaving, the young man invited us to come any time to his apartment. We thanked him.

Attending Synagogue Service That Evening

The synagogue was located in the Keilstrahse. It had not been destroyed since it was a tenant house with the synagogue occupying the first floor and basement. It was small with benches on each side of the room. Women sat on the left side of the wall; men sat in the middle and on the right side of the room. The President of the Jewish Federation, speaking German with a heavy Polish accent, led the service. It lasted only a short time since he did not present a sermon. This small crowd was mixed. Some were Jews, some were German non-Jews, and a few were Russians who spoke German quite well. The husband of the lady sitting next to me offered to bring me some documents belonging to my parents and my sister. They were stored in the basement in the file cabinets. Each document had the name of my father, mother, and sister Margit, their birthdates, and the date of January 21, 1942, when they were deported to Riga.

Saturday, November 6, 1993
Leipzig Railroad Station

In the early afternoon I walked in the brutally cold rain from the Guesthaus to the railroad station to meet my former classmate and friend, Hilde. She was arriving from Cologne to spend four days in Leipzig with me. I had to ask directions two or three times, and I could not believe how friendly and helpful people were. Some offered to go with me to the station, but I declined with thanks.

Not remembering exactly how the station looked in 1934, I found the rebuilt one very beautiful. It had 26 tracks leading to all destinations in Germany and Europe. It was clean and had the usual hustle and bustle. Since I had time before Hilde's arrival, I sat down in a little cafe and watched the traffic and the people. It was then tears came and overwhelmed me. By the time Hilde arrived, I had regained my composure.

Spending The Evening With Hilde
in Frau Irma Theissen's House

Irma lived on the main floor of an apartment complex that was slightly more elegant than an army barracks. The apartment was so clean that I would not have been afraid to eat off of the floor.

Irma was a pleasant lady and did not look her age of 81. She told me how, with much difficulty, she and her husband were able to get this apartment. She once paid 36 German marks a month and now pays 360 a month. During the construction of this apartment complex, her husband spent many hours laboring on the construction—for no pay at all—just so they could get this place. Now, after so many years of living here, with the unification of Germany she is fearful of being evicted some day.

When she put in for a telephone three years previous, she was told she would not get one until 1995 even though she is 81 years old. The nearest phone is in a booth on the street eight long blocks from her home.

Sunday, November 7, 1993

Hilde and I went to the street where I had lived, and we visited that nice couple on the fourth floor. After being served coffee by the lady of the house, we left and I knew this was the last time I would visit my childhood home. That night my thoughts turned back to this episode of my life and how fate had dealt with me, bringing me the roundabout way to Oklahoma. Why I was spared the fate of my father and mother—why I was kept alive—I could never come to a reasonable answer. Yet, with mixed feelings, I was grateful to have the opportunity to see and partly relive my past.

Monday, November 8, 1993

We went to a townhouse for a meeting with town dignitaries and the mayor of Leipzig. One lady in our group asked if the Hitler era was taught in history classes in school. The answer was "No." Another member of our group asked how they were financing all the rebuilding that is now in progress. The answer was from the residents' taxes and from what once was the West German government.

After a short intermission the mayor of Leipzig made his speech. The nature of the speech, as with all the others, was regret and apology for the happenings during Hitler's time. He concluded with hope for world peace.

After signing our names in a big book called the "Golden Book of Leipzig," we walked back to the Guesthaus.

Hilde and Eva told about many events that happened during our school years. I confess I do not remember these at all. The name of our school was "Dr. Smitt'sche Higher Daughter School." That was misleading because I have a picture of my class when I was 10 years old, and there are boys in the picture. It was a private school and rather expensive. I remember only a few of the teachers and a Protestant preacher who taught religion.

We Jewish students did not attend the Protestant class. We went out into the hall, and in the afternoon we went to Hebrew school. Usually during Christmas time and on very cold days, we Jewish children remained in the classroom during the Protestant class. I know all about the Christmas festivities and how they are done, and I know most of the Christmas songs—in German.

In April 1933, shortly after Hitler came to power, I, as well as all other Jewish children, was forced to leave this school. Besides, my parents were not financially able to pay since we had no income. What I did until December 1934 when I left for Palestine I do not remember. I asked Hilde and Eva why they never contacted me from 1933 until 1934. They both said they do not remember, but I think it was much too dangerous for German children to be in contact with Jewish friends. They also claim that they did not know about all the atrocities that were done to Jews or that Jews were sent to concentration camps. I want to believe this because I know they had no access to newspapers or radio and that there was hardly any news. Both Eva and Hilde say that they learned all this—the fate of six million Jews-after the war.

November 9, 1993
Commemoration for the November 9, 1938, Crystal Night

At 10.00 a m., accompanied by the president of Leipzig, Mr Magurus, and others, our group walked to the Gottsched Strahse, where once stood the largest Synagogue of Leipzig, for a memorial service to commemorate the Crystal Nacht. Flowers were laid at the monument, speeches were made, and the president of the Israelitisch (Jewish) Federation led us in reciting the mourning prayer, the Kaddisch.

From there we proceeded by bus to a large Jewish cemetery. The graves were neat and well-kept. Quite a number of people in our group had relatives and loved ones that died before the Hitler era here. I visited the grave of my uncle whom I remember visiting in the Jewish hospital in Leipzig.

From the cemetery we went again by bus to another memorial. Leaning over a fence, we saw a ditch, rather steep with grass growing around it, and a very small river running the length of it. The fence was all around the ditch. Jews were thrown into the river and ditch and deported from there. My cousin mentioned to me that my father was taken there. How many Jews were taken there she did not know except they were all men, and it happened in October.

The men were sent to various places, my father to the police station in one of the suburbs. My cousin does not remember how my mother found out which station, but she went there to take him his winter coat. It was a cold day, and in the hurry of being picked up he had left without it. The policeman brought him to the front office, left, and when my mother realized that they were alone, they quickly fled.

My cousin's family helped make arrangements with the mother of a woman named Ruth Priesel to help smuggle my father into Poland from Beuthen, Germany. The Nazi's thwarted this attempt. They conducted a raid on the Beuthen train station just as my father attempted his escape. After hiding for two weeks he somehow returned home.

My cousin was in touch with my family until America entered the war and no more mail came. After the war we tried to find out about my family, but to no avail.

In 1957 my cousin met a young woman from Leipzig. She cannot remember her name. In talking to her, she learned that the woman and her parents had been sharing an apartment with my parents and my sister until all of them were deported to Riga, Latvia, in early 1942. Soon after arriving in Riga, the men were immediately separated from the women. My mother later found out that my father had been shot the next day. This young woman my cousin met was the same age as my sister and was her friend.

In the fall of 1944 the Nazis dissolved the Riga ghetto, and the woman never found out what happened to her mother and my mother. She and my sister, Margit, were sent to Stuttof where they both developed typhoid. Margit died, but this woman survived. After the war it became known that the Nazis had put the Jews in Stutthof on old, decrepit ships and sent them out to sea where the ships sank.

This location and story had a great emotional impact on me. I walked to the bus and watched as again the Kaddisch was recited.

We returned to town and, after dinner and a rest, attended the church service at Nikolai Church, a Protestant church. We received a candle when we left and joined the procession to Thomas church. It was about a 12-block walk, and the candles remained lit in spite of the cold rain. I walked next to a young mother who told me that she had walked this route with candles every Monday night for many months. In 1989, she and 20 people met at the Nikolai Church under the pretense of attending services. This small group met to work on a strategic plan for the reunification of Germany and freedom from the Communist regime. That is how the candle march started. Months after doing this, the followers were in the thousands. Finally, the wall that separated East from West came down.

I asked her if she feared for her life, taking such a risk all that time. She replied that she was very much afraid, but having a better future for her children was worth the risk. As we reached the Thomas Church, I lost her in the crowd.

I was absolutely astonished to find this church as I remembered it. It is almost impossible for me to describe this monumental structure of a church inside and out.

The pastor of the church made a lengthy presentation, talking again, as had all the others, of the sorrow he and all of humanity felt for the brutal and inhumane actions the Jews suffered in Germany and other European countries, as well as his sorrow for the Gentiles who defied the Hitler regime and sympathized with the Jews, only to lose their lives for this cause.

At the conclusion of this service, Hilde, Eva, and I took a cab to the Hotel Deutschland where we met Edith, another of my former classmates. I had not the vaguest idea who she was. She told me to look at our class picture (when we were 11 years old), and that she was the one with the braids. We had dinner there and spent almost three hours talking and reminiscing. At midnight, Edith's son-in-law picked us up in his car and took each of us home. Edith is a resident of Leipzig and owns a fish store.

It truly was a memorable and enjoyable evening, one that I never, ever in my wildest dreams thought I would see. We said good-bye since Hilde and Eva were to return to their homes the next day.

Wednesday, November 10, 1993
Reception at the American Consulate

The next day at 11 30 a m., we walked to the office of the American Consulate. The American Consul, a young man about 40 or more who spoke German fluently, greeted us. He told us about the work he does in Leipzig. He mostly handles the task of keeping relations stable between the United States and Germany. He also helps Americans who are going to school in Leipzig with some of their problems. Because Leipzig is not only known for the World Trade Fair but also for its contributions to music, the majority of those students are music majors.

Thursday, November 11, 1993
Departure from Leipzig

The next morning I got up at 4:30 to begin my journey home. I was taken, along with five other people, by car to the Leipzig airport.

Summary

I appreciated the invitation to Leipzig. It was an experience that made an impact on my life; it was an experience I shall never forget. It left me with the sad thought that the world has not learned from that experience and that atrocities, cruelty, wars, and fighting continue.

AT DACHAU PRISON
WHEN I TRIED NOT TO SEE

I see the statue representing
victims
I see the sign,
"Blood Ditch."

My daughter looks so nice
in her new chemise, so chic.

I see the ovens, see the forks,
see the horrible ovens, see the ashes.

She is the first in her class to wear
the new chemise. Poor thing, she is
crying.

I stare in horror at the forks,
the forks they thrust in the crotch
to shove the bodies in the ovens.

My son looks so cute
in his new beret. We bought it in Paris.
He is a little man.
Now he looks sad.

These are the shower rooms.
Showers that are not showers, but
gas chambers!
Inside my ears I hear screams.
I don't want to see, I don't want to hear,
I want to enjoy this small
interval of peace between wars.

My beautiful children are walking
on the grass.

Are they thinking of all
the skulls under
the grass?
I won't see, I won't hear!

Come, children, we must go.

by *Betty Wedel*
Fairview, OK.

CHAPTER FOUR
ON THE FRONT LINES

'Lest We Forget' Our Heroines
in the armed forces
who gave their all
and faltered not
when came the call.

LOVE AFFAIR WITH THE AIR

by

Elaine M. Dodson

Five-foot-two, brown-haired Mary Jones has been in love for over half a century, and World War II made the love affair possible. However, unlike many successful marriages begun during the war, this was not the union of a lovely lass and a handsome military man. Mary fell in love with the airplane.

Like a lot of women who served in WWII, Mary enjoyed a special privilege during the war. Many women had gone to work in factories, taking the places of men who were needed in combat. But women like Mary who loved to fly were also fortunate to play a crucial role during the war. Pilots of the Women's Air Service Patrol (WASP) performed flying duties that military women fought for several decades to reclaim after World War II.

Mary's flying career actually began in a department store in Cleveland. "There was a very handsome, young blond fellow who was working in the same department I was working in. I heard that he was a pilot," recalls Mary. One day he asked me if I wanted to go for a ride. I said 'Absolutely.'" That was the beginning of a love affair, but for Mary it was not the traditional kind. Girl did not meet guy. Girl met airplane.

No one in Mary's family had ever flown in—let alone piloted—an airplane. "In fact, our family didn't even own a car," recalls Mary. "They didn't own one until I was an adult. I learned to fly before I learned to drive."

Because she had scant financial resources, Mary had to figure out a way to finance her airplane fever. She managed to get a job as a clearance officer at Willoughby Airport, near Willoughby, Ohio. She earned $25 a month plus her flying time. Mary's first solo flight was in a J-3 Cub. Taking the job at Willoughby proved to be a critical decision in her life.

At Willoughby, Mary became acquainted with other female pilots. Eventually, Mary and three other women purchased an air-

Mary R. Jones in uniform and as a WASP trainee flying a Stearman PT-19.

plane—a Taylorcraft. One of the women was Marge Hulburt, a woman who was to become very important to young Mary Jones. Eventually, Marge enlisted into the WASP and began to write to Mary telling her about the "exotic aircraft" she was getting to fly. Even though Marge urged her to join the WASP, Mary was unable to sign up. "Since I didn't meet the age requirement of 21 years, I had to wait. I was finally accepted in April 1944," says Mary.

Although recruitment for the WASP program was unofficial, word of mouth attracted 20,000 women to apply for admission. The Air Force graduated 1,038. "Everything about the program was military except the way we were paid. Because it was an experimental program, as an expedient we were paid like civil servants," Mary said. The civil servant status proved to be a disadvantage.

Even though they were serving their country like other military personnel, WASPs did not enjoy the benefits of military service. WASP pilots paid their own way to Sweetwater, Texas, where they had to buy their own uniforms. Although they had no rank, they took orders just like enlisted men and were subject to military discipline, even courts-martial. They did not receive military insurance, and the 38 WASPs who died were not entitled to military burials. Their families were not even allowed—officially—to drape a flag over their caskets.

In 1944 a bill was introduced into Congress to militarize the WASP program, but heavy lobbying prevented its passage. After the war, the Women's Air Service Patrol was disbanded. Almost 20 years later, in the 70s, WASP alumni petitioned Congress to give WASP members recognition for their service.

"I got my discharge from the Air Force in 1978," says Mary. "The discharge shows that I had honorable service in the Air Force. I saved the envelope because the envelope is postmarked 1978, and the discharge shows 1944."

Despite the disadvantages of their civil servant status, WASPs realized that few women of that era were able to enjoy the freedom and exhilaration they felt when they took to the air. During the war, WASPs had their primary training in the Boeing PT-17 (commonly know as the Stearman biplane), basic training in the Vultee BT-13, and Advanced Training in the North American AT-6. Mary trained at Avenger Field in Sweetwater, Texas. "Our training was comparable to that given the male aviation cadets," remarks Mary. "The exception was that, since we would not be performing combat duties, we didn't get training in formation flying and acrobatics, now called aerobatics."

However, the flying was certainly not all fun and games. The hours were long and grueling, and, although no one was shooting at them, WASP pilots faced danger just like their male counterparts. Some WASPs flew experimental planes and many were killed or injured. Mary was more fortunate in her one close call.

Doing maneuvers over the skies of Sweetwater, Texas, Mary made her first—and, to date, only—forced landing. She was flying a PT-17 (Stearman) and found herself with only idle power. "I made a forced landing in a cabbage field," remembers Mary. "The old farmer came out with his daughter. The airplane was fine, and I wasn't hurt. The only casualties were the cabbages."

Upon her graduation from the program in November 1944, Mary

was assigned to Waco Army Air Base as an engineering test pilot. This duty involved flight testing aircraft after repairs and "slow-timing" engines, which meant taking off at reduced power and flying for a specified period of time on reduced power to "break-in the repaired engine.

Mary was officially a WASP far too briefly. On December 20, 1944, the entire program was disbanded.

For 33 years, the closest Mary got to an airplane was her room number—747—in her job with the Cleveland Federal Executive Board, a kind of federal chamber of commerce where she was executive director.

After her retirement Mary decided to rekindle her love affair with the air. She enrolled in the Spartan School of Aeronautics in Tulsa, Oklahoma, in 1982. Mary's interest in the sturdy Stearman biplane, which she had force-landed in a cabbage patch years before, led her in another direction. "Once you've flown a biplane, it just kind of stays with you," explains Mary. "I wanted to see if I could do it again."

In 1984 Mary bought a yellow biplane, a Navy N3N. A year later, with her new friends in Tulsa, Mary inaugurated the National Biplane Association which, since 1986, has held a fly-in at Bartlesville each spring.

Although Mary's flying career during the war was brief, many women—and men—benefitted from her military career as a WASP. Mary's enthusiasm for flying still draws people to her and fuels the enthusiasm of many pilots—men and women alike. Her small stature and quiet demeanor camouflage her determination. Like other women of war, Mary is a woman who simply doesn't know the meaning of the word "can't."

ALL HANDS HIT THE DECK

by

Estella (Tillie) Knapp Kernan, Lt. Jg., USNR

The Japanese attack on Pearl Harbor, December 7, 1941, plunged the United States of America into World War II. The lives of millions of Americans were affected directly or indirectly by this single act of aggression.

World War II was not foremost in my mind during 1941; I was in college, and war seemed far away and unreal. I was in my senior year at Oklahoma University, and the year before I had been elected beauty queen. Although the draft was in effect, many of the college boys vowed they weren't going to war.

I knew things were bad, but I still didn't focus on the war until some of the boys started coming to class saying, "We're going!" and "We're leaving school; we have to go tomorrow." Attitudes seemed to change almost overnight about enlisting and serving in the military.

Graduation was marred by the knowledge that some of our classmates who had joined up earlier had already been killed overseas. Walking down campus after the ceremony to return our caps and gowns, the topic of conversation inevitably turned to the war: which of our friends were leaving for the Army almost immediately, and how devastating the bombs had been at Pearl Harbor. One of the boys in the group suggested, "Why don't you join the WAACs?"

"The what? I never heard of that. What is it?"

The year 1942 was the beginning of WAAC, The Women's Army Auxiliary Corp; WAF, Women in U.S. Air Force; and WAVES, Women Accepted for Voluntary Emergency Service (Navy). To enlist in the WAVES, a woman had to be between the ages of 18 and 25 and unmarried.

I signed up for the WAVES shortly after graduating from Oklahoma University in 1942 and was immediately scheduled for testing at the 8th Naval District in New Orleans, Louisiana. On arriving in New Orleans, I checked into the St. Charles Hotel—it led the list

Tillie Kernan

of hotels included with my orders. I met two other enlistees who had picked the hotel for the same reason. We were all a little nervous about being in a strange town, so we decided to stick together. Testing was scheduled for the next day.

After we located the testing site, we learned there were three sections to the tests: the personal interview, the physical, and a written test—the same tests given to the men at Annapolis. I knew I'd never pass. The math exam alone would kill my chances, but I was determined to see it through.

The physical caused some anxiety. The doctor taking my blood pressure said, "If you want to get in the Navy, you're going to have to calm down. I'll just let you stay here for a few minutes, and I'll come back." I took a few deep breaths, and by the time he returned my blood pressure was in the acceptable range.

After giving the required urine samples, several of us sat around in our medical gowns chatting and waiting for the next battery of tests. A sailor passed by carrying a cardboard box. Written on the side was "TNT EXPLOSIVES—DO NOT DROP." It was our urine samples.

A Naval officer conducted the oral interviews. He asked questions about why we wanted to get into the Navy and questions that explored our personal feelings and personalities. I assumed the questions were designed to judge whether we could cope under stressful conditions even though women were not allowed in combat.

After the testing we were all called together for the results. I knew the written test would be my failing. As the names were called off, it was hard to determine how the selections were made. Some of the applicants who had not been selected appeared to be well qualified.

On the train going home, some of the ones who had not passed went around asking, "Did you get in?" When one asked me and I answered in the affirmative, she said, "Well, what was your degree?"

"Psychology," I replied.

We decided the Navy wanted women just out of school who could be trained for a specific purpose. In Communications or Administration, we could replace men, freeing them for active duty. Although we were considered active duty, we stayed ashore while the men went to sea.

I received my orders to report to Northampton, Massachusetts, a week before Christmas in 1942. At the train station, we piled aboard a train already filled to overflowing with soldiers and people who had made reservations. There weren't enough places to sleep, and with so many soldiers waiting in line at the dining car, by the time we reached it, there was no food left. It took three days and two nights to reach our destination. We arrived after dark, hungry and tired, to a snow-chilled Northampton.

Some of us were loaded on a bus and told we were being sent to Mount Holyoke College for a month's training. Mount Holyoke turned out to be a girls' school—closed because there wasn't enough heat. The girls had been sent home until the school could get more fuel. Little signs on the windows and mirrors warned, "If you get cold, put on your sweater. If you get too cold, put on your coat."

My roommate's name was Lou. She was from Ohio and a recent graduate of St. Mary's at Notre Dame. That first night she and I put away our clothes, grabbed our nightgowns, and started down the hallway to the showers. A young woman in uniform stopped us and said, "You've got to hit the bunk now." We protested that we hadn't had a shower for three days. "Too bad," she said unsympathetically. "Just put your gown on, or whatever, and get in your bunk."

Stretched out in the bunk trying to keep warm, I thought drearily, "Why did I do this? I don't know anybody, I'm miles from home, and it's almost Christmas!"

Next morning, even before light, I heard, "All hands hit the deck." I was learning Navy lingo. There was little for us to do in the days before Christmas but learn Navy expressions. Then Christmas was over, and the training began.

We wore civilian clothes because our uniforms had not been issued. I had packed a pair of oxfords because my mother warned, "You can't go in there in high-heeled shoes; you won't be able to walk. And take your galoshes." I was thankful I had taken Mother's advice. I never would have made it marching around in the heels.

There was a small circle we marched around during training. Sometimes it was snowing so heavily you couldn't see the person in front of you. It was bitterly cold but we marched on.

After our month at Mount Holyoke, we were sent to a hotel at Smith College in Northampton where we began studying in earnest. In the course of our stay at Smith, we had to have another physical, this time with a pelvic exam. Most of us had no idea what a pelvic exam was; there were a lot of suppositions and rumors among the girls that made us even more scared and upset. Finally, to allay our fears, we were shown a film on exactly what to expect.

It was discovered during the exams that one of the girls was pregnant. This was a bad thing. She had been married secretly— to a Naval Officer. This was another bad thing. As part of our pledge when we signed up, we agreed not to marry anyone in the Navy. However, even though she had broken two major taboos, she was treated like a delicate piece of china until she was eased out; the Navy didn't want to be responsible for anything happening to a pregnant woman.

We had to make formation each morning at seven o'clock a.m.

at the back of the parking lot of the hotel, the temperature usually below zero. We marched to all our classes, the taller girls to the front of the line. Cotton stockings were regular issue, reasonably warm, and held up with garters. One girl, shorter than me, later said she spent most of her time marching behind me and watching my stockings slowly slip down and hoping we got back to the hotel before her own fell around her ankles.

During one of our marches, an Army commanding officer was present. We were lined up according to height, marching in formation, first one way, then another. Suddenly we heard laughter. We marched eyes forward, backs ramrod stiff, the shorter women now leading. We heard the voice of the commanding officer call out, "Would you little girls back there like to march with the rest of us?" Some of us had made a bad turn and were marching all by ourselves, straight into a wall, waiting for someone to say, "Halt!"

Despite marching every morning in severely cold weather, followed by demanding class work that was punctuated by difficult tests, we managed to keep going. There was no time off for headaches or cramps. We had to tough it out; we were Navy Waves.

We finally got our uniforms. They were designed by Mainbocher and made at Filene's of Boston. Someone from Filenes' came and measured each of us for a fitting. When the finished uniforms arrived, we were thrilled with the fit, the look, and, most of all, the comfort. They even included things like covers to keep our hats dry in the rain and warm trench coats to wear over our uniforms.

After about three months we received our commissions. Lou and I remained roommates all through training and got our orders to Washington D.C. We were given 48 hours leave, not even enough time to go home.

When we got to Washington, we had one more short stint of training before we reported to the Chief of Naval Operations. We were assigned to Communications. With dismay, we looked at the machines we would be working with. I was glad I had learned to type, a skill essential in Navy communications. The commanding officer in charge of Radio Washington dashed our self-esteem when he blatantly stated, "Now we didn't want you girls here, but since you are, I hope you'll do the best you can". We'd had the impression we would be needed.

In sealed coding rooms we learned to operate the encoding and decoding machines and systems. Messages came through a tube from a room downstairs and were put in baskets classified as ROUTINE, PRIORITY, TOP PRIORITY, or URGENT depending on how fast they needed to be acted upon. Messages were sent to various coding rooms labeled RESTRICTED, CONFIDENTIAL, or TOP SECRET. Early in the war only men cleared TOP SECRET messages.

My first duty was in CONFIDENTIAL. Any message in or out was signed by the person handling it and the person who checked it. Mistakes were critical; we were told we could sink a ship if we were careless about numbers.

NSS Radio Washington was open *365* days a year, 24 hours a day. We worked 12-hour shifts: on at 8:00 o'clock, off at 8:00 o'clock. The shifts were devastatingly long and hard, and even the men were feeling the effects. Our off-hours in Washington with its traffic and having to stand in line for everything, like getting your laundry done or getting your meals, were calamitous. Some women were so unhappy they married just to get out. When the Navy realized what was happening, the rule against marrying Navy men was rescinded, and the shifts were cut to eight hours.

Eventually, I was cleared for top secret work and sent over to SECRET. Thousands of messages came and went continuously. There was never a time when the baskets were cleared. Some messages, after being decoded or encoded, had to be copied. There were special messages that demanded to be encoded or decoded in only minutes. We were instructed not to talk about any messages, although we rarely had time to study any of them. Going to the head (bathroom) for more than a couple of minutes meant getting sarcastic remarks like, "We really missed you; how long were you gone?"

The amount of work and the noise from the machines made conditions almost intolerable. Another WAVE and I made a list of things we felt needed improvement and went to a female lieutenant commander for help. We didn't think of it as mutiny, although it could have been misconstrued as such. She came down to the coding rooms, made notes, and agreed things were pretty bad.

The lieutenant commander went to our male commanding officer with our complaints and advised him that, with the present noise level, a person could become deaf. She told him it was "...so noisy in there, these women can't even think." His reply left little hope that any corrective measures would be taken: "They don't need to think; they just need to do what they're told."

We were told we couldn't have leave in communications. The women decided we would all ask for leave at the same time. The commanding officer called us in and asked why we requested leave. We told him we felt we deserved time to go home for visits, that we wanted to show our family and friends our uniforms. We were finally allowed to have leave, but we had to work seven of our days off to make up for taking one week's leave.

It took my whole leave to get home and back. If you had a seat on the plane and a higher ranking officer wanted that seat, someone tapped you on the shoulder and said, "I'm sorry, but your seat's been taken." I kept getting put out of my seat so often I wound up taking the train.

A rumor made the rounds in CONFIDENTIAL that our commanding officer was leaving. We all liked him and were a little anxious when we heard the new commanding officer would be a lieutenant who had been a member of Admiral Halsey's staff, served on the *Enterprise*, and participated in several major sea engagements from December 7, 1941, to 1943. He had been in Washington for rest and relaxation and now was put in charge of our coding room.

Lieutenant Phil Kernan walked in wearing all his ribbons. One of the girls, unaware of his presence, was working away and happened to make a mistake in her typing. She jerked it out of the machine and threw it in the wastebasket. Lieutenant Kernan turned to his guide and asked who she was. When told her name, the Lieutenant said, "Well, if she can't control herself any better than that, she'll have to be sent to St. Elizabeth's." Knowing that St Elizabeth's was the mental hospital, we all groaned inwardly and thought, "Uh oh, he's going to be bad news." We all walked carefully around him.

One day I had a message to deliver to him, and he asked me if I would do him a favor. I responded, "Aye, aye, Sir." He turned around and asked what I had said. I was taken aback but replied, "Aye, aye, sir. Isn't that what I'm supposed to say?"

He agreed, "Well, yes, it is." He thought I was being smartassy with him. The staff continued to be a little wary of his intentions. He was our first contact with an honest-to-goodness seagoing Naval officer.

When we put a communication in the coding machine, we put in "padding" at the beginning and ending to prevent the enemy from breaking the code or deciphering the message. One day Lieutenant Kernan, who usually sat at his desk and supervised, went to one of the coding machines and began to type. Since we routinely checked each other's messages, he asked me to check this one. At the beginning he had written, "How about a date...." The ending read, "...let me know." Without acknowledging the padding as unusual, I signed off on the message as the reviewer. He asked if I had read the entire communication and I replied, "Yes, sir. I did."

"Is that it?" he persisted.

"Yes, sir. That's it." I said blandly. I wasn't about to attribute special meaning to words that may have been only subterfuge for the enemy.

During one of my days off, I had visited a teenaged cousin, who had the mumps. A few days later, feeling feverish and swollen, I went to the infirmary and reported my suspicion that I, too, now had the mumps. The doctor felt my neck and declared that I was mistaken and could go back to my duty station. The next morning there was no denying the fact. I had the mumps!

When I called the Naval department head and reported my ailment, he contacted the doctor at the infirmary. The doctor recommended I come in prepared for a trip to the Bethesda Naval Hospital. When I stopped by to tell Lieutenant Kernan, he said, "For God's sake, get out of here! We've already been exposed for eight hours."

Bethesda Hospital was not prepared for female officers as patients and didn't know what to do with me. They put me in a room that shared a bath with other Naval officers. The men had a lot of good-natured fun throwing things at me across the bathroom. I felt too sick to appreciate their amusement.

While I was in the hospital, Lieutenant Kernan visited me with flowers and a card. I'd forgotten it was my birthday. He asked if I would go out with him when I was well enough. I figured the question left no room for misinterpretation this time.

The Lieutenant—Phil—and I had been dating for some time

when he learned he was being sent to Nobi, Trinidad. He asked me to marry him. My answer was a resounding, "Yes." At the Washington, D.C., airport, I promised I would wait for him to return to take my leave. On his return from Trinidad, he gave me a ring.

His next assignment was to the *USS Ticonderoga*, where he remained for a short time, then to the *USS Tulagi*, an aircraft carrier. Not long after his transfer to the *Tulagi*, the *Ticonderoga* was bombed. Phil, in his position in communications on the ship, would surely have been killed.

Phil finally got shore duty, and we confirmed our engagement and set the date. It was futile to request leave, so I was on duty until almost the last minute. I hurried home, changed uniforms, and my roommate changed hers. She was my best woman. My brother, an Army captain stationed in Washington, was best man. We drove over to Bethesda with my cousins and got married in a small, wood-framed Catholic Church.

We spent our honeymoon in Philadelphia, but I had to report back to work in 72 hours. Phil spent the rest of his 10-day leave without his bride, who was on duty!

After Phil received orders to Norfolk, Virginia, he went to my commanding officer and requested that I be transferred to communications in Norfolk. Overriding protests from Washington about losing personnel and in light of Phil's Naval background and service record, the commander approved the transfer.

It was like going from night into full sunshine in the communications room in Norfolk. The workers sat around reading books, went out for coffee, or just sat. They were astounded at how fast I operated the machines even though I told them about the masses of priority work done in Washington. I was surprised that there were so few messages coming and going in Norfolk.

It wasn't long before I was pregnant and, as a result, discharged from the Navy. Phil and I were at a cocktail party for officers one evening and I was wearing civilian clothes. During the war you wore your uniform every place you went except when playing sports. One of the officers asked me what I was doing out of uniform. I replied that I was out of the Navy. "How did you manage that?" he asked.

"Well, I'm sorry, but it won't work for you," I answered.

Phil and I are proud of the years we served as officers in the United States Navy and for the opportunity to help our country during a time of need. Our only son, Phil, Jr., was born December 5, 1945, in Ft. Worth, Texas. I've spent my life as a civilian being a wife, mother, and a volunteer. I chose the kinds of volunteer work I considered might make a difference and would be a needed contribution. My Navy experiences were an excellent addition to my college education, and military discipline has been helpful. And, in a way, the war gave me my husband and my son.

Author's Note:

Tillie and Philip A. Kernan sneaked a beat on other Navy veterans to become the first couple to receive their American Defense and Victory medals from the 15,000 ready for mass handout. Noting that Friday begins right after midnight Thursday, the former lieutenant commander and his wife, once a lieutenant junior grade in the WAVEs, got a Navy recruiting officer out of bed for a special presentation. The scheduled presentations were held the next morning.

Among the many achievements of Tillie Kernan, the one she is most proud of is her involvement as a Reach To Recovery volunteer. In 1975 Tillie had both breasts removed, and some years later she lost a kidney to cancer. She says, "It helps to say, 'I am a survivor.' For three years, through the American Cancer Society, she visited women in hospitals suffering from breast cancer. Tillie could tell a woman about her own experiences and had answers for some of their questions.

On Memorial Day 1995, Tillie's son, Phil Jr., drove his mother and father to Bethesda, Maryland, where Tillie and Phil had been married. They found the little Catholic church, now brick, and a handsome young priest wearing shorts invited them in. He found the records of their marriage, put his marriage raiments on, and after 50 years, in their casual clothes and with their only son, Phil, Jr., present, renewed their wedding vows.

A SOUTH PACIFIC SCRAPBOOK: JESSIE VIRGINIA BOLING RIDGEWAY

as told to

Virginia Ridgeway McCombs

This has been a nostalgic journey back in time. I've often looked at pictures and other memorabilia of the war years and, of course, our wedding anniversary always takes us back, but this is the first time I've made an effort to put the events in sequence. Things happened so quickly during the war years, and yet frequently time seemed to stand still. There was either a great deal of activity, or we were waiting for what came next.

Our generation believed it was our duty to serve; this was something we owed our country. As the political structure of Europe deteriorated in 1940 and war seemed imminent, we prepared to enter the work force.

In June 1940, I graduated from the School of Nursing at Washington University in St. Louis. After graduation I worked one year at the St. Louis Children's Hospital; pediatrics was my specialty. My plan was to work one year there.

During the summer I worked in St. Louis, I interviewed to be a United Airlines stewardess and at the same time applied to the Navy Nurse Corps Reserve through the Red Cross. My orders from the Navy Reserve and my acceptance from the airline came the same day. At the time I was at home in Terre Haute, Indiana. Once my orders came from the Navy, there was really no choice to make. I had a skill that was needed now that we were at war. Most young people my age felt the same way. Of course, a quest for adventure could have entered into my decision.

Thirteen days after Pearl Harbor I had my physical, and on March 2, 1942, I reported to Great Lakes Naval Station, Great Lakes, Illinois. I was now a member of the Nurse Corps, U.S. Naval Reserve. Our lives suddenly became regulated, both on and off the base. Our uniforms were prescribed, even to the height of the heels

177

Virginia and Ridge Ridgeway

on our shoes, and no jewelry except watches could be worn. Naval regulations were equally specific concerning our professional and social lives. Professionally we were regulated by the Navy's standard routines and also the Navy Nurse Corps rules. Although we were not officially officers, we were subject to their code. The number one rule was no socializing with enlisted personnel. There were orientation sessions on these rules as well as those relating to the war, especially the rule "loose lips sink ships." Our travel was restricted to within 75 miles of the base.

Being in the service meant learning to drill, and I still have a soft place in my heart for the Marine sergeant who tried to teach us. We must have become somewhat proficient because we were to have been included as part of an honor guard when President and Mrs. Roosevelt came to Great Lakes. Unfortunately heavy rains canceled our appearance. The Navy also required gas mask drills, training we fortunately never used.

Our pay was $70 per month plus subsistence, which the Navy

valued at $690 a year. Our quarters were cottages. As more nurses arrived, our single beds were replaced with bunk beds, and we had roommates. We had our own dining room, similar to the officers' mess.

I was assigned to a contagious disease ward. I assume this was because of my emphasis in pediatrics during nursing school. My patients were all young men in various stages of the mumps, from those flat on their backs to those sitting out their contagion for a boring two weeks. The wards were huge, and I think I shall never forget my first view of them. Our nursing duties were fairly routine. We were the charge nurses with corpsmen assisting. These were well-trained young men who would not only work in the Naval hospitals but also be assigned to various ships in the fleet as well as hospital ships. They were taught all of the nursing as well as emergency skills. Our patients were very young men, sick and away from home, a good combination for homesickness. We nurses became surrogate mothers, sisters, and girlfriends. As a result, we often had letters, poems, and, most frequently, sketches given to us.

This was where I tried for the first—and last—time to be "salty." The ward became very noisy, and I came out of the nurses' station, stood at the door, and said in my loudest Navy voice, "All right men, knock it off!" Little did I know the corpsmen had just passed out bedpans.

We had monthly inspection and also unannounced "white glove" inspections of our wards. We had to keep them shipshape—woodwork and furnishings polished, supply rooms cleaned, floors scrubbed with steel wool, waxed, and buffed. The horror of getting a bad inspection was very real, and great the celebration when the ordeal was over.

Our duty uniforms were the standard nurse's whites, all very heavily starched, with caps sporting Navy gold braid. We had summer white dress uniforms with white hose and shoes (in Navy parlance these were called fatigues), and Navy blue wool with black hose and shoes for winter. Also, we had heavy Navy blue capes, sweaters to wear on duty, and top coats, all of which we received just before leaving for the South Pacific! We thought our uniforms were pretty neat and didn't mind wearing them. I know we thought our uniforms were much better looking than those of the Army Nurse Corps. "Civvies" could be worn when not on duty.

Great Lakes Naval Station was a great place to be as far as recreation was concerned. We not only had access to base facilities, such as tennis courts, bowling alleys, bicycles, and entertainment by U.S.O. troops, but we also benefitted from the nearness of Lake Michigan and Chicago. One of my lasting memories is church on Sunday with a huge choir, all the men and women in uniform, singing the Navy Hymn.

In October of 1942 several of us, including two of my good friends, were ordered to San Francisco. We made more friends on our train trip to the coast as most of the passengers were military personnel heading west for a similar purpose. Our excitement was mixed with nervousness when we wondered about our next assignment.

My two good friends and I stayed at the Sir Francis Drake Hotel in San Francisco. As at Great Lakes, we were restricted to no travel beyond 75 miles. We were required to report to the Navy every three days.

We saw the sights of the city, were given tickets to the ballet and theater, and, because we were among the first nurses to go overseas, we were interviewed on an Office of War Information radio program.

Fortunately, I had second cousins in San Francisco and was able to spend time with them in their homes. Being with relatives on Thanksgiving helped dispel the homesickness that would creep in once in a while. I had a visit from my beloved Navy uncle from San Diego. The first thing he did after our meeting at the train station was to take me to have my shoes shined up to Navy standards. This was the same uncle who, in answering a complaint from me about the Navy, replied in a letter, "Did the Navy invite *you* to join?"

We sailed on November 30th aboard the *USS Polk*, which was quite an experience for someone whose only boating experience had been in row boats on Indiana lakes. It didn't take us long to get into the ship's routine and learn the new shipboard vocabulary, such as "port," "starboard," "the smoking light is out," and "ladder," not stairs. We 50 nurses also had sessions regarding our eventual destinations and more Navy rules and regulations. We practiced routine boat drills and had an occasional alert. Ships sailing back to the U.S. picked up our mail, all of which was censored and stamped "unknown date, unknown destination."

We spent our days on ship walking and exercising on deck, jumping rope, watching the flying fish, playing bridge, making new friends, and talking, talking, talking, talking. We also had "happy hours" with entertainment by shipmates, both officers and enlisted men. There was a daily news bulletin, thanks to the ship's radio, a calendar of events of the day, and a review of the previous happy hour. Since we traveled in a convoy, ship watching was another pastime. We observed airplanes taking off from accompanying ships and listened as various ships (including ours) checked gun batteries. All of these diversions helped to dispel our apprehension regarding what lay ahead.

Midway to our destination we nurses were told that half of us would go to New Zealand, and the other half would go to a destination farther north. We three from Great Lakes volunteered to go north. That resulted in even more lecture sessions to prepare us for tropical living and for working in a war zone.

The first stop we made was New Caledonia, which was a supply depot for the South Pacific fleet. We who were to go north to Project Roses were temporarily stationed at the Naval hospital to await transportation. Once again we found new experiences. A tropical island!! We awaited transportation, but spent most of our time at the beach.

New Caledonia was fleet supply for the area, and many ships were in dock at this time. We were the first female Navy personnel in the South Pacific, so consequently each ship requested that some of our group come to breakfast, lunch, or dinner each day. The command posted sign-up slips in our quarters, and, of course, we were thrilled to go. The sign-up sheets stated, "Captain So and So of the ...... requests the pleasure of your company...." We went aboard cruisers, battleships, destroyers, and aircraft carriers. There were many, many lonesome men eager to see women from stateside and hear any news from home. Christmas 1942 was one I'm sure none of us will ever forget. Christmas Eve we went to a dance followed by my first Roman Catholic Mass.

New Caledonia was exciting, but after two weeks of waiting and traveling we were ready to be settled. Orders and transportation came December 28 for us to travel to Efate, New Hebrides. Our transportation was the hospital ship *Comfort*. Three days later we arrived at our destination.

Efate was one of two islands in the New Hebrides on which the U.S. had bases. The Navy had been on the island since May 2, 1942, and the first hospital was set up in tents. The medical unit later moved to the French hospital on the island while the Seabees built roads and hospital base #2 know as Roses. It had a full staff of doctors and surgeons along with specialists, including psychiatrists and dentists. The purpose of the base was to care for the Guadalcanal casualties who were flown in by planes that then took fuel and supplies back to the war zone. The Japanese tried to destroy the supply line from New Caledonia to Guadalcanal and islands farther north.

We landed at the small port of Vila, where natives in their dugout canoes greeted us. When we got to our quarters, we were again warmly greeted by smiling native girls offering large bouquets of flowers. They serenaded us with "You Are My Sunshine," "God Bless America," "She'll Be Coming Around the Mountain," and "I'm Happy When You're Happy." Missionaries had educated these young women years before and had taught them to wear muumuus. Imagine my delight in seeing one of the native workers reading *Pride and Prejudice* while on his lunch break! The natives lived on their own island, Mele, in the harbor and came to work each day in their dugout canoes. Word of our arrival got around, and soon we were not only seeing the male patients, corpsmen, and doctors, but also a variety of Army and Marine officers as well.

Our hospital was built on a coconut plantation. It was constructed of Quonset huts all connected with covered walkways. Sandbags surrounded the surgical rooms. Our nurses quarters also were Quonset huts, complete with indoor plumbing, hospital type beds with much needed mosquito netting, individual tables and chairs, and maid service. Our quarters were at one end of the compound with the officers' quarters at the other and enlisted men to one side. We had a guard on duty. We ate our meals at the officers' mess.

The officers' club was the center of our social life. A screened porch had card tables where there were always bridge games in progress, a slightly out-of-tune piano, and a phonograph with a few records. Outside stood a volleyball court. The Seabees constructed this all in a few months. Although this was a war zone, the Navy provided us many comforts.

On January 20 we finally received our rank of Ensign and an increase in pay. Now we were officially officers in the United States Navy Nurse Corps. I don't remember a grand celebration, only a feeling that it was about time.

Work was much the same here as stateside. Again we had inspections once a month. The tropics created their own set of housekeeping problems—humidity, mold, and insects. We were assigned to wards: I rotated among postoperative, surgical, and medical wards. I believe my favorite ward was a surgical ward of patients who had suffered facial, nose, and throat wounds. We worked eight to ten hour shifts. By the time we got to Efate, the battle of Guadalcanal was winding down, and the war was moving north. In spite of this, we were kept busy with casualties. Not only did these men have battle wounds, but malaria was rampant. Malaria was no respecter of persons—corpsmen, nurses, and doctors also fell victim to it. The work was hard and at times could also be boring. We overcame boredom by remembering from whence the patients had come. In more practical ways we broke the routine by doing things such as making fudge for the patients using Bunsen burners and cans from the galley.

My letters home read like a copy of the social news along with a shopping list. Although the Navy had certainly anticipated and taken care of our creature comforts as none of the other services could, the ship's store was not prepared for women on board. We had been warned and brought supplies of sanitary pads, white shoe polish, and hairnets, but not enough for a year. These items were always on the shopping lists home, and they were later available in the ship's store.

My first shopping list included one dozen diapers. What for? I cannot remember. Later I requested more uniform shoes because the coral roads and paths really cut up the soles of our shoes. Our mail was heavily censored; my first few letters attest to that as the censor excised not only words but entire sentences. We soon found out what was acceptable, and the Navy sent out our mail regardless of its condition. When we first arrived in early 1943, the command limited letters home to two per week. As more convoys successfully arrived, the Navy relaxed the number restriction but not the censorship. As far as the mail we received was concerned, it was often feast or famine. We received Christmas cards at Easter time.

The island of Efate was unique in that it was governed by a condominium, a combination of French and English rule. The influence of each was evident. Both governments were most cordial to us, as were those families who remained on the island. We had tea in their homes, played tennis on their courts, and spent many leisure hours walking to an orphanage run by Catholic nuns. Air alerts did not occur too often after we arrived on Efate, but we did have them. An occasional Japanese plane would honor us with a "fly over."

As supply ships came in, the most coveted items were new or different movies, ice cream, and, most of all, mail. Our movie theater was a screen and benches under coca palms. The theater also served as our church, weather permitting, and we had both Protestant and Catholic chaplains. But in spite of all of our options, we spent our most important time at mail call or in letter writing.

We nurses enjoyed both work times and leisure times. After we had been in Efate a short time, we realized we needed a fatigue uniform. We had only our nurses' white work uniform, which were our dress whites. These had to be worn off base except when going to the beach or playing tennis. We designed a khaki uniform—skirt and blouse—that was casual but also very tailored in the military fashion. Four of us modeled our uniforms for a photograph that was sent to the Navy department, but our efforts were to no avail; our summer whites continued to be our fatigues. We did have a good idea and a great picture.

Days were long in the Southern Hemisphere. Despite our long workdays, we had lots of daylight left for leisure activities. We passed the hours with letter writing, playing tennis, and taking walks in the beautiful countryside. We also enjoyed many beach parties, always with men carrying side arms. After a certain period of time, we had a jeep at our disposal. Even I drove one! We drove to the town of Vila and to the orphanage. We always ventured on any excursion in groups of two or more, and curfew was usually at 11 p.m. Occasionally curfew would be 9 p.m., but we never knew why. Dating was usually a movie (if a supply ship had been in), socializing at the officers' club, an occasional trip to town to dinner at a restaurant, and daytime dates of tennis, jeep rides, and picnics.

I met my husband, Elmer "Ridge" Ridgeway, at Roses. He was one of the youngest doctors and also one of the few bachelors at the base. He had been in his residency in OB-GYN at Touro Infirmary in New Orleans when he volunteered for the Navy. We had plenty of time to get acquainted since talking was a major pastime. Although we started being interested in one another about a month after my arrival, I didn't want to hear another proposal from a lonesome, eligible man. I continued to socialize and play tennis with other doctors. I did not mention Ridge in letters home until February.

By spring of 1943 Ridge and I were engaged. My first engagement ring was a gold cigar band received shortly before I received orders on May 27 for my new duty station in New Zealand. My second was a native-made ring of mother of pearl and abalone shell. Ridge was anticipating orders stateside. Departure for New Zealand was a tearful affair. Eight of our original group and one doctor sick with malaria departed on a mine sweeper for Auckland on June 11. The seasons were changing—the day was very gray, cold, and the sea rough. We much appreciated our top coats and blue wool dress uniforms. For the first and only time many of us were seasick. The captain suggested we stand forward on deck against a bulkhead. Unfortunately, the bulkhead was the site of the galley exhaust that only made things worse.

We knew winter was on the way when we arrived in Auckland the next day. The further south we sailed, the colder and rainier it became. Our orders were to Mob #4, a naval hospital built by Seabees. The Navy had not finished construction of our nurses' quarters, so they housed us in a hotel.

In Auckland we discovered what war was like in the civilian world. This country had been at war four years, and the Japanese had cut off naval supply lines. Fuel was in short supply, and nonessential public buildings were no longer heated. Store shelves were virtually empty, and the government rationed goods.

Four of us stayed in a third-floor room of the Hotel Stonehurst. Our only heat was a small fireplace that burned briquettes. We felt ourselves very lucky to have our own bathroom that, by the way, was the only entrance to our room. One of the first things we noticed in the bathroom was a prominently placed sign that stated:

TOILET PAPER
Is almost unprocurable.
Please economize in this matter
very strictly.
Otherwise there will be none.
If guests would provide their own
It would be greatly appreciated.

We followed the latter suggestion thanks to the Navy.

Being cold was always on our minds, and keeping warm occupied a lot of time and effort. Our days started with a cup of the darkest, strongest tea ever. The hotel staff carried it up three flights of stairs and served it to us in bed. Oh how we hated getting up in the morning in those cold rooms! We lived in that hotel for two weeks while the Navy finished our quarters, which were luxurious compared to the Hotel Stonehurst. We had baths, laundry facilities, etc. As more of our "Roses" were transferred south, we were housed on the third floor of Navy quarters, which we referred to as the "penthouse." We were once again a close-knit group.

The hospital work was much the same as it had been on Efate. Our wounded patients were more often than not sent stateside. Once again the Navy assigned me to a medical ward with many patients suffering from malaria. We also relieved the nurses who had recurring bouts of malaria.

Working ten-hour shifts still gave us time to explore the city once the weather became better. Until then our exploring consisted of going downtown to a movie. Our moods were rather in tune with the weather. Once the sun started to shine and the flowers to bloom, they took a different tack. We had to adjust to cars driving on the left side of the road, reversed water faucets and light fixtures, and most importantly the money exchange. We found the local people most gracious, frequently inviting us to their homes for tea.

Letter writing still consumed a great part of our time. Mail from home continued to be a sometime thing, and we could go as long as two months without a package or letter. When we first arrived in New Zealand, the cancellation on outgoing mail was stamped, "Japs Now Look Sick." Of course, the Navy still censored the mail, but the only word cut out of all the letters I sent home from New Zealand was "Maori," which I used to describe a native-carved souvenir. One of our assignments in quarters was telephone duty, which on a quiet night was a good time to catch up on our correspondence. Within a short period of time all of the nurses from Roses rotated to New Zealand. Our communication to Efate proved easy as there were frequent trips between the islands.

Eleanor Roosevelt inspected the Naval hospital in Auckland, and once again we were subjected to drill as nurses joined the honor guard. She also inspected our nurses' quarters; this created a little more activity than our monthly inspection.

While at Roses I had applied for a discharge from the Navy to be married, and I received discharge orders on September 17. Females could not be married and stay in the Navy. My orders were interesting in that the discharge is "honorable" with an aside, "for her own convenience."

My transportation home was aboard the *New Amsterdam*. It was still on its maiden voyage having just been commissioned when the Nazis started bombing Rotterdam. She had been used as a troop ship and a floating prison camp (Nazi prisoners of war were in her hold) without returning to home port. Despite the wear and tear, she was still an elegant ship. Our accommodations were considerably better than on the *USS Polk*, and our shipmates represented quite a mix. There were at least eight nationalities aboard: women and children (families of missionaries); people who had lived abroad for years; survivors from torpedoed merchant marine ships; and military personnel going stateside for the first time since Pearl Harbor. My cabinmate was an English journalist.

The trip passed uneventfully until our arrival in San Francisco. We had just crossed under the Golden Gate Bridge, and what a thrill that was, when we hit a sand bar. The ship rolled to one side, greatly disturbing those still at breakfast. Their food ended up all over the floor, and their chairs slid to another table. Oh the thrill of being in the United States again! I arrived on my birthday, October

17, 1943.

My orders from San Francisco to Indiana were not processed for three weeks. I said my good-byes to my very good friends and shipmates, all of whom were either going home or off to future assignments. I arrived home in Terre Haute, Indiana, in early November. Ridge arrived in the states just before Thanksgiving. We were married on December 10, and shortly thereafter we reported to Norfolk, Virginia, for his next tour of duty. I then began my education as a civilian in wartime, but that is another story.

AUTHOR'S NOTE, by Virginia Ridgeway McCombs:

As children, my sister and I grew up looking at pictures of our parents, Virginia Boling and Elmer Ridgeway, on a South Pacific island during World War II. A particular favorite of mine was a photograph of the two of them, hugging, on a windswept beach, my dashing father with his Navy hat cocked at a jaunty angle and my beautiful mother at his side. We heard stories of their South Pacific romance and the war years in general; what baby boomer did not hear such stories or see them immortalized time and again on film? But the enormity of the World War II experience largely escaped me until many years later after I had children of my own. I chanced to read Anton Myrer's novel, The Last Convertible. Myrer's story of a group of young friends caught up in the rising storm of World War II was an epiphany for me, and my parents' youthfulness and idealistic devotion to duty became clear through the characters of the book. I now have a deepening appreciation for that generation of young people. They were born during a period of national prosperity, matured during the hardship of the Great Depression, defeated forces of undeniable evil during World War II, and then helped build the United States into a formidable economic, diplomatic, and military power in the postwar years.

Consequently, when my mother asked me to help her record her war experiences for this book, I was delighted to do so as an historian and especially as a daughter. Because my Grandmother Boling saved all of her daughter's letters, they serve as the basis of this story which is told in my mother's own words.

OF LIFE AND LAND
1982

For without life, there is no value;
And without value, there is no glory;
And without glory, there is no God;
For God is life;
And God is glory.

by *Dr. Hanna A. Saadah*
(From *The Loves and lamentations of a Life Watcher*)

REQUIEM FOR JOAN

Like her banner, bold, unfurled.
The soul of Joan adorns the stake.
Then lit, the fiery smoke upcurled
And she became a torch to make
Bright our soul's lost womanhood:
She chooses God before the good.

She chooses heart instead of mind.
She chooses truth and shuns all lies.
With love so deep in her enshrined
When love breaks forth she fairly dies.
Then at Christ's feet is nobly laid
The blazing soul of Joan the Maid.

Dr. Stan Cosby

NOW

THE CLOUDS LOOK DARK IN TIMES LIKE THIS—THE
    DAYS ARE BLACK
AS NIGHT—MISERY AND PAIN THE WORLD MUST
    FACE—BLOODY,
HORRID, DEATHLY SIGHTS—EACH FACE YOU SEE POR-
    TRAYS THE
TIMES—EXPRESSIONS BLACK AS PITCH—SEEING FAR
    AWAY CROSS
WATERS BOLD—THROUGH JUNGLES, FOX-HOLES, A
    MUDDY DITCH—
WHY LOOK SO BLACK, YOU'RE SAFE, YOU'RE SAFE—
    YOUR BROWS ARE
KNITTED LOW—EACH SHOT THAT'S FIRED, EACH BOMB
    THAT'S
DROPPED—PIERCES DEEP INTO YOUR SOUL—THE
    SUFFERING OF
THE WORLD TODAY—SPREADS OVER THE UNIVERSE—
    EACH NIGHT A
MILLION PRAYERS ARE SAID—TO END THIS
    WRETCHED CURSE—
BEHIND EACH CLOUD WE HOPE TO SEE—A SKY THAT'S
    BLUE AND
BRIGHT—NO MORE MISERY, NO MORE PAIN—NO MORE
    DEATHLY SIGHTS

by *Bernardine Buyez Sydner*

IN GOD I TRUST

by

Susan M. Bickford

It was late winter, 1940. I was young and happy-go-lucky. I worked at St. Ann's Hospital in Chicago along with 20 other girls. We boarded in a dormitory there. Hitler was running rampant in Europe, and one day I could hear the girls chatting away. They all believed, "No one would dare attack America."

I was troubled because I sensed arrogance and haughtiness in their attitude. Finally I jumped into the conversation and said, "Don't be too sure that America won't be touched." All hell broke loose. I was accused of being a Communist and a traitor. And the word soon got around that I was the enemy.

That was ironic since I felt that the real enemy was counting on this kind of American apathy. I felt concerned that our country was asleep at the wheel. December 7, 1941, confirmed for the whole world the stark, cold reality that, yes, even America was vulnerable to a surprise attack.

I was born and have lived in America all my life, and I would gladly lay down my life to protect her. Our country fought a costly war. Of course, it cost our country money and personal comforts. But much more valuable and tragic was the number of people, young and old, who lost their lives. Money and personal comfort were easily recovered after the war, but those human lives established a debt that we cannot repay.

I joined the United States Marine Corps in early 1944. My brother was in the Army and was very upset with me. But I was happy in the Marines. I served as a mail clerk in Quartermaster Battalion at Camp Lejeune, North Carolina. I enjoyed my work, although there was a sad side to my daily tasks. Some of the mail I handled were bundles of possessions that had to be returned to the families who had lost loved ones killed in action.

Today America is strong in some areas, weak in others. We must not forsake or take for granted the Creator and His Word, the

Bible, and the principles our forefathers honored. They founded this nation the way they did because they believed that God and His principles would keep safe and guide America well. With our faith consistent with God's word and leading, we cannot fail. If we walk away from these foundations, we will once again pay dearly. In God I trust.

BE STILL AND KNOW

"Be still and know that I am God."
 Throughout this earth where loved ones trod
My presence can no more be hid,
 Than can the world of space be rid
Than can the sun refuse to shine,
 Even tho' sometimes a cloud behind,
Can I refuse a plea of thine.
 Although it tarries—it will come,
In Jesus name it shall be done.

That I am God be still and know
 Where rain doth fall and wind doth blow,
Where mountain peaks stand tall and bare,
 In desert stillness—I am there
And thy petition sent to me
 Can answered be across the sea.
Thy Heavenly Father cares for thee
 And in my care are all of thine
For they are yours and you are mine.

by *Lela N. Turner*

THE STORY
OF NURSE DORA J. STOHL

as told to
Rosemary Eckroat Bachle

When Dora J. Stohl's tall, willowy body uncurled from the heli-copter that landed her at the Mobile Army Surgical Hospital Unit 8055 in Korea, the exact location of the "4077" Mash unit, she was as excited as ever to once again serve her country in time of war. Korea was just one of her three war experiences in the Army Nurse Corps. The conditions in Korea, long hours of intense work under less than ideal situations, did not surprise Dora Stohl. Before Ko-rea, there was Africa and Italy in World War II.

Imagine having a thousand-bed hospital consisting of tents out-side of Constantine, North Africa, where camel caravans passed by each morning and evening. Imagine temperatures so hot that thermometers could not function properly. Imagine living in a tent infested with insects while coping with water shortages, 18-hour days, and bad-tasting food. Picture air raid sirens blaring through the night followed by a bomb that sank 17 U.S. ships in the harbor at Bari, Italy. All were routine experiences for Army nurses.

Dora was born January 29, 1918, in Dresser, Wisconsin, and grew up in Minneapolis, Minnesota, a sheltered only child. She was influenced by her mother to become a nurse. Dora received her five-year Nursing Education degree from the University of Min-nesota. When the Japanese bombed Pearl Harbor December 7, 1941, she, like many of the young women in those days, was deter-mined to use her talents for her country. She heard of the need for nurses in the "26th General Hospital," organized and staffed by the University of Minnesota. She went on active duty in February 1942 and was promptly sent to Fort Sill in Lawton, Oklahoma.

Lieutenant Colonel Dora J. Stohl tells her story:

We landed in Fort Sill, Lawton, Oklahoma, on a Sunday after-noon in early February of 1942. I remember clearly. We trans-ferred from the train to a bus to take us to the Cantonment Hospi-

Dora J. Stohl (center) and friends the day after the bombing of Bari, Italy.

tal, and three nurses, supposed to be our sponsors, stood with arms folded on the steps of the hospital. They didn't come running to the bus to meet us. They watched as all 40 of us struggled off the bus, claimed our luggage, and started wandering up the path. And we were not met with greetings, "Welcome to Fort Sill," but "What are these GD Yanks doing down here?" That started our Army career for nine months at Fort Sill. We fought the Civil War and re-fought the Civil War the whole nine months.

We had classes on how to wear the uniform and certain policies of the Army and close order drill. Our uniforms were white, but our off-duty uniforms were navy blue wool. In the summer we had white seersucker and a field uniform, and then a blue seersucker, kind of a fatigue uniform, and the eternal white cap, white hose, and shoes. We did have some time on the wards working with patients to learn regulations, policies, and how to function as Army nurses.

Because I had my degree in nursing and my classmate Mary Hodgin had graduated with the baccalaureate in science and a major in nursing education, several enlisted men from the state of New York were assigned to us as corpsmen. So we had some allies in the Civil War fights. Four nurses were appointed to teach them patient-care techniques they would have to use on the wards. So most of the summer Mary and I were teaching.

They told us that when we left the U.S. we would be out of the country for five years and to plan accordingly. At that time Kotex was one big problem that immediately came to mind. One of the interesting anecdotes, which some may enjoy but which may shock others (remember that your active nurses in those days were young women and you have that young woman's affliction every month) was figuring out what in the world we were going to do. Obviously, a five-year supply was out of the question. Then word got around that we could use Birdseye diapers and wash them out. And then, some wit said, drape them over any nearby bush. So we invaded Lawton, Oklahoma, and bought out their Birdseye diapers. They really didn't have any left. I don't know what the babies in Lawton, Oklahoma, did then.

We were allowed only one suitcase, so they taught us how to roll our clothes in a bedroll tight enough to fit in train baggage cars. We had to get our clothing organized. Choosing was painful. Some of us had Kotex, and we stuck those in shoes and the diapers were easy enough. But we could not roll those bedrolls. We had everything but the kitchen sink in them. So they sent the enlisted men in to help. What was humorous was when they got to our shoes the Kotex kept falling out. So this becomes quite a production. We laughed a lot about that. The doctors found out about it, and they immediately dubbed us "the Birdseye Corps." We carried that title from then on.

When it was time to leave Fort Sill in September of '42 to strike out overseas, they had a dry run for us. They say "bug out," and you're supposed to get packed and get out waiting for transportation. We had a little advance notice, so we were ready, thinking this was going to be a dry run. So we cheated a little bit. We decided we had to eat. We were always eating, so we raided the mess hall and got some cold pork chops and a salad. We stood and ate that cold stuff at midnight, and there weren't any garbage cans, so we hid the bones behind the door. It's awful to think of now, but this was our dry run.

Now, a few days later, we had the real Mccoy, and that night we behaved ourselves. We got out of there in good order and got on our troop train. We'd been there nine months, remember, fighting the Civil War the whole time. We were ready to leave Fort Sill and go out and fight the real war. So when we got on the train, we were a jubilant group. We were on our way to fight the war. We got to Chickasha, Oklahoma, and got sidetracked. And as we called them in the Army later, "latrine rumors" started flying through the train that we would "set up" here, and that's where we were going to spend the rest of the war. We were ready to—I don't know what we would or could have done, but we got "unsidetracked" and headed east. They never tell us where we're going or what we're doing. They certainly wouldn't give anyone as lowly as us any information.

We headed to Camp Kilmer where we spent five days. Our chief nurse told us to go to the PX (Post Exchange) and buy slacks. Women weren't wearing slacks much at this point in time, and Nylon was not available. Well, as tall as I am, this was a problem. I managed to get one heavy, wool pair and a lighter, cotton pair of navy blue.

At the end of five days we boarded a ship (the *Mariposa*) and headed out. One day we went one direction and the next day another. We had an escort with us. The third morning we looked out and there were no ships around us. We were all by ourselves on that big Atlantic ocean still going one way, then another. We got up into the North Sea, and it got very rough and this is October now, and the North Sea in October is no place to be.

We found out we were in the English Channel. They told us not to undress that night because we would be in mined waters, and we might have to abandon ship. They gave us a musette bag and told us to put our emergency rations and other emergency equipment in it. What to take? Well, it wasn't difficult at all. We abandoned the emergency rations and put in our silk hose and our perfume, naturally, and that's what was in our musette bag. If we'd ever had to abandon ship, we would have the important things. We had rationing already, and so we couldn't get this type of thing. We survived that. We didn't have to abandon ship, thank goodness. We finally arrived in Liverpool sometime in October of 1942. In Liverpool we found out what lorries meant, these great big English trucks. They

loaded us into them under blackout conditions. We'd never experienced blackout before, so this was very eerie and exciting because
here we were in a foreign country. We knew England had been
bombed with B Bombs, all kinds of nasty things going over England
by the time we got there. And, so, we are finally in our war, and
this was pretty impressive for a bunch of youngsters. We rode
most of the night getting down to Birmingham, England, where we
stayed for three months. The English say Bra-maa-gen, not Birmingham. They mumble everything, tight upper lip.

We lived in row houses that England is famous for with two
rooms upstairs (the hot water tank was upstairs), one big room and
a kitchen downstairs, and no heat. We had two nurses to each
room, even in the kitchen. We were beastly cold. There was a tiny
little fireplace way over in a corner. We were not used to that after
central heating. So for three months, we did suffer, and some of us
got respiratory infections bordering on pneumonia as a result of the
chilled and clammy walls. England in November, December, and
January is gray most of the time and cloudy and rainy.

We had folding cots with newspaper between the sheets, if we
could get newspaper. Remember, this was a war, so England didn't
have newspaper. Their daily paper was the pub where they drank
their ale at the end of the day. We put more blankets underneath us
to keep the cold air coming up from the floor. You think you are
never going to survive this, but you do.

One thing did help; we found a pub nearby, and in the evening
from eight o'clock until ten o'clock, we drank spirits and we'd found
some enlisted men. Now, this was forbidden in the Army in '42 and
'43. Officers did not even look at the enlisted men, but that made it
good, challenging fun. The fellow I was paired off with—we didn't
say dating—was a tall baker, so he provided us with food from the
kitchen whenever he could get it. That helped. They had good
cheese from Australia, then he would provide the bread, so we
toasted cheese sandwiches in those little fireplaces. Makeshift, but
when we did something we shouldn't be doing, it was always fun.

We weren't working. We were what is called "staging." We
had road marches and some close order drill in the morning, but
then we were on our own. It was miserable sitting around in cold
rooms, so we'd go out and explore the neighborhood. One of the

things we had to do was get coal and sticks for the fireplace so we wouldn't freeze to death. We'd do anything to keep warm. So we found a coal yard, and this is amusing when I think back on it now, because one of our duties was to keep our nails polished, and so we would dig under this coal with our fingers, and fish two or three hunks of coal out for our fireplace. Then if we could find any twigs or wood, we'd get that too. It looked strange to see a well-manicured female out there picking up hunks of coal.

In the evenings we found refuge in the "pubs." The pubs are public houses where the British gathered to exchange news of the day. They would have their ale and spirits and sit around and talk with some dignity. When the Americans came in, they wouldn't settle for this. They had to mingle and sing. Well, the British looked at as down their noses, and then they started joining us. Traditionally, they never did this. They didn't have that kind of thing in their pubs, but they may now after the Yanks, as we were called, have been there.

They started inviting us to their homes. There was a shopkeeper, a dear couple that invited us one night for some refreshment. It was a special day November 11, Remembrance Day they called it, which we call Armistice Day. Now the British were rigidly rationed on everything. Sugar was one of the things they cherished for their tea and could not get, so we would always take sugar when we were invited to tea.

The English don't celebrate Thanksgiving, but a gracious lady invited some of us into her lovely Manor home. She was used to a lot of hired help. They had just one person left. They were people of means, but they had to undergo rationing just like everyone. At the time I know I was thinking, as young and foolish as I was, "I can't see any Americans taking this."

At the end of January 1943, we learned we were waiting for an invasion to take place in North Africa. A British cruise ship, the *Stratnaver*, converted to a troop ship for wartime, took us from England to Oran, North Africa.

We spent about six weeks in tents on so-called Goat Hill at Asi Amour, outside Oran, and again just staging, not working, and we lived in ward tents with about 20 nurses to a tent, sitting on the edge of a desert, isolated, in a wheat field. An Arab camel caravan went by each morning and returned in the evening to a little town where they purchased their wares in the open market. The nights were bad.

One night while doing road marching and close order drill just to keep busy, we had a call from a unit up the road from us. They said they'd heard the nurses were there and would we like to come to a birthday party with food and dancing. So sure, I wanted to go. They came with transportation, and we went to their unit for this party.

At the end of the evening, four of us, two couples, sat at a table, with four empty bottles of champagne. I'd never had champagne before. I don't know who drank all that champagne, but nobody was drunk! We danced and sang and ate. There was a big birthday cake decorated with roses and whipped cream writing on it. We had been severely rationed on anything sweet. Since we arrived in Africa, we hadn't seen anything fresh at all. We ate very dull C rations. We thanked them and said how wonderful it was to get something sweet and asked how in the world they got it decorated. They said the cooks baked it and the writing was shaving cream. We blamed our heads the next day on the shaving cream and not the champagne. I remember leaving the unit that night. We went in armored Jeeps with anti-aircraft guns sitting on them. The North African night was beautifully clear. There was a crescent moon with a star at the corner. You don't see that star in the east too often except around Christmas time here. I remember that clearly so I wasn't drunk.

The next morning we were expected at chow. When I woke up, oh, my head! It was huge. I couldn't move. Everything rocked, rolled, and shook. I thought, "What in the world is wrong with me?" Then I heard moans all around me, one by one. Nobody made it to chow that morning. And the fellows from the night before called our unit to check on us. There was only one phone. Unfortunately, it was in the headquarters building. Later we learned our officers discovered our escapade through the phone call. They said some nurses were seen fraternizing with the enlisted personnel. No names were mentioned, but they decided they had to do something about that.

When we finally set up our all-tent hospital unit outside

Constantine, North Africa, the officers were in tents to one side with the enlisted men behind them in tents. The nurses' tents, some distance away, were bordered by white rocks that went into never, never land. We were not to cross the line at all. Quite a to-do was made of that because it looked so foolish for adults to be treated this way.

Our hospital established quite a reputation because it was a 1,000-bed hospital in tents. That had never been done before nor has it been done since. We expanded to 1,500 beds in tents, and I heard the top census was 1,550 patients. Our accolades were extensive to the type of work done by our surgeons and the staff. It was remarkable that we had so low a mortality rate, and it showed the medical care and mercy given. The front was east of us. Our troops, the Allied Forces, were running Rommel out of North Africa, and our casualties came from that fighting. We were acting as an evacuation hospital, rather then a general hospital, because we had so many patients for whom we'd do what we could and then evacuate them. A general hospital usually can hold patients longer, but not under these conditions. Rations were poor, and there was no air conditioning. It was blistering hot during the day. The engineers poured concrete floors and then wet them down to help keep the patients cool. They would lay on the floor under their beds with the mosquito net down on them. Checking pulses every four hours was a routine job. If you didn't see a patient on the bed, there would be an arm come up from underneath. Taking a temperature in the heat was a real challenge. We'd cool the thermometer in alcohol and then pop them in real fast before they had time to rise. Hypodermic procedure was interesting. We used C ration containers to put fuel in. We would light this and melt tablets in a hypo, syringe, put it over a little flame, then expel the amount that was needed.

Nursing was never like that in the textbooks. We took antimalarial pills, Atabrine, and we were all yellow from that. None of us got malaria, but we did get dysentery. Even though we had chlorinated water, dust and germs were flying around. So we frequently were as sick as our patients and had to make a run to the latrine, which would be two or three blocks from the ward, and then come back and take care of patients. Quite a challenge!

After leaving our nine-month sojourn in Constantine, North Africa, we set up our hospital in Bari, Italy. The hospital had been built by Mussolini for his military patients. It was operated by the sisters with the high headdress, the flying nuns. When we moved in, the nuns still lived in their quarters. We thought we could move into the chapel and use it for services immediately and did.

December 2, 1943, two nights after we landed in Bari, the air raid sirens went off, and we heard a terrible bombardment. The shutters blew open, and everyone ran to the windows. We saw a big cloud of smoke and fire down towards the port. We learned later that the port was four miles from where we were. The rest of the night was quiet. The next morning we were settled in our quarters, but we had no equipment so we couldn't work. The place was so filthy we couldn't take care of ourselves, much less patients. There was grease that had to be chiseled off before we could even start to use our equipment. Our hospital could not begin operations until the X-ray equipment, beds, drugs, bandages, and other items were delivered. Our supplies were still on the *Samuel J. Tilden* in the harbor.

The next morning after the bombardment, our 26th General Hospital detachment was still trying to get accustomed to Italy. We had already seen a lot of the world. About five of us, acting like young giddy girls, decided to walk to port where the smoke was coming from. Nurses did not have cars. Just the WAC's had cars. The MPs (military police) caught up to us almost by the time we got to the port and wanted to know what we were doing there. They said, "Don't you know you are under a gas alert? Where are your gas masks?" We didn't think there was any real danger. We answered, "Back at the hospital."

They said "Well you can't go down there."

So one of our little nurses, who was pleasing to behold, blinked her big, blue eyes and said, "Oh, please, we walked all this way. Can't we go down and take pictures?" So they took us close to the port, and I have pictures of us and all the smoke. We still didn't believe the gas alert deal. We thought it strange to see people leaving with their earthly possessions piled on little carts going the opposite direction. After we had a good look and took a few pictures, the MPs loaded us in their cars and took us back to the hospital among thick columns of smoke.

It wasn't until much later that we learned the merchantman ship *John Harvey* was spewing her deadly contents, mustard gas, into the bay water. Seventeen ships were in the harbor, including the one with all our supplies. They were badly damaged, and some sank as a result of the air raid from the Luftwaffe. Some said afterward they thought that the Germans probably saw us crossing, because a hospital ship is always lighted, and that we may have led them to Bari.

A British hospital unit in Bari called for our help. They had a lot of casualties from the bombing, so many of our doctors and nurses, including me, went to help for a few days. We found out the gas alert was no joke. There were blisters, external burns, also burns in the respiratory tract. We did what we could for them. It was tragic. We treated the survivors for shock and exposure, not realizing that they had been subjected to a chemical agent. We learned that the bombs had not exploded on the ship. The ship had been damaged, and the bombs cracked and leaked out gas, spewing her deadly contents over both town and harbor and into the bay waters.

More than 1,000 military personnel and an even larger number of civilians lost their lives as a result of the air raid. The disaster at Bari, Italy, was called "The Second Pearl Harbor" and kept top secret for many months. It was hard to believe that we, Americans, were ready and willing to use mustard gas.

Thank goodness we could still laugh. One night one of the girls went on a date to a fancy place with an officer. She went into the restroom and was introduced for the first time to that extra fixture. We didn't know what to do with the extra fixture when we were first introduced to it, which was back in North Africa, French style. We thought first that it must be something to soak our clothes in because there was a plug in there. So we plugged it, then thought, no, that wasn't right because when we turned the faucet it sprayed water up and not down like the wash basin. So we experimented until some one enlightened us as to what the douche bowl was, a bidet. So here was our chum telling us all about this blue porcelain thing. Well, you guessed it. We dubbed her the '~queen of the blue porcelain douche bowl."

Army style, a Bell Chopper brought Dora Stahl to her MASH unit in Korea.

When the war in Europe was over, the doctors rotated home because of the point system. In WWII, points were allowed for the area of campaign, number of months on the line of duty, for decorations, a Purple Heart, etc. Once a soldier received the required number of points, he was rotated back to the U.S. for a 30- to 90-day duty, then he was assigned to the Pacific theater. The nurses were not rotated. They stayed on and changed the number from the 26th to the 45th General Hospital, and a new group of medical officers came in. We remained the 45th until September 1945 when the war ended in the Pacific, and the hospital was shut down.

I have been asked if I was ever frightened. I've never felt fear. I don't know why except I was young and didn't know what was ahead of me. I remember patients saying, "My God, what are you women doing up this close to the line?" In fact, in Korea we could hear small arms fire at night. That is pretty close. When we were busy doing our jobs, we didn't think of fear.

After World War II, I returned to Minneapolis General Hospital where I worked until my reserve unit was called up in June of 1951.

I served at Ft. Leonard Wood in Missouri until April of 1953 when I went to Korea.

MASH is more than just a TV show to me. It stands for Mobile Army Surgical Hospital, a place where everything is an emergency. I landed in a helicopter at hospital unit 8055 in Korea, the exact location of the "4077" MASH unit, on the 38th parallel, just like in the TV series. I was told I was to be head nurse of the post-operative ward, a new challenge for me. We lived in a tent with cots in three corners. The fourth corner was the bar with treats from home as well as drinks. The doctors and nurses had 12 hours on and 12 hours off—and no days off. I was in Korea four months during the winding down of the war.

Among my fond memories was the nurses' Korean dog "Knuffels"—Dutch for "lover boy." There were so many dogs in the area that a limit was set at one dog for the nurses and one dog for the doctors. Knuffels looked like a Husky with yellow dots over his eyes and a heavy coat of brown and black thick hair. Well, Knuffels was a Korean dog. The Koreans eat dog. We had Koreans walking guard around the compound, and we couldn't hear them but Knuffels could and the ruff on his neck would stand up. He'd utter a low growl; then we knew the guard was close by. We didn't want him landing in the boiling pot.

Lover boy would go to the club with us and, as we finished our drinks, some wits would put their half empty glass down and Knuffels would lick the sides of the glass. He got tipsy one night and almost fell off the steps.

We landed in March and it was still cold. I had packed for a 30-day leave, sort of in between clothes, and I didn't have anything warm to sleep in. So here I was in a tent with a little potbellied stove and a sleeping bag with blankets wrapped around the bag, and I was freezing. They stoked up the stove at night. The next morning when the sun came up, there were holes all over the tent roof where sparks had burned through. We didn't try that again.

We were so close to the front lines that a soldier with a less severe wound might be wounded in battle, be transported to the unit, go into the operating room, and be in a ward bed in a 45-minute period. With a less severe wound, emergency surgery and basic treatment only was given in a MASH unit, and then the men were moved out, usually within three days. We worked over 12 hours many times because we just kept working for as long as the wounded came in. The groups came in so fast it was hard to keep up with them.

I don't believe it is necessary for the nurses to be so close to the front line. We could hear the shooting close by. The whole thing was a logistics nightmare.

There wasn't much to do on our hours off but sleep, so we would go to the club, a Quonset hut, and entertain ourselves at night, much as in 4077 on TV. The tale of grisly battle wounds and highly humorous flirtations with nurses sounds about right. I have shared my story so much that, when someone asks if I'm "HOT LIPS," I say "sure," so I acquired the nickname Hot Lips. The TV series is true to the life and times of our unit, and I am especially fond of the cease fire and 24-hour countdown episode which is exactly as it happened, countdown and all, in July of 1953.

When the war ended, I was transferred to Sendai, Japan, about 250 miles north of Tokyo for the duration of the two years I had remaining. I was Educational Coordinator and assistant Chief Nurse.

I spent six months in San Antonio at Administration School after returning from Japan and went on to get my Master's Degree at the University of Minnesota. I spent four years in Denver as a Clinical Technical School teacher and did a 1961-1963 tour in Germany where I really got into administration. I was three years at Ft. Knox, Kentucky, and then an assignment to Okinawa in 1966, where I nursed patients from the Vietnam War. And finally, closing the circle, I came back to Fort Sill, Oklahoma, as Chief Nurse for the Medical Center from September 1968 to March 1970.

Author's Note:

Does that sound like a full enough life? Well, we're not through yet, for Dora was awarded the Legion of Merit for her work as Chief Nurse at Ft. Sill, Oklahoma, where she reorganized the entire nursing system to compensate for the shortage of nurses in the Army. The Legion of Merit is the Army's second highest non-combat award. So rarely do they give this award to women, the inscription on the Legion of Merit award reads "Awarded to Lt. Col. Dora J. Stohl, who distinguished

Him self for exceptionally meritorious service. "

In 1978 after 28 years of duty, Dora retired from the Army, but was asked to head up a new program in Oklahoma developed by Lloyd Rader: non-technical medical care for state welfare recipients in their own homes instead of nursing home care. She is proud that she was responsible for hiring registered nurses to teach and supervise the "providers" to care for the homebound patients.

Since her second retirement, has 77-year-old Dora slowed down? No, not at all! She makes her home in Oklahoma City, Oklahoma. She is currently in docent training at the Cowboy Hall of Fame. She gives one day to the Kirkpatrick Museum and one day goes to the Lyric Theater. Her other interests include genealogy, oil painting, and travel. I had to catch Dora in-between trips to get her story. Dora J. Stohl's life is an incredible story of a dedicated women who makes us all proud to have women like her to look up to.

Talking with Dora is like being there, and this writer is exhausted just to relate this lady's exciting and active life. Several times during her interview, Dora said "We were just a bunch of young, giddy girls doing what young, giddy girls do." Thank heavens for all the young, giddy girls who risked their lives for all Americans. Thanks.

Author's note:

A paperback book, Disaster at Bari, *by Glenn B. Infield recounts, "One of the best kept secrets of World War II is the fact that on the night of December 2, 1943, over one thousand Allied military personnel and unprotected Italian civilians died at Bari, Italy, when one hundred tons of poison gas were unleashed. It was mustard gas, the deadly chemical used so successfully by the Germans in World War I and still regarded at the time as the ultimate in hideous weaponry in a world as yet unacquainted with the horrors of the atomic mushroom cloud.... The bombing at Bari was the worst shipping disaster suffered by the Allies since Pearl Harbor. Seventeen ships were totally destroyed by the Luftwaffe bombers that night and eight others were damaged. "*

PARACHUTE SILK AND POW RICE: NURSE JEAN WILLIAMS HAYES, UNRRA, WORLD WAR II

as told to

Rosemary Eckroat Bachle

Germany invaded Poland on September 1, 1939; two days later Britain and France declared war on Germany. This sparked the beginning of World War II. On September 10, 1939, for the first time in history, Canada declared war in her own right.

For Jean Williams, a native Canadian, the war began in September 1940 when she returned to the University of Toronto to do postgraduate work in Public Health Nursing. She had been working at the University of Michigan Hospital in Ann Arbor because jobs were more plentiful in the United States, and the pay was better.

Jean shares her memories of that time, confiding that, "Butter, sugar, and men were scarce, and nylons were practically non-existent. I wore my one and only pair for four years."

Like many others, she knitted scarves for "ditty bags" (military care packages) while riding back and forth to the university on the streetcar.

After graduation in 1941, Jean worked as a visiting nurse for the Victorian Order of Nurses (a Canada-wide organization of visiting nurses started in 1896) in Toronto and in Cobalt, Ontario. Cobalt was a ghost mining town, a one-doctor, one-nurse town with no hospital. "Babies were delivered at home; tonsillectomies and other minor operations were done in the doctor's office. The Red Cross Bloodmobile would come to town twice a year, and I did all the advance work, rounding up equipment, volunteers, and donors."

One of her duties was administering guidance to families of military men. The soldier overseas worried about his family's welfare. "Some of the wives would rather use their baby's sugar ration to make wine instead of formula," Jean acknowledged.

208

Jean Williams Hayes

In 1942, the Hylander Regiment from Jean's hometown of Hamilton, Ontario, was decimated in a commando raid on Dieppe, a French port located on the coast of the English Channel. The raid left Britain and Canada with heavy losses. Jean felt compelled to contribute her services to the war effort, but public health nurses were not permitted to enlist in the Armed Forces; they were too valuable on the home front.

After three years as a visiting nurse, Jean was eager for a new challenge, although one had not yet appeared. In November of 1944 she agreed to accompany another nurse to a meeting of the Canadian Association of University Women. The speaker that night was the president of the group, and she spoke on varied and interesting subjects. Jean listened as she told about the positions available overseas; one in particular was with the United Nations. Since the Germans were in retreat in Europe and the end of the war seemed imminent, Jean filled out an application with the United Nations Relief and Rehabilitation Administration (UNRRA).

In April of 1945 she applied for a transfer to the West Coast with the Victorian Order of Nurses. During preparations for the transfer, her application with UNRRA was accepted. Before she could leave her present position, however, she had to find her own replacement.

Jean was assigned to the Displaced Persons Mission in Germany, started by General Dwight D. Eisenhower. When American soldiers entered Germany, they found many people of different nationalities being used as slave laborers in factories and building roads. The Autobahn, paved with stones measuring four cubic inches and fitted together in a semi-curved mosaic, was one result of such labor. Since these people were not prisoners of war, the displaced-persons camps were set up to house them until they could be repatriated.

The largest camp in the American zone was at Wildflecken in North Bavaria, sometimes called the "poor man's Switzerland," and held 25,000 Polish and 400 Baltic States people. A team of 12 (like Jean, assigned from Allied countries) directed the camp. The team was housed in the deserted 55th Panzer officers' quarters which boasted of luxuries such as parquet floors and heated towel racks, a far cry from the tents and canvas cots that were expected. The new residents found Christmas tree ornaments and children's toys left by the former inhabitants.

The displaced persons were settled in barracks. Nurses were assigned to the barracks to oversee the rooms and attend to the needs of pregnant women, infants, and school-aged children. They insured that each room contained a stove and the required number of blankets and guarded against single girls living with men. Some barracks were used as hospitals. Each building had its own laundry room with huge stone tubs and stone washboards. A large supply of synthetic white material, originally used to make ski uniforms, had been left behind and was now used to make sheets. It contained wood fibers that, when wet, were stiff and boardlike. Fortunately, when it dried, the material became soft and pliable again.

Some of the skilled Baltic States people were transferred to their own camp and the hospitals staffed with a German prisoner of war medical unit. Because of the deep hatred between the Polish people and anything German, armed GIs were stationed on each hospital floor. Nurse Elizabeth Petrie, a fellow Canadian in charge of the obstetrics hospital, told her GI guards, "If you see a stork circling, scare it off before it can land."

While in Germany, Jean met Lieutenant Dan Hayes who was with the Third Army Battalion guarding the camp. Love bloomed, and he asked her to marry him. Since Germany was no longer a country, permission had to be obtained through General Lucius Truscott, Commander of the Third Army. Permission was granted and Lieutenant Hayes reenlisted for an additional three months so they could marry.

The couple refused to let red tape tangle their wedding plans. Jean acquired five yards of parachute silk and arranged for a German girl to make her long white dress for five dollars. The girl supplied a white bone zipper in exchange for one from a GI skirt and furnished cream lace for the trim. Jean traded a pair of brown oxfords for silver sandals. Dan made her ring from an American quarter: hammering, then smoothing it with a rat-tail file. Jean gave him a Canadian quarter, and he repeated the process for his ring. Her wedding bouquet was made with a premula bloom surrounded by greenery and encircled with a paper doily. Flowers for the church were cut from cyclamen plants rescued from a bombed out greenhouse, and music flowed from the church organ even though it had been damaged by shell fire and some of the keys were missing. After the wedding they were showered with rice from an Indian prisoner-of-war parcel.

At the reception in the Officer's Mess, champagne flowed freely, supplied by the Post Exchange when everyone cashed in his or her liquor rations. In true tradition of weddings everywhere, the bride's table offered another proof of Murphy's Law. The wedding cake's three tiers, beautifully decorated by a German baker, had mistakenly been arranged side by side instead of on top of each other by Polish DP girls helping out in the kitchen. Jean and Dan had to walk alongside the table cutting the layers one by one.

Jean and Dan honeymooned in Switzerland courtesy of the Army's rest and rehabilitation (R&R) program. When they returned to Germany, they attended the Nuremburg Trials.

As newlyweds, Jean and Dan came home to Oklahoma. Dan finished his last year at Oklahoma University, and Jean worked for the Cleveland County Health Department. One of her duties was to visit families for maternal and child health. Well-baby clinics were started on the North Navy Base in one of the large dormitories for men. No one gave a thought to having a group of babies, many crying, in a men's dorm. That's the way life was in 1946 at Oklahoma University.

Jean celebrated her 82nd birthday on November 16, 1997, with memories of a wartime love story that continues.

AIR RAIDS IN LONDON,
WORLD WAR II
by
Martha Kay

This is the most difficult task I have ever undertaken. I have always wanted to forget those ghastly years for so many reasons: the continued thoughts about my family's well being, my brother in the Air Force, my husband in the 8th Army and another brother in Burma. Words are hard to find to describe the horror of those nights, and, later on, it became days as well: going off to war and wondering if I would be alive another day, going home in the evening and wondering if my house would be there.

Since all young, able-bodied men were away, the tasks fell on the women who were left at home. Everyone was pressed into action, and I chose to be an air raid warden. It was during the time of the phoney war as it was called in those days. I never imagined what was to come eventually, but during this lull I joined the Red Cross and found that time rewarding.

I would read to soldiers and airmen. I would read the news to them, write letters for them, and, most of all, bring the outside world to them. They were so grateful and the thanks of their families was so rewarding, but this quietness did not last too long and then came the raids which were nerve-wracking. And worst of all, we were not prepared.

I lived in an old Georgian house in a delightful area surrounded by fields on either side, and so we were spared blasts and bombs for some time. Much later we were blasted, and the damage was not too bad compared with the devastation of other places in London.

After training for bomb disposal, I was raring to go—but what an awakening. Armed with buckets full of sand, my job was to pick up incendiary bombs which were dropped in clusters and put them in the sand to stop them from blasting and catching alight.

Actually, they were looking for the balloon barrage in the fields

213

across from the house. I often wondered how the Germans knew all this information. I used the station which was completely manned by women to leave my bombs, which these brave girls destroyed.

Working all day and all night on alert or till the all-clear came, life was rather hectic. The only sleep I got was a few hours in our Anderson shelters. These were steel shelters issued to every household. They were partly submerged and afforded shelter in case the house had a direct hit. My mother and sister spent every night in the shelter, and, as my headquarters was not too far from our house, I would look in to see if they were okay.

I always thought a bomb was small until a dud came down outside our house, and it was enormous. Then I understood why so much havoc was caused. The Army took the bomb away, and all through the war it stood outside the local Town Hall. We all bought war stamps and stuck them on the bomb. It was covered very quickly. It was our way of saying, "Bomb away; you will never break our will!"

Every night as soon as the air raid siren sounded, I had to report to the warden's post. I always said goodnight and goodbye to my family just in case I did not return. Looking back, I don't see how we survived. We had a wonderful little dog named Pluto who became the neighborhood pet as he barked and let everyone know an alert was coming. He then wasted no time in running to the shelter.

Rationing never bothered us as there were so many other things to worry about. My mother would stand in a queue for hours for a banana or an orange. By the way, we were allowed one egg a week. I personally didn't care about those things after seeing death firsthand and having to keep pulling people out of the rubble. This changed my whole outlook on life forever. I must say we certainly had a lot of guts.

My oldest son was evacuated. I did this to spare him any trauma and also to enable him to attend school safely, but I made a mistake. After a few years he made up his mind to come home. He worried about us, so one day he took the train back to London. Naturally with no ticket, the police took care of him and called me. They fed him and made a big fuss of this young hero. He grew up to be a dear considerate person in spite of all the turmoil and horror he endured.

Because of all the bombing, drains were opened. One night on duty, to my horror I saw this black path approaching, and I realized there were rats running for safety—me included. I am even scared of mice, but the worst horror to stomach is a direct hit and having to keep the injured or pull the dead out of the rubble. Such sorrow is hard to explain—it's heartbreaking. I wish the world could live in peace, but that seems impossible by events today.

Life went on, if one could call it a life. People lived in the underground stations with absolutely no privacy. One night there was an awful accident: people panicked during a bad raid. Many lives were lost at the exits. Young children, women, and old folks were crushed to death. We were all called out to help. It was devastating. I cannot remember how many incidents were just as awful through the war years, but eventually it was over. It took another two years before my husband came home.

When the war ended in Germany, I went out with the Red Cross to bring the children that were still in Belsen, but that I will not go into—it's still too painful.

We of that generation lost many years, and it's my opinion there will never be a braver bunch of folks. I salute each and every one of them.

The Japanese affected us as well. My brother was in a POW camp and was killed when the Allies bombed the Burma railroad which the prisoners were forced to build. So I have no qualms about dropping the bomb on them—none whatsoever. In my lifetime I have seen many wars, starting in 1914, and each one saddens me. Why? I question. All anyone wants is to live one's life in peace.

TEA CEREMONY

During the war in Britain, they said
The cat and I were found under a table,
Hiding together from noise that sounded
Like thunder.

The childhood litany was suddenly clear,
I could hear the ring of it in my mother's voice
And the small thwack of a jump rope
In the garden.

Mummy please just halfway down the lane—
I promise to come straight back again.

Listen to ne young lady or
I'll show you what this hand is for.
Wicked girls going off to play
Are blown to bits in the middle of day.
Good children stay home where they belong.

I spilled the tea, spotting
An embroidered cloth, the one covering
A child in the dark hole that would save us
Beneath night grass.

Sirens. The clatter of cups.
In trouble again, pulling down black curtains.

I didn't do it! And anyway
There were no aeroplanes today.
Can we please have lace instead?

Lace is for brides and for them that's dead.
The black one's so the Jerries won't find us.
If they come, no use making your silly fuss.
They do terrible things to girls who tell lies,
Especially ones with brown hair and dark eyes.

Precisely what things, I could not imagine,
Nor she, trying so hard to keep us alive
She had to frighten me every day
into breathing.

Reflecting on the nature of peril
I changed the cloth to handmade lace,
Obedient to dark-eyed daughters,
Standing in their body. The sound of doors
Bolted. It might have been thunder
Or fireworks, almost anything.

by *Sandra Soli*

Author's Note:
*Born in the middle of an air raid in Birmingham, England,
Sandra Soli uses war and loss as recurring themes in her po-
ems.*

LETTERS HOME
by
Irene Sturm Lefebvre

As the daughter of Merle and Loyde Sturm, wheat farmers of Grant County, Oklahoma, I am the oldest of their six children. I attended the rural Prairie View grade school, but in order to attend high school it was necessary for me to board in Medford. This I did, returning home on weekends. I graduated at the age of 15 and, after completing a one-year course at Enid Business College, became a secretary in the law firm of Ridings and Drennan.

On my 21st birthday in 1943, I enlisted in the Women's Auxiliary Army Corps. I served at Camp Lee, Virginia, in New Guinea, and on Leyte and Luzon Islands in the Philippines from March 1943 until October 1945. I was fortunate to have had a mother who not only kept a constant flow of letters following me but thoughtfully saved all my letters as well. From this collection of letters home, I can retrace many of my steps.

After basic training in Fort Des Moines, Iowa, I was assigned to duty at Camp Lee, Virginia. Although we had no advance notice of our destination, the reception was memorable. In my first letter from Camp Lee, I reported: We were met by a band and a photographer. There are 15,000 soldiers here—everywhere men were staring at us. We were weary after two days and two nights on the train but stood retreat at Post Headquarters, then marched two miles to our barracks, dropped our coats, and fell out for mess.

My letters home were filled with items about friends at Camp Lee, frequent mention of KP (Kitchen Police), and, because of security, no information about my job as secretary for the Trial Judge Advocate. Social life was basically movies on base. One letter indicated my sending $20 a month home and a $12.50 deduction for bonds—all out of the $50 monthly pay. Then I always was mindful that a furlough train fare home would be $35.50, which I managed every six months while at Camp Lee.

218

In September 1943 the WAAC became a part of the regular Army and I enlisted in the Women Army Corps (WAC). Life seemed to continue routinely until a detached service assignment connected with the Fifth War Bond Drive resulted in very exciting duty for a Quartermaster Corps open air extravaganza. My assignment was as secretary for Russ Matthews, the civilian head of the massive mobile exhibit. This "Weapons of War" presentation of military equipment and simulated battle scenes was shown in the largest parks of Washington, D.C., New York City, and Chicago.

It was at this time that I met Technical Sergeant Paul Lefebvre from Camp Lee, Virginia, also assigned to the Command Post for public relations duties. Romantic sparks were evident but were interrupted upon our return to Camp Lee with my overseas training assignment to report to Fort Oglethorpe, Georgia. Paul and I each took furloughs to Oklahoma to meet each other's families and for me to say good-bye.

The days moved forward as dictated by military orders. The memories of overseas training were overshadowed by one brief visit from Paul. I was able to get a pass of four hours duration and meet him at the gate of Fort Oglethorpe to go into Chattanooga, Tennessee. Paul brought a diamond ring to signify our engagement. I remember the next day adding my tears to the lye soap sudsing of the mess hall floor as I scrubbed to fulfill my KP assignment.

From this point, I quote excerpts from my letters to my family in Medford.

> 24 September 1944 (Somewhere-Blue Pacific) Twilight is falling—I'm on deck, and all I can see is light blue sky meeting the inky blue water—haven't written prior to this as we had to get used to the motion of the ship. I haven't been seasick, just woozy and dull. Our rooms get warm during the night; we are told as we near or cross the Equator the temperature may reach 110 degrees on deck.
>
> Usually it's so crowded on deck—we all squat down, sitting on our life preservers. We eat twice a day—morning at seven and afternoon at four. I've had KP once. We have good food; the tables are high, and we stand to eat.
>
> I attend church services every day. We wear or carry the life preservers constantly plus a canteen of water. Every day we have "abandon ship" drill.

A letter to my brother, Donald Sturm, begins:

At Sea, 28 September 1944: Today we crossed the Equator. It is the custom to have a ceremony for those crossing for the first time—some of our men officers had their heads partially shaved, their faces painted, and water sprayed on them. I caught part of the water; we now automatically belong to the "Royal Order of Shellbacks."

All we see is water, horizon, and sky. We get up at six and, until it got so hot, we went to bed at ten but now eleven-thirty, enabling us to stay on deck in the fresh air as long as possible. We still don't know our destination and our curiosity increases.

Twenty days later we landed—Hollandia, New Guinea. My letter home dated 12 October 1944 identifies the location as Netherlands East Indies. Our assignment was the 5205th WAC Detachment of General Headquarters. We represented the Radar and Radio Countermeasures Group of the Signal Corps with "top secret" classification. Our office was high on the mountain, and the upper portion was screened. The clouds came through the office at times, blocking the view of portions of the office. Our sleeping quarters were units for six on a concrete slab with burlap around the sides for privacy. The entire WAC area was encased in burlap.

Upon our arrival at Hollandia, we turned in our winter uniforms. We were asked to turn in our gas masks so that the male soldiers might have access to them wherever needed. Mail call netted me 18 letters which was a great boost to my morale. We were cautioned not to go anywhere alone and that WACs should go in pairs and each be accompanied by two armed U.S. male soldiers.

We found we needed trousers for the convenience of riding in trucks, and there was no GI issue for the women after arrival in the Southwest Pacific. This explains one excerpt in a letter from New Guinea, dated 15 October 1944, that I gave a GI my beer ration for which he was to get me a couple pair of men's khaki trousers.

Letter of 17 November 1944 mentions getting paid in Dutch money (230 some guilders—about $123).

An article forwarded from the *Camp Lee Traveller, WAC Silhouettes*, by Sergeant Irene O'Connor, featured "LEE WACS IN LEYTE."

The Women's Army Corps has added another locale to its

This Army photograph noted, "THE FIRST WACs IN THE PHIL-IPPINES arrive at Tacloban by air." Sergeant Irene Sturm is second from left.

itinerary, the Philippines. Two Lee WACS, dressed in khaki trousers, heavy field shoes, and steel helmets, were among the first group climbing down from the transport that flew them from New Guinea to Leyte. They are Sgts. Irene Sturm and Ada Rathvon. Excerpts from a letter sent by Sgt. Sturm to her fiance, T/Sgt. Paul Lefebvre, ASFTC PUBLIC RELATIONS OF-FICE are quoted:

Flew up last night from New Guinea [referring to Tacloban, Leyte Island]. Mud everywhere. Some places we walk through mud as high as our field boots; we just roll our pants legs up and splash through. The little Filipino girls wear pretty colored dresses and usually go without shoes. They say that the Japs made them paste paper over all the pages of their school books that referred to the United States. Two evenings ago we hit the foxholes a couple of times. At the office we have air raid shelters just for us girls.

Xmas Eve we will be allowed to stay up until two a.m. so we can attend midnight Mass. The children's party on Christmas morning is to be broadcast to the States. For the children's party, we can make a gift item using the material from our striped seersucker GI-issue robe—they were ankle length and we are authorized to use the amount of material that would still maintain the knee length. My efforts to make a doll weren't successful; a WAC friend, Irene Wolan, studied it and said, "If I put ears on it, I could develop a stuffed rabbit." The design turned out so well that it was given to President Osmena's grandchild who attended the party with him. Christmas Eve and Christmas night were almost total blackouts.

A letter home revealed that in the town of Tacloban, Leyte Island, we were quartered in a boy's school. There were U.S. soldiers at the other end of the school that were assigned to R & R for a short time. We had a military-constructed latrine outside at the back of the school building.

> We wash our faces in our helmets, then wash our underwear in the same water. There are shower facilities, but we watch how much water we use as we only have a tank in the yard but soon we'll be attached to the town's water system.

I never did write my family about the experience of going to the latrine early one morning to hear the sound of enemy strafing. I immediately fell to a prone position on the cement floor, grateful for training to follow this procedure. The sound soon became distant, and my experience became an indelible memory.

To continue with quotes from my correspondence home:

> The native women come in and ask to do our laundry. They charge very little. There is a price fixed by President Osmena, and we are not to pay more so that we won't upset the standard of value here. They don't want money as there is simply nothing they can buy; instead they want dresses or soap. We include soap with our laundry as they have none. They can't understand why we don't wear dresses. Don't know when our laundry will come back as the natives have few clothes lines, and it rains all the time and they have no way of getting it dry. I see them put a lot of their clothes out on bushes or grass in the yards.
>
> In almost every house window, one can see a Singer sewing machine. I am told that in peace time sewing machines from the United States were their most heavily imported item. When we can secure a pair of GI trousers, we give our cigarette ration to a laundry lady to alter them to size, remove the fly in front and make a side, button opening.
>
> Traffic jams are terrific as the roads are so narrow—only

made for walking or light rickshaw carts. Our GI trucks, Jeeps, and ducks have torn them up. We have one truck just for our transportation and the driver's name is Smoky—he knows all the little kids and the Filipino soldiers by name. All of the boys you see have a truckload of little kids or a Jeep full. The boys say that here they feel more like fighting than in New Guinea because the natives back there weren't educated enough to show any feelings, but here the people are so appreciative and they feel there's some good being done.

I might mention that on two occasions we encountered General MacArthur—he was in a Jeep, and we were also. We saluted, but he answered the salute with a wave. On one occasion his wife, Jean MacArthur, came to our very tiny post exchange to shop.

To my brothers, Raymond and Melvin, I wrote on 2 January 1945:

We have just been informed that after a couple days we will no longer be allowed showers—guess the scarcity of water is serious, especially now that the rainy season is about over. My helmet will now be a bath tub, wash tub, and a protection for my head.

The Nips came over last night—once we got up, about two A.M.; our ack-ack guns were making a lot of noise. We went out and stood by the foxholes, but nothing happened.

We moved to a coconut grove near Tolosa on Leyte Island. A letter home dated 30 January 1945 stated:

Yesterday we moved to an adjoining town some twenty miles away—we're living in a camp area just outside of this town. Back to huts, but this time no floors, but the soil is extremely sandy. Also no electricity again, so back to candles. We're six in a tent temporarily and as soon as enough tents are put up, there will be four. All our buildings are made of a slight wooden frame, and the sides are woven bamboo or thatch, with a good tin roof and a concrete floor. Our mess hall is such an improvement and so is the food. We are just a short distance from the beach. This is my first time in the ocean and I enjoy it immensely.

Often I find remarks in my letters that I received more mail than any of the other girls, and they make a big to-do about it but I love it! I tried to answer letters promptly which encouraged additional letters. I appreciated all those loyal hometown friends and relatives. My mother wrote every day, and so did Paul so that accounted for a constant source of mail even though sometimes their letters arrived in bunches.

The only medication I ever took in the Southwest Pacific was a daily tablet of Atabrine, which was prescribed for malaria prevention. Soon our skin showed a yellowish tint and remained this way until some time after returning to civilian life. Each night we tucked in our mosquito netting, which formed a screen around each cot. I was never at any time conscious of mosquitoes. At Tacloban on Leyte Island I was glad to have the netting around my cot as many chameleons were on the walls, visible and non-visible as they changed color.

As General MacArthur's headquarters moved north, so did our office and its personnel—we were called Section 22 for security. Everywhere in Manila were the ruins of buildings. A letter to the family states:

> We live in a large college building [later this could be identified as the LaSalle College on Manila Harbor]. This is the residential, university, and business part and naturally the section that was most heavily bombed. Buildings were as beautiful as our own legislative and college buildings; they are now crumbled to dust with parts of the walls still standing. The glass in the windows are shattered or completely gone; frames standing with the insides gutted out—black and smoke stained. The bodies have been removed from the sections we occupy, and the areas have been cleared of mines. The streets are marked if they are clear. Some places we drive by smell from the bodies buried under the debris.

Letter from Manila dated 8 May 1945:

> Among the military personnel, there is deep regret for President Roosevelt's death. I was surprised at the lack of elaborate services of mourning. Of course our flags still fly at half-mast.
>
> We ride in trucks—they come after us for work and bring us home—we must be a couple miles from work, and the mess hall is some two or three miles the other way from our living quarters.

A letter from Manila, dated 9 May 1945, indicated:

> We have electric lights now and the engineers are working every day fixing the plumbing so we will have inside latrine and shower facilities. Also the mess hall is about complete and if enough Filipino people can be secured who can pass the Food Handlers' test, then we will have Filipino help and won't have to do KP. Water is coming out of the fire hydrants and people are bathing in the gutters, washing their vegetables or even their clothes. At night especially and sometimes during the day we can hear the firing from the front lines.

A letter from Manila, dated 9 May 1945 related some gruesome sights:

> Two Japs were caught in our area—one accosted our guard during the night—was carrying a bag of hand grenades but the guard fired at him, wounding him. He was taken to the hospital but has since died—some Filipino kids spotted a Jap in the ruins across the street from us. He was killed about seven a.m.—we all went over to see him. The Filipinos had cut a diamond shaped piece out of the middle of his stomach, had stuck sticks into his mouth and through his ears - an American guard came along, however, and made everyone leave.

Later I saw a Japanese officer who had committed suicide only a little over a block from our office. Irene Wolan and I walked down to see him; some soldiers had taken his shoes as souvenirs. I could see the side of his head where the bullet had penetrated—that together with the fact that some Filipino had sliced the officer's left ear completely even with the side of his face, made me very squeamish!

Letter dated 1 June 1945 reports an all day trip to Clark Field—about a three-hour drive through lovely Midwestern country, the fields all green like our wheat fields, only they are rice. The highway was good, and you could see the railroad tracks and the telephone lines. Clark Field was quite a battle point, but of course now it looked just like the average airfield except there are many wrecked Japanese planes lying everywhere. Traveling in the countryside one saw water buffalo as the beast of burden.

One trip with the Navy as the host gave me an opportunity to go to Corregidor. In the tunnel under the road there were bones of humans and a slight stench remaining.

When the cessation of the war with Japan was announced—August 14 in Manila—we were at first conscious of fireworks in the harbor (actually tracer bullets), and then from somewhere the news came. I remember we went to the mess hall, and the hysteria was reflected in our spontaneous yelling and yelling and dancing with each other for joy. We were confined to quarters for two days as protection from the intoxicated celebrants in the streets. The song, "Sentimental Journey," that had been played for months in the mess hall now meant the reality of going home.

We started back to the States on a small troop ship called the *Evangeline* and spent much of the 20-day voyage on a rough sea ahead of a typhoon. A letter to my family: Blue Pacific *USAT Evangeline*, 8 October 1945:

> We're stopping at a small island to refuel and mail is to be taken off at that time—boarded the 2nd but didn't set sail until the evening of the 4th as one day we filled with water and the next refueled. All of us have been seasick—this is a very small boat and it has been stormy and the ocean rough. The Skipper is trying to make the trip in eighteen days.

Approaching the Golden Gate, it was suggested that we yell to give vent to our emotions—the suggestion was unnecessary because that was the natural reaction. We were temporarily quartered at Camp Stoneman, and the emotion of saying good-bye to our WAC buddies with whom we had shared some 13 months of overseas duty was made easier by the anticipation of getting to our respective homes and families.

I was discharged from the military at Fort Sam Houston, Texas. Remembering that my daddy, Loyde P. Sturm, had been discharged from that fort in World War I, I hired a taxi and asked to be taken to any of the old locations or buildings on the fort of World War I vintage so that I might report having seen them.

November 1945—Back in Medford and Grant County where the citizenry had networked a communication system with their family service men of my possible locations in the Philippines so that I received many visits from hometown service personnel on the island of Leyte or in Manila. This special bonding has remained strong through the years with Hardy Abbott, L.H. Anderson, Donald Hott, Glen Ray Taylor, Everett Cooperider, Bennie Kilian, Louis Yunker, Victor Dailey, Paul Harper, Clarence Krittenbrink, and Dilmond Postlewait (who married my sister, Evelyn).

Paul was discharged the next month at Indiantown Gap, Pennsylvania. We then made plans to be married in a simple ceremony at the First Christian Church of Medford on January 8, 1946. Having traveled so much, we both preferred to settle in Oklahoma and be within visiting distance of our families. Paul launched his commercial art career in Oklahoma City, and I took a secretarial position with a tax attorney. Later I retired to become a full-time mother and homemaker.

WARS OF THE 40'S

The wars of the 40's were against all
of us, the young and the old
The enemy was all around
but all the women were brave and
true to their loved ones in the city
and in the towns

The bombs came down with destruction
with terror in the trenches and on
seas, yet old glory waved in the cities
and in the towns proud and true
that one day our loved ones would be
safe and coming home again to their
loved ones in the cities and in the towns

Our flags color still waving the red
white and blue
Our memories of World War II are
so sad for
the brave service men that gave their
lives so others could live
and live their lives with destiny
in God's plan

by *Dorothy Myers*
From *Poetry and Sayings*

BOOT CAMP: CAMP LEJEUNE, NORTH CAROLINA WORLD WAR II, JULY 1943

by

Mary Louise Courey Glann

My indoctrination into military life began in boot camp at Camp Lejeune, North Carolina. We sat through classes learning Marine Corps history and traditions, physical fitness, and, of course, the marching drills to prepare us for dress parades and ceremonies. The discipline in boot camp taught us patience, endurance, tolerance, loyalty, and true patriotism among other things.

One highlight I remember was suffering the effects of a tetanus shot which inflamed my arm from elbow to shoulder and caused many intolerable days. Each evening my bunkmate, a tall pleasant girl from North Carolina who occupied the lower bunk, would be kind and gentle in giving me, a short Yankee from Iowa, a boost to the upper bunk since my arm hurt to use it and I didn't have the strength to do it myself.

I met women from all over the United States and was rewarded with very enlightening history lessons. Some of the Northern girls in our bunk area would debate the Southern girls on the outcome of the Civil War. My "bunkie" and I thought the girls totally silly for rehashing old history, but our bunk shook and swayed with repressed laughter as the conversation became pretty heated until lights out. The evenings of hilarity helped ease the pain.

After taking a battery of aptitude tests, I hoped to get into radio school and become a radio operator. Much to my disappointment, I was sent instead to Aviation Machinist Mate School at the Naval Air Technical Training Center (NATTC) in Memphis Tennessee for a month, then to NATTC in Norman, Oklahoma for about five months.

Traveling by troop trains proved to be quite a geography lesson, and training at different bases became a mini cultural education.

Our soil in the North is black; I couldn't get over the red earth in the Southland. I didn't like Memphis' hot, humid climate, but Oklahoma's rural settings and trees were so different from my home state. Being city bred, the beautiful sunsets were a novelty. We went to classes with Sailors and Marines. You could tell a Navy man by the way he walked at a 45-degree angle. The women Marines were a small group with our own barracks. The WAVES had their own barracks too.

For five days a week I gained aeronautical knowledge, inside and out, and learned how to use tools. We worked on skeletal Piper Cub planes to familiarize us to the practical purposes and workings of aircraft. Of course, we still had daily march drills to and from classes, even to the chow line. The evenings and weekends were spent on trolley rides to Oklahoma City where we danced to the music of Tex Benecke and his band, who were stationed there, and great music are such pleasant memories.

After completion of the course, seven of us were shipped via troop train to the Mojave Desert Marine Air Station in Mojave, California. This would be our home for the duration of the war. The rest of the unit was scattered to other bases.

We seven girls were assigned to Women Marines Aviation Squadron #1, about 200 strong, among thousands of male Marines training for South Pacific duty or aircraft carrier duty. We worked in flight section at the airfield alongside the men. As aviation mechanics, we wore men's work clothes and "boondockers." I was issued the smallest size they had, and the boots were still too big for my feet. So I wore heavy socks. The clothes were too big, but we made do for there were no tailors on base. Our female uniforms and oxfords couldn't stand the daily use of gas, oil, kerosene, and jumping up and down off airplane wings.

One Easter morning while waiting for the base bus ride to a nearby town, I looked up to the mountains surrounding our base to see a B-24 hurl out of the clouds. Before my eyes it crashed into the mountainside and exploded into flames. Standing all alone, a chill overcame me and I cried out. At Mass in the little Spanish Church, I offered up the Mass and Communion for the men aboard. On return to the base, I learned one of our girls on duty at the field had gone with the crash crew on a truck to the site and helped look

Corporal Mary Louise Courey Glann in her dungarees.

for survivors. There were none, and the scene was pretty grisly. It was a big shock to her. To this day the memory of it is vivid.

There were 48-hour passes to Los Angeles and Hollywood or 72-hour passes to San Francisco to sightsee or to attend programs of interest. Other times, I would visit the towns in the area. In Hollywood we girls would go to Earl Carroll's show, the Brown Derby, Schwab's drug store to see what stars were there, radio shows, and numerous other events. One morning at "Breakfast at Sardi's" (a place where the movie stars would go), I was chosen along with other service men and women to be interviewed on the air. In my hometown, relatives, friends, neighbors, and strangers called my parents or stopped by to say they had heard me on the radio. You know the days of radio.

At the Hollywood canteen, big-name actors and actresses entertained the service men. Service women weren't allowed on the main floor but relegated to seats in the balcony to watch the performance. I did get to see Bette Davis from the balcony. Supporting actors or those making their start in movies would come up to the balcony and sit with us. Our base being 100 odd miles north and east of Los Angeles, we were fortunate to be entertained by Hollywood stars such as Bob Hope and his cast, Kay Kyser and his band, Veronica Lake, and Brian Donlevy to name a few. We had a girls' softball team and would fly to other bases to play their teams.

The flight section took care of incoming and outgoing aircraft as well as making sure the station aircraft were tuned and ready at a moment's notice. Officers in administrative duty, in order to collect their monthly flight pay, had to put in a certain amount of actual flying hours in those planes. Once in a while, we could go on a flight to some other city with the pilot while he completed some business. Our job was to stay with the plane until his return, then fly back to base. Each of us mechanics on duty would take turns for these assignments. It was refreshing to leave our desolate surroundings and see other places.

Our base had a PX (post exchange), bowling alley, and a building shared for Sunday Church Services in the morning and converted to evening movies. At our barracks we had a volleyball court and a few bicycles to check out. One of the squad rooms had a Ping-Pong table and a radio.

In the little town nearby, a couple of the bars or lounges had swinging doors like one sees in western movies. Also, one building had the upper balcony hanging over store fronts like in cowboy movies.

One Christmas, the most popular saloon or lounge gave a very festive Christmas party with all the trimmings to those of us who couldn't go home for Christmas. In appreciation, everyone tossed coins into its very fancy crystal chandelier with inverted bowl.

MY LIFE
IN THE WOMEN'S ARMY CORPS
by
Mildred L. Brezic Setterberg

Way back in 1942, I got the sudden urge to do something different and exciting. Perhaps it was a patriotic feeling for my country,
or it could be because I had been dating a fellow for three years
and suddenly he wanted to get married to avoid going into the service.

The forgoing is not too important to anyone but myself, but let
me tell you that on the morning of November 28, 1942, in Colum-
bus, Ohio, when I raised my right hand and was sworn into the
Women's Army Auxiliary Corps, there was moisture in my eyes,
and a lump in my throat.

I couldn't help thinking of my father, who had been in the Aus-
trian army, and my mother, who came two years later through Ellis
Island. I thought about how brave they were, leaving Europe to
come to a new country not knowing or understanding the language.
They met in the U.S. and married and had my brother, sister, and
me. I'll never forget when my father got his U.S. citizenship papers. He was so proud he invited all his friends for a party. Everyone brought their children, and, while we ran around and played,
the men were in the basement drinking wine and singing. The
women were in the kitchen drinking coffee and eating pastries. But
more importantly, I remember my father telling me how lucky I was
to be born in America.

My mother and father died when I was small, but the rest of my
family and friends saw me off as I boarded the train on my way to
Daytona Beach, Florida, for my basic training.

During the first few weeks, we got shots every day, it seemed.
We were fitted for clothing, classified, and tested. Then I began
the routine of daily classes in military matters, customs and courtesy, map reading, calisthenics, first aid, and drill. There were nights
when I was dead tired, wondering if I was going to like this new life

233

with the bugle blasting every morning at 4:45 a.m. and "falling out" in the cold Florida mornings to another long day.

However, I loved every minute of it and looked forward to that day when I could be sent out to a company in the field and do that which I had come into the WAACs to do—release a soldier, a man, who could go into the battlefield and fight as I could not.

The next six weeks I attended Administration School learning military correspondence. We were transferred to "Tent City," a remote area not too far from Daytona, and put on hold, waiting to be shipped out. There were rows of tents as far as you could see with six women in each and a potbelly stove we had to feed to keep warm at night. We took turns going to the coal pile to fill our buckets and carry them back to our tents. After breakfast we went back to our tents to clean up. Nothing could be left laying around. We were always subjected to inspections.

Finally, in February 1943, we shipped out on our way to Fort Benning, Georgia. We piled into Army trucks and were off to the train station. At last I was sent out into the field as a replacement to a company which had been activated two weeks before. Tired and hungry and depressed, we stepped off the train and met our new officers. We later heard that all of Fort Benning had waited for us for three months. They needed replacements badly because we had lost so many men overseas. We were the first WAACs to arrive at Fort Benning.

The day passed, and our spirits lifted as we met and talked with our new "GI" sisters. In the evening the company went en masse in Army trucks to a buffet and dance. What fun! This event climaxed our day, and, riding home in our Army trucks singing army songs and laughing, I decided right then that all those weeks of agony when my arms were sore from shots, my feet burning from drilling, and my head aching from study were now just thoughts. I was going to love this Army life!

Our officers took bed check at 9:30 p.m. every night. We had four soldiers patrolling our three barracks. They just kept going around and around, so there was a soldier on all four sides of our barracks. They all carried guns. Of course, we couldn't leave either. We were guarded 24 hours around the clock.

We drilled, had company meetings, training films, paraded, and pulled kitchen police (KP). We each had jobs that kept us busy eight hours a day and longer with no time-and-a-half for overtime either. Our pay was $15 per month the first year in the WAACs until President Roosevelt made us part of the Regular Army in 1943. From then on we were under the same regulations as the men. Since there was a change in our status, all of us were discharged from the WAACs and had the option of returning to civilian life or reenlisting, which I did for the duration of the war plus six months. Many who quit and went home were sorry. Some tried to reenlist, but it wasn't easy. They were rejected. Those of us who reenlisted weren't kicking. We had a job to do.

My company commander chose me to be her company clerk. I was responsible for keeping records of everything that affected 180 women. Later our 1st Sergeant was shipped overseas so I assumed her duties also as Acting 1st Sergeant.

In September 1944 I got orders from the War Department, Washington D.C. I was picked to go to Recruiting School at Fort Sam Houston, Texas. After graduation I was sent to Charlotte, North Carolina. They issued me a staff car, and I commuted back and forth to Columbia and Florence, South Carolina, and back to Charlotte. We worked out of the Post Office.

To this day, I have enjoyed it. Not once have I honestly regretted reenlisting in the WAC (Women's Army Corps) instead of returning to civilian life. I knew that one day I would be leaving all this, saying good-bye to friends, women like myself. I shall never forget my "Tour of Duty" in the WAC, Army of the United States. It's been an experience I wouldn't have missed for anything. I stayed in the Corps until the last shot was fired and peace again was ours in 1945.

Mildred L. Setterberg

A WAC IN NORTH AFRICA, WWII

by

Irene Isaacson Ward

After a year of marriage and following my husband from Texas to Massachusetts, to New York, and finally to Camp Patrick Henry, Virginia, I joined the first company of the Women's Auxiliary Army Corps (WAACs) being activated in Virginia. In uniform I felt like I was doing more for my country and felt closer to my husband, Amos G. Ward, a sergeant in the 45th Division.

Basic training was in February 1943 at Daytona Beach, Florida, and, being the first WAACs there, we lived in tents with wooden bunks. Then one day I had a wonderful surprise; my husband was not on his way overseas, but right there in Daytona on a pass. It was a wonderful two days, and this time we were sure this would be the last that we would see of each other until after the war.

Before I left Daytona, I, along with approximately 75 other girls, ended up in the hospital with food poisoning. After four days we were shipped out to assignments. I ended up at Fort Knox, Kentucky, went to typing school, and then was assigned the job of company clerk. A large, hot room with no cool air or fans held around 50 WAACs who were typing pay rolls for companies of men doing their overseas training at nearby Camp Campbell. Then the first of June, another happy surprise: there was my husband again for two days. That lifted my morale sky high, and I didn't mind all the tissue and carbons it took to type a payroll on that manual typewriter.

In August we were told that the WAACs was to become the WAC (Women's Army Corps), be part of the Regular Army, and that the "Articles of War" would apply to us as it did to the men. Since women were not drafted, we did not have to join the WACs. Most of the girls got out, but many of us stayed. I stayed on the condition that I be transferred far away from Fort Knox. Little did I know how far that would be.

I was sworn into the WACs and transferred, by way of Fort

Irene Isaacson Ward sent this photograph home from Fort Knox, Kentucky with the caption, "A view of the buildings we not only worked in but attended typing classes."

Oglethorpe for overseas training, to Hampton Road Port of Embarkation. There I sailed for North Africa the 28th of October, 1943. In the excitement, I didn't notice until we were out in the harbor that a British flag flew overhead. That's when I learned we were on the *Empress of Scotland*, a converted British pleasure cruiser, formerly the *Empress of Japan*. Our company and 5,000 paratroopers were on the top decks, plus a lot of GIs on the lower deck. In eight days of sailing we had one incident I'll never forget. One night an American destroyer wanted our ship to identify itself, and with no answer they turned bright lights on us and we shot them out. They made us break radio silence, and, to make sure we were safe from German U-boats, they followed us the rest of the way.

We landed in Casablanca and then went by a train to Algiers. We made several stops to let troop trains come on through. They were men returning from the front line who were ill or wounded, who had fought the German General Rhyme, and chased him back to Germany. We traded our C-rations for their K-rations, and, boy, was that a mistake. A little of the rich chocolate bar went a long way. We decided our cans of hash weren't bad after all. Every time we stopped, we would get off the small train and walk around. One day another girl and I came upon a couple of Military Police (MPs) eating French bread and apple butter as they stood by an open boxcar. They offered us some, and we accepted gladly; the bread was every bit as good as it looked. As I grew up on the farm, I never liked apple-butter, but I must say this was the best-tasting food I ever ate. The taste didn't stay with me, for to this day I still don't like apple butter.

After several days we finally arrived in Algiers. Our new home was a large museum with several floors of cold, hard marble and an elevator that didn't work and was never fixed. We were a communication company, and I was assigned to work in the Message Center of AFHQ (Allied Forces Headquarters). General Eisenhower came in and out on the day shift. We rotated three shifts round the clock. The U.S. Army took over the St. George Hotel, and British soldiers and our WACs worked one each to a desk. We sat through lecture after lecture on security and what top-secret meant every day before every shift.

I soon learned the importance of my work as I logged in messages from the front line listing all our men killed or missing in action each day, airplanes lost, and etc. I also learned that the 45th Division was fighting in Italy across the Mediterranean Sea from us. It was exciting and satisfying to know that Amos and I were not far apart. Our V-mail letters couldn't say much, but it let us know that each was okay. Before I left North Africa, besides Personnel Clerk, my discharge had three more Army specialty classifications: Clerk Typist, Medical Attendant, and Message Center Clerk.

Time flew by for I liked my work, and knew I was really doing something vitally important for my country, but our living conditions were wild. We slept on a double bunk nailed together out of wooden boards. The spring was a flat chicken wire stretched across, the corrugated mattress was stuffed with straw, and two wool blankets were issued. When it was cold enough to freeze water, we slept in our flannel pajamas and used the extra blanket for a pillow When it was hot as "Hades," we used the cotton seersucker pajamas. That's when the giant mosquitos were in season, and we had to sleep under an olive-drab tent of netting, which made it even hotter, but no one wanted to get malaria from those "dive bombers," as we called them, and we took our "yellow pills" regularly to help prevent malaria.

A few days after Thanksgiving my husband surprised us all when he showed up in my commanding officer's office. I happened to be in the building and not at work, and Captain Buetell (the only name I remember besides my bunkmate's), was very happy for me and wrote out three one-day passes. We were the only couple in NATO (North African Theater of Operation) that was married before we were sent overseas. Amos hitched a ride on a cargo plane, and when he got back to his company the *Stars and Stripes* published an article about him visiting his wife, and they sent the news to our hometown papers. My sister sent me the clippings.

From my work I kept up with Amos's company as it fought its way through Italy. After I left work, I had no problem keeping top-secrets, I knew my husband was right in the middle of it. Even in the museum, no one ever mentioned work.

As busy as we were, there were times when no messages came through, especially between 2:00 a.m. and 5:00 a.m. More than once someone pulled a prank on someone to keep us from going to sleep sitting up. One night we folded paper into small hard wads and using a rubber band to flip them and hit the head or shoulders of another person. That kept us awake and busy as bees making the little paper wads. No one managed to see who hit them, but they made sure they didn't get caught while targeting some one else. The officer in charge, who pretended nothing was going on, finally stopped us. He told everyone to lean over and start picking up the "snow balls" that covered the floor because General Eisenhower would be coming in later that morning. Then he decided the floor needed to be swept also, so he told me to get the broom and Cook to get the dust pan and clean up the floor. When I got through sweeping, Cook was still looking for the dust pan. It was nowhere to be found. Cook decided she would solve that problem. She poked the dust and paper wads that I had swept in a pile into a knothole in the wooden floor. She worked several minutes and finally got rid of it all. I put the broom up and went back to my desk.

In another minute or so, a British Captain came stomping, not walking, into the room and stopped in front of our officer's desk.

He looked up and asked if he could be of some help. The British officer was so agitated that his face was all red as he described, in his fast-talking way, and rather loudly, too, what had happened to his officers. Their offices were on the first floor under us, and they were having tea and tarts when a lot of dust and hard bits of paper fell down on their table into their tea and tarts. He wanted to know how that could possibly happen. Our captain told him that he would look into it and promised it would not happen again. The British officer whirled around and left the room. It was so quiet that you could hear a pin drop. I looked at the British private that I worked with, and he didn't blink an eye. Although he hadn't taken part in the paper wad shooting, he had watched me.

We all liked our captain for he was a good Joe and certainly knew how to get along with the British soldiers and the American WACs that he supervised. The next shift we came to work the knothole had been filled with wood and finished so smooth that if we didn't know better we wouldn't have known there was ever a hole in that board. Other pranks were played on the graveyard shift but no more paper wads were flipped

The next year by Easter of 1944 the front, which included my husband, had moved up to north Italy, and when my CO sent for me the day before Easter I nearly fainted when I walked into her office and saw him standing there. She had already written five one-day passes and given them to Amos with instructions to give me only one pass at a time and make sure it was for the correct day, for if an MP caught me with the wrong date on a pass, I would get in trouble and then she would be in trouble. He assured her we would watch the dates. As we left her office, I remarked about how beautiful her large vase of white lilies were. "They are from your husband," she told me smiling. "He is a very thoughtful person." Later I told my husband that he would make a good politician, and, again, little did I know!

As we ate Easter dinner in a cafe overlooking the sea, two carrots were the only food on our plates that we recognized. Amos allowed that the meat might be monkey, but I told him it could be dog, for the MPs had told us that none could be seen in the city because the natives ate them. I'll never forget that Easter dinner. We talked ourselves out of eating it and went to the Red Cross building and ate French rolls and meat rolled in dough and baked. They were good and safe to eat. Much of the week we ate in my mess hall, C-rations heated and flavored by the cooks, so it wasn't bad at all. I even ate the powdered eggs scrambled for breakfast. Amos felt bad that we in the rear echelon had to eat C-rations, but I didn't mind. I knew the fresh meat and food went to the front line. My 1st Sergeant loaned Amos her mess kit each day. She and the noncommissioned officers in the kitchen remembered him from his visit the previous fall and for sending me a box of fresh almonds from Italy, which the cooks roasted and used cocoa to make the best fudge I ever ate.

As before, the trip Sergeant Ward made to North Africa to see his wife in the WACs made the Army's *Stars and Stripes* and hometown newspapers.

After the war Amos, part Cherokee Indian whose father was on the Dawes Roll and had a land allotment in Rogers County, Oklahoma, was elected Sheriff of Rogers County for 32 years. We have one child, a daughter, who is an Agent for the FBI. After 40 years of marriage and "up and down" politics, Amos, still sheriff, died of lung cancer in the middle of a four-year term.

I am writing a book on the many years he served as sheriff, for it spanned three decades and parts of two others.

I was born in Temple, Oklahoma, in 1919 on a wheat ranch. My parents, who were born in Norway, purchased a farm in Rogers County when I was three months old. I have lived here ever since and in this same house 49 years.

SERGEANT MELBA JO GAITHER: SURVIVOR OF DESERT STORM

by

Opal Hartsell Brown

Sergeant Melba Jo Gaither and her husband, 1st Sergeant David Gaither, had been in the air 24 hours when they stepped off the C-5G Galaxy Transport on December 27, 1990, at Dhahran Air Base, Kingdom of Saudi Arabia. They and 69 others had boarded the plane on Christmas Day at Altus Air Force Base in Oklahoma.

Attached to 1345 Transport Company, Oklahoma National Guard at Ardmore, they all were in Saudi Arabia as part of President George Bush's "Desert Shield" operation.

The Gaithers talked about their experiences to visitors in their home near Gene Autry, Oklahoma. "I wasn't ready for the shocks," Melba Jo said, "as the heat from the tarmac hit me in the face like a blazing furnace! The odor of burning jet fuel from fighters and transport, as we passed in review, stiffled me.

"Aircraft pallets stacked high with war supplies," she continued, "faded into miles and miles of sand. I wanted to cry. What was I doing here—leaving my girls when they needed me? Of course, they were in good hands with David's parents, but I was shaken."

Melba Jo picked up a poster of pictures. "These," she said, "will give you a better idea of our experiences. David and I use them when we talk to schools and organizations. The chocolate chip uniforms always set our minds awhirl with miles of sand-covered lava, veiled women, and things that happened in Arabia."

Melba Jo identified the pictures and answered questions. "No," she said, "we did not live together over there. The men and women had separate quarters." She smiled. "But it was like dating again for us."

Melba Jo admitted it was comforting for them to be there together, yet tremulous. "The enemy could have wiped us out with one blast. And you would think, with David being my first sergeant, I would have had it easy. It was just the opposite. If someone couldn't do a job or there was an extra duty, I did it."

242

Sergeant Melba Jo Gaither on the shifting sands of Saudi Arabia, 1991, which she noted was the "Land of legendas, lava, rock, and shifting sands."

Everyone was laughing when David entered. Dark, healthy-looking, and as handsome as Melba Jo was beautiful, he joined the conversation. "We had only two or three alerts in the desert," he said, "and none of them were close. Sometimes in the night, though, it got spooky. We could watch a SKUD headed for Riyad. That's one of the capitals. We always hoped our Patriot Missiles got it and thanked God we weren't the target."

The couple talked about other dangers: plane crashes and accidents on the job. "Either one," David said, "could have left our daughters Brandy and Dava without either parent."

"The day we left for the Middle East," Melba said, "was not only Christmas, but Brandy's birthday. That made it more difficult for all of us."

"Three weeks before that," David said, "Jo was their mom, a wife with a job as parts and tool attendant for the Guard. Suddenly, she was in full combat gear—with flack vest and M-16— subject to action. She had no idea of how long she would be gone or whether she would ever get home."

There was a moment of quiet meditation, then Melba Jo suggested, "Let's talk about something else." She turned to a guest, Lavon Rivera. "You asked for more about SKUDS and native culture. After the 'Storm' began, SKUDS and missiles were everywhere. About the first month of the unit's advanced detachment, I was part of it. We lived in tents, ate T-Rations, something like TV Dinners, and bathed out of a pan.

"And cold," she shivered. "I almost froze on mornings when we had to break the ice on the water. It was a cold I never felt before. We wrapped up in anything we could find. There were no trees for wood, so we built fires with packing crates and tent pegs. The pegs were useless as tent anchors, because the lava was too hard for them to penetrate.

"The days got warm," Melba continued, "and toward the end of our tour, the temperature got to a 115 or 120 by noon."

"There was one good thing," David said. "About daytime at the camp, we didn't need much security. We could see almost forever. If anything moved, we knew it. We spent our days filling sandbags. But that wasn't easy.

"We had to hunt for drifts to find enough to shovel and fill our sacks. We stacked them around the camp for fortification at night. And you talk about dark!" David frowned. "The only light was the stars and the microwave tower about 15 miles away. And nighttime saw all of us pulling guard duty."

Melba Jo chuckled. "We had another protection," she remembered, "a long black scorpion, dug up in the desert. He caused quite a stir, especially by the girl holding our bag. We took him back to camp and secured him in an open cage as a chemical detector.

"We fed and monitored him closely," she added. "We knew if he died, we were in trouble. We had a regular chemical detector, but we trusted the scorpion's senses more. We called him 'DARTHVARDER'."

"What about toilet facilities in the desert?" someone asked. Both Gaiters chuckled. "At first," Melba Jo began, "the men got behind the vehicles. We women made screens for one another with our bodies and ponchos."

"That was before we got the latrines dug," David explained. "We had to burn the waste to keep the latrine halfway sanitary. We had a black cloud of smoke every day for about a month. After that, the commanders ordered us to the rear near the Port of Dammon. We packed up and took off on a cold bus ride."

"Yes," Melba Jo agreed, "and the air war was in full bloom at the Port. Due to the mystique of women soldiers there, we women weren't even supposed to drive. But that didn't last very long. We continued our jobs there, but lived in an apartment complex about 20 miles away. The complex had been built for Bedouins, but they wouldn't live in them. They stayed in their tents."

David talked about the turbulent action in that area. "Almost immediately we realized we were in harm's way. We were hemmed in by a major Allied air base, a seaport, and the Persian Gulf. Days were long, but uneventful. SKUDS usually began coming in about six in the evening. Sometimes every hour. Other times there was no rhyme or reason for their coming. Dhahran-Kobbar-Dammon was their target."

"Worse than SKUDS," Melba Jo said, "were the sirens. They grew from faint sounds to loud wailings that pulsed our ears and sent chills down our spines. We knew a SKUD was coming."

"Now," David said, "imagine the radio's announcement of that crisis! 'SKUD impact, one minute! SKUD impact, 30 seconds!' That's when even atheists start talking to God. In 30 seconds we all could be wiped out.

"Then came the 'THUD, THUD, THUD' of Patriot Missiles. Our hearts pounded faster. Should we go out, or sit, wait, and hope? As the sky lit up like a Fourth of July Celebration, we knew our Patriots had done their jobs. At first, when the "All Clear" sounded, we took off our gear. Before long, we got so used to the warnings we went to bed in full MUPP gear to save dressing so many times."

During the Gaithers' seven months in Saudi Arabia, Melba Jo found the culture almost as intriguing as the war. "One day?" she said and smiled, "I asked an Arabian woman where the toilet was. She turned her veiled face and hurried away. Her husband stepped up and told me. Their wives aren't allowed to speak even to strange women.

"At prayer time each day," Melba Jo continued, "businesses

close and everyone prays. I wonder whether their customs are more religious or political. For instance, when girls reach the age of 12, they have to wear the veil. When they get married, they tattoo or paint their hands and feet for their wedding night to make them softer. But women and some men want more freedom for the women.

"The Arabian people," she continued, "now have satellite dishes and watch TV from America. The men like 'Bay Watch.' That's the one where women wear scanty clothing. Some officials want it stopped, but they aren't about to get that done."

David remembered a day on the road. "Way down on the horizon," he said, "came four cars abreast at breakneck speed meeting us. There was no other road, so where were they going? Where were we going? As I sat in that truck with a Saudi driver and cars came nearer, my heart began to pound.

"I was ready to jump out," he laughed, "when the four cars split in the middle, 'WHOOSH!'" He demonstrated with his hands. "Two cars came on each side of us, stirring up a storm of sand, then wheeled back into the road, four abreast. It was several minutes before my heart settled down."

Both Gaithers found the custom of eating amusing. "We became acquainted with one family," Melba Jo said, "and went to their home for a meal. It was served on a cloth on the floor. The host knew we used plates, knives, and forks, so they gave us some.

"But they ate with their hands," she said, "from a big single dish. They had the best Italian food and bread I ever ate. The bread was rolled flat and cooked on the sides of the oven. They served a lot of fruit, such as dates and mangoes."

Wanting to see the country for which she had come to help rescue and defend, Melba Jo took a short trip to Kuwait. An independent sheikdom, it is encircled by the Persian Gulf, Arabia, and Iraq. Only 5,000 square miles, that little country was somewhat of a "sphinx" to both contenders: rich, coveted, and torched. Its blazing oil wells were "a patch of hell, strangling and foreboding." One glimpse was enough for Melba Jo. Another of her unusual experiences in the Middle East was a fishing trip with some friends for barracuda. She had no luck.

The lady sergeant did have luck during one of her tours to Ger-

The lady sergeant did have luck during one of her tours to Germany. "David and I met there," she said and smiled at him. "Germany was a beautiful country, especially at Christmas, but we waited until we got home to be married."

"In 1992," Melba Jo said, "we both decided our daughters, Brandy and Dava were at the age when they needed me with them. We also decided that both of us could not leave them again for war, so I left the Guards. When the girls get older, I may return and stay until I can retire. I'd like to go back to Germany and Arabia to see how much they have changed."

EPIGRAPH

The use of history is to give
value to the present hour.

—R.W. Emerson

APPENDIX:

A: WOMEN'S SERVICE ORGANIZATIONS

Women's Army Corps:

On May 15, 1942, President Franklin D. Roosevelt signed the bill authorizing the formation of the Women's Auxiliary Army Corps (WAAC), which would function with the U.S. Army, but not be a part of it. The purpose of the WAAC was to utilize women's talents and abilities in the war effort and to provide women an opportunity to serve as Army support staff, freeing men for combat duty. It was the first military service during World War II to enlist women and the only one to offer overseas duty.

With the announcement of the formation of the WAAC, women flocked to enlist, eager to serve in any capacity, at any place. Training began at Fort Des Moines, Iowa, in July 1942 with 440 women enrolled in the newly created six-week officer candidate school. At the same time, some 125 enlisted women took a four-week basic training course. After training, the women were detailed to almost every branch of the Army.

The first detachment of WAACs sent to an overseas post arrived in North Africa in January 1943 to be a part of General Dwight D. Eisenhower's staff. The following September, President Roosevelt established the Women's Army Corps (WAC) to replace the auxiliary organization, thus giving the women full military status. By this time, some 60,000 women had enlisted to serve in the Army.

After the war, on June 12, 1948, a law was passed making the Women's Army Corps a permanent organization to provide a nucleus for expansion in case of emergency.

U.S. Marine Corps Women's Reserve:

The U.S. Marine Corps was the last of the four major services to organize a women's reserve in World War II. The establishment of the Marine Corps Women's Reserve was made possible by an amendment, dated July 30, 1942, to the U.S.Naval Reserve Act of 1938. The women reservists were called Marines. They were the only women's service that did not have an acronym designation or semiofficial nickname. They were not an auxiliary group, but rather were accepted as a full-fledged part of the U.S. Marine Corps Reserve. More than 20,000 women were in the Marine Reserves by the time the war ended. And somehow, they left the Corps with a feeling of "Once a Marine, always a Marine." Semper Fidelis.

All units of the Marine Corps Women's Reserve were disbanded by September 1946. On June 12, 1948, Congress passed an act establishing the Women Marines as a permanent part of the Regular Marine Corps, as well as granting them permanent reserve status.

WAVES (U.S.Navy):

On March 17, 1917, the Navy Department authorized tbe enrollment of women in the Naval Coast Defense Reserve. At peak enlistment, there were over 10,000 yeomen (F) serving the U.S. Navy during World War I.

In 1925, after the war, the Naval Reserve Act was revised, and women were denied admission to the Navy. By the end of 1941, however, the Navy again became interested in the recruitment of women. In July 1942 congress passed a bill creating a Women's Naval Reserve. Thus the WAVES (Women Accepted for Volunteer Emergency Service) was born.

The Navy women who served in World War II fulfilled their avowed purpose by freeing men for overseas duty. According to the Navy, these women released 50,500 men to sea duty and filled 27,000 other jobs.

The Women's Reserve was detached from active duty in September 1946. On June 12, 1948, the Waves became an integral part of the Regular Navy as well as the Naval Reserve, providing a nucleus of officers and enlisted women to fuel any future expansion needed in time of war.

Army Nurse Corps:

American nurses began serving in the military as early as the

Revolutionary War. During the Spanish-American War, contract nurses were appointed in the Regular Army although not actually commissioned as officers. In July 1918, during World War I, the Nurse Corps was redesignated the Army Nurse Corps. During World War II, the Army Nurse Corps reached a peak of 57,000 nurses and functioned in the United States and in the European and Pacific theaters of war. According to the book, They Also Served by Olga Gruhzit-Hoyt, 211 Army nurses died during World War II.

In April 1947, by an act of Congress, the Army Nurse Corps became a part of the Regular Army of the United States.

Navy Nurse Corps:

In May 1908, Congress passed a bill establishing the Nurse Corps as an integral part of the United States Navy. These nurses did not have official status as either officers or enlisted personnel. They were under Navy regulations but did not receive any retirement benefits.

During World War I, 1,835 navy nurses served. In 1938 the Naval Reserve Act was passed, enabling qualified nurses to be recruited for the Nurse Corps Reserve. The nurses of the Regular Navy and the Naval Reserve served in hospitals and overseas; they worked on air evacuation planes and hospital ships. At the time of peak enrollment in 1945, there were 11,086 nurses on duty with the Corps. The Navy nurses endured long hours and often miserable conditions. They proved that they had the training, the will, the heart, and the stamina to help the fighting men of their country in their time of need.

After the defeat of the Japanese, a grateful nation welcomed the Navy nurses home. In 1947, in recognition of their service, the Navy Nurse Corps was nade a full, permanent, commissioned staff corps of the U. S. Navy.

U.S. Coast Guard (SPARS):

On November 23, 1942, the U.S. Coast Guard Women's Reseeerve was established. Known as the SPARS—derived from the Coast Guard's motto, Semper paratus, "Always ready"—the Women's Reserve would grow from a few recruits to approximately 10,000 enlisted personnel and 1,000 officers by the end of World

War II. In December 1942 twelve WAVES volunteered to be SPAR officers. Enlisted SPARS started boot camp at stations at Oklahoma A & M at Stillwater and elsewhere. The SPARS' slogan was "Release a Man to Fight at Sea," and the women who joined did just that.

After the war, the SPARS were seperated from the service, although a few years later a reserve training program was established that allowed women to participate in the Coast Guard.

On December 3, 1973, legislation was passed allowing women to serve in the Regular U.S. Coast Guard; three years later, the Coast Guard Academy in New London, Connecticut, became the first branch of the servise to admit women itito its ranks.

American Red Cross:

The Red Cross had its roots in the Geneva Convention of 1864, when the delegates sought to establish national organizations to aid the sick and wounded of wars.

After the Civil War Clara Barton went to Europe and served with the Red Cross in the Franco-Prussian War. She returned home and worked successfully to secure government adherence to the Geneva Convention (1882) and to found a Red Cross Society in the United States.

During World War II, the American Red Cross operated all over the world. The Red Cross established over 1,800 recreational facilities for the soldiers overseas. The war was very real to the women of the Red Cross. They all gave of themselves to make the life of the U.S. fighting troops a little bit easier. That they did so is of great credit to them. They too were women of courage.

The American Red Cross, with its 2 million volunteers, continues its peacetime service, but is ready to expand into wartime duty whenever and wherever needed.

B: CONTRIBUTORS

Dorothy Almen wrote about her wartime experiences in three stories: "Remembrances of My Tour of Duty in London, England, on the Secretarial Staff with the United Nations Organization (UNO, now UN)," "Experiences in the War Department During World War II, 1941-1946," and "Christmas Memory." Dorothy, now over 80, is writing her autobiography while serving as a Deacon, pianist, and historian at St. Stephen's Presbyterian Church. She is a member of the National Republican Senatorial Inner Circle, an exclusive group including only 20 Oklahomans. Dorothy is married to Harold W. Almen a retired businessman. They are worldwide travelers and now live in Oklahoma City, Oklahoma. They have a son, a daughter-in-law, two grandchildren, and three great-grandchildren.

Rosemary Eckroat Bachle, author of Women's War Memoirs, wrote "Los Alamos-the Secret Place in the Sky," a poem: "Witness," "On the Home Front," "Bring Back Daddy Club," and many of the stories from interviews. She is a writer, poet, business owner, artist, wife, mother, grandmother, and great-grandmother. She lives in Oklahoma City, Oklahoma.

Blanche Barrymore wrote "Remnants of War." She is a writer and still attends classes at the University of Central Oklahoma Creative Studies department. She has two grown children and lives in Oklahoma City, Oklahoma.

Susan Bickford was in the United States Marine Corps and wrote "In God I Trust." She is a member of the Women in Military Service for America Memorial at Arlington National Cemetery. Susan lives in Claremore, Oklahoma.

Pollie G. Blanton wrote "The Vietnam Years." It is from a forthcoming book by Pollie entitled Blanton's House of Havoc. She is an artist, a writer, and President of the Norman Branch of the National League of American Pen Women. She and her husband, Duane, adopted an international family: three girls—Chinese, Aztec Indian/Spanish, and Korean; and two boys—Cherokee Indian and Amerasian. They now live in Noble, Oklahoma.

Lillian C. Boland wrote "Serendipities from World War II." Retiring from the University of Central Oklahoma in 1987 as faculty member in the communication and humanities department, she has continued to lead a busy life as a book and play reviewer and serving as a volunteer in many organizations. She was inducted into the Alumni Hall of Fame at the University of Science and Arts of Oklahoma in the summer of 1996. On March 14, 1997, she was one of The Oklahoma Hospitality Club's "Ladies in the News." She is married to John L. Boland and they have two children.

Opal Hartsell Brown wrote "One Civilian's Connection with Three Wars" and "Sergeant **Melba Jo Gaither**: Survivor of Desert Storm." She graduated from East Central State Teachers College in Ada, Oklahoma. She taught civilians and military personnel for 36 years and is now a freelance writer and journalist.

Opal is the author of seven published books including Indomitable Oklahoma Women. She is listed in *Personalities of America, Foremost Women of the Twentieth Century*, and *Who's Who of Intellectuals*. She lives in the Arbuckle Mountains of southern Oklahoma.

Glenda Carlile wrote "Colonel **Rosemary Hogan**: 'The Angel of Bataan.'" As a writer she has published two books, *Petticoats. Politics. and Pirouettes* and *Buckskin. Calico. and Lace*. As an entertainer she has become familiar to audiences across Oklahoma as, in period costume, she brings to life the stories of exciting early day women. She is the Executive Director of the Oklahoma Center for the Book and an officer for the Oklahoma County Historical Society. She lives in Oklahoma City, Oklahoma.

Colonel Rosemary Hogan is buried at Arlington National Cemetery.

N.E. (Nora) Chapman wrote "God Said It's Not Time Yet." Nora is a writer of children's stories, inspirational stories, and everything in between. She has won more than 200 awards in writing contests and has had more than 70rticles and short stories published. She is a member of several Oklahoma, national, and international writing clubs.

Dwane E. Cline wrote "The Military Years of Rosie E. (Marshall) Laird." He is a member of the Oklahoma City Writers club and lives in Watonga, Oklahoma.

Dr. Stan Cosby lives in Durant, Oklahoma, and his poem,

"Requiem for Joan," won first place in an Oklahoma Poetry Society competition in 1997.

Janiece Ritter Cramer wrote "Remembrance and War." She is a writer and lives in Norman, Oklahoma.

Jean Waiter Dabney is the WAC in "Los Alamos Love Story." Winston Dabney supplied the information that helped get this story written. The Dabney's still live in Los Alamos.

Mary Louise Courey Glann wrote about her experience in the U.S. Marine Corps Reserve in "Boot Camp-Camp Lejeune, North Carolina." She was an active participant on dedication day of the Women in Military Service for America Memorial at Arlington, Virginia. She is the historian for the Heartland Chapter, OK-2, Women Marines Association. Mary lives in Oklahoma City, Oklahoma.

Dena R. Gorrell is a member of the Poetry Society ofOklahoma. Her poem, "Long-Awaited Homecoming," was a winner in a 1997 contest. She lives in Edmond, Oklahoma.

Carol Hamilton is both writer and poet. She wrote "Sweet Secrets," a story about her aunt, and a poem, "Patterns." Carol was Poet Laureate of Oklahoma in 1995-96. She lives in Midwest City, Oklahoma.

Ora Harris in "Leipzig After Sixty-Two Years" shares her diary with us. Dignitaries of Leipzig had invited Ora and ten others who had lived in Leipzig under the Hilter era to visit the city. Ora lives in Oklahoma City, Oklahoma.

Jean Williams Hayes was a nurse in Germany with United Nations Relief and Rehabilitation (UNRRA) in World War II. Her story "Parachute Silk and POW Rice" was written as told to Rosemary Eckroat Bachle.

Jean has many interests in her busy life. She paints with the Oriental Brushwork Society of America. She teaches a back exercise class at the YMCA, travels with her husband Daniel, and has been a visiting nurse in Cleveland and Oklahoma Counties. The Hayes' contributions helped start the Designated Endowment Fund at the Community Foundation for the Visiting Nurses Association.

Mary Jones' story, "Love Affair with the Air," written by **Elaine M. Dodson**, shares with us her experiences in the Women's Air Service Patrol (WASP) as a pilot in World War II. In October 1993 she received the Clarence E. Page Memorial Trophy for outstanding individual contribution to aviation sponsored by Oklahoma Air Space Museum and Hall ofFame. Mary lives in Tulsa, Oklahoma.

Elaine M. Dodson lives in Tulsa, Oklahoma and is Associate Editor for Nimrod Magazine.

Martha Kay was an Air Raid Warden in London, England, during World War II. Her story, "Air Raids in London, World War II," was written by Rosemary Eckroat Bachle. Martha now lives in Alexandria, Virginia and donates her time working as a volunteer at The White House in Washington, D.C.

Lieutenant J.G. USNR WAVE **Estella (Tillie) Knapp Kernan** was a coder and decoder in World War II. Her story, "All Hands Hit the Deck," was written as told to Rosemary Eckroat Bachle. Tillie and her husband, Philip A. Kernan, are proud to have served as officers in the United States Navy during our country's time of need. They live in Oklahoma City, Oklahoma.

Pat Krikorian was "A WAAC in Los Alamos" and was proud to know that the scientists were working on "something very special" that would end the war. She served from August 1943 and was discharged in January 1946. In 1948 Pat married a scientist, Nerses H. Krikorian. She has traveled with him to China and Russia to visit laboratories.

They have one daughter who also is a scientist. The Krikorians still live in Los Alamos, New Mexico.

Irene Sturm Lefebvre is an author and wrote her own story, "Letters Home." She was a WAC in the 5205th WAC Detachment GHO in the Southwest Pacific.

Irene, in collaboration with her husband, Paul E. Lefebvre, as artist and photographer, is the author of"Cherokee Strip in Transition," "Tales and Trails of the LeForces," and many articles featuring Oklahomans. They live in Oklahoma City, Oklahoma, and have two sons and a daughter.

Irmgard Marchant was a coder and decoder under the Hitler regime during World War II in Germany. "My Son Grew Up in a Bunker," as told to Rosemary Eckroat Bachle, is the story of a young woman's survival in war torn Europe. Irmgard lives in Midwest City, Oklahoma.

Billie Marsh's powerful poem, "Long Live Peace," brings us all down to earth about war and peace. Billie belongs to the Poetry Society of Oklahoma and lives in Tulsa, Oklahoma.

Flo Mason packs a punch with her poem, "Flashback." Flo was president of the Poetry Society of Oklahoma and her poem, "A Woman of World War II," placed first in the "Women's War Memoirs" category at the Poetry Society of Oklahoma Awards March 8, 1997. She lives in Oklahoma City, Oklahoma.

Marj McAlister wrote "A Day That Made a Difference" and a poem, "Global Warfare." Marj taught poetry for several years at St. Lukes in Oklahoma City, Oklahoma. She lives in Edmond, Oklahoma.

"Willing Followers: **Lee Gummer McDonald**'s Story," was written by **Kathleen Gummer**, Lee's daughter. Lee lives in Edmond, Oklahoma.

Louise Lord Miller tells her story, "The Tiny Riveter," and lives up to what Rosie the Riveter said: "Give me the right tools, and I will hand you an airplane." Louise is an Oriental Brushwork Painter and lives in Midwest City, Oklahoma.

Dorothy Myers wrote a poem, "Wars of the 40's." She is a member of the Poetry Society of Oklahoma and lives in Bethany, Oklahoma.

Joan Naylor lets us look into the mind of a child in her story, "Dog Tags for Kids." Joan is a civic leader and prolific writer. Joan and her husband, Earl, have lived in Oklahoma since 1955. They have four children and 21 grandchildren. They live in Edmond, Oklahoma.

Madalynne Norick is the "World War II Working Mother" in this story written by **Rosemary Eckroat Bachle**. She remembers World War II well. She worked at several jobs during the war years, cared for her young son, and followed her husband from base to base when he was stateside.

Madalynne is an artist and among her many accolades she is a recent recipient of the Oklahoma City University Distinguished Philanthropist Award. She and her husband, Jimmy, have two children and live in Oklahoma City, Oklahoma.

Virginia Ridgeway's story, "A South Pacific Scrapbook," was written by her daughter, **Virginia McCombs**. Virginia and Ridge Ridgeway have been married over 50 years, have two daughters, six grandchildren, and two great-grandchildren. They live in Oklahoma City, Oklahoma.

Virginia McCombs is the director of the Honors Program and an associate professor of history at Oklahoma City University. She is married and has three children.

Billie Riggs in her story, "The Wives Who Wait," tells us of her big adventure in life as a military wife. Her husband, William G. Riggs, was in the military for 30 years. She had many moves and said, "In looking back over all our years in the military, I must admit I enjoyed every one of them—good and bad. The experience for our children was priceless."

Billie and William live in Oklahoma City, Oklahoma.

Ida Green Ritchie was a Los Alamos WAC. In her story, "The Giants on the Hill," she says, "Since I had no technical background, I hadn't a clue as to what was going on in the lab until Commander Bradbury announced that one of our units was dropped on Japan."

In 1953, Ida and her husband, Ernest Ritchie, left for Denver and other moves including Oklahoma. The Ritchies now live in California.

Dr. Hanna A. Saadah's poem, "Of Life and Land 1982," is from one of his books of poetry. All proceeds from his books go to charitable organizations and cancer support in Oklahoma. Dr. Saadah, M.D., S.A.C.P., has an internal medicine practice in Oklahoma City, Oklahoma.

Mildred Brezic Setterberg wrote "My Life in the Women's Army Corps." She is a retired corporal. She was a host on a local radio station's emphasis on Men in War and was in the Color Guard of the Disabled American Veterans. She is a member of the Women in Military Service for America Memorial at Arlington National Cemetery. Mildred resides in Oklahoma City, Oklahoma.

Sandra Soli writes her poem, "Tea Ceremony," about her life in London, England, as a child in World War II. Sandra is an excellent editor. She lives and teaches poetry and other writing classes in Oklahoma City, Oklahoma.

Patty Croft Kelly Stevens, the Japanese Prisoner of War in "Four Came Home," enjoys life to the fullest. She plays golf, is active in many civic and social clubs, and she and her husband, Q.O. Stevens, enjoy traveling. Patty lives in Oklahoma City, Oklahoma.

Dora J. Stohl, the Army nurse in "The Story of Nurse Dora J. Stohl," is a busy person. She is a decent at the Cowboy Hall of Fame, and she gives her time to the Kirkpatrick Museum and to the Lyric Center. Her other interests include travel, oil painting, and genealogy. Dora lives in Oklahoma City, Oklahoma.

E. Bernardine Buyez Sydner's poem, "Now," is one of many poems this award-winning poet has won. She is a civic leader n Oklahoma City, Oklahoma.

Doris N. Taylor wrote her story, "A Teacher's Story: WWII USO Volunteer." Doris was a well-loved teacher in the Oklahoma City schools for many years. She lived in Oklahoma City, Oklahoma until her death in 1997.

Lela N. Turner's poem, "Be Still and Know," was written in World War II and came to her while praying for her brother. Lela belongs to the Poetry Society of Oklahoma and lives in Oklahoma City.

Al Waintroob is a member of Oklahoma City Writers. He wrote "A Mother's Story of the Five Blue Stars." Al lives in Oklahoma City, Oklahoma.

Irene Isaacson Ward writes of her experiences as "A WAC in North Africa; WWII." Irene is an author and is writing a book about her husband who served as Sheriff of Rogers County in Oklahoma for 32 years. Irene was born in Temple, Oklahoma. She now lives in Claremore, Oklahoma.

Betty Wedel is a member of the Poetry Society of Oklahoma. Her poem, "At Dachau Prison When I Tried Not to See," is very moving. Betty was in the Women's Auxiliary Army Corps (WAAC later WAC). She lives in Fairview, Oklahoma.

Betty Butler Wiseman wrote "Prewar China" and "The Battle for Europe, World War II." She is a retired biochemical research worker from the Oklahoma University Health Sciences Center in Oklahoma City, Oklahoma. She is an aspiring writer and poet. She lives in Edmond, Oklahoma.

Mina R. Zentz wrote a poem, "It was a Matter of Curiosity," about a bundle of old letters she found in an attic. Mina lives in Oklahoma City, Oklahoma.

BIBLIOGRAPHY

The Art of Creative Nonfiction. Writing and Selling the Literature of Reality: Lee Gutkind: John Wiley & Sons, Inc. New York 1997.

They Also Served: American Women in World War II. Olga Gruhzit-Hoyt. A Birch Lane Press Book published by Carol Publishing Group 1995.

The American Woman's Cook Book WARTIME COOKERY 1944. Cornell University. The Blakiston Company, Philadelphia.

Standing By and Making Do: Women of Wartime Los Alamos. Jane S. Wilson and Charlotte Serber, Editors. Los Alamos Historical Society Los Alamos, New Mexico 1988.

Never to Forget: The Jews of the Holocaust. Milton Meltzer. Harper Collis Publishers 1 976

Loves and Lamentations of a Life Watcher: Poetry by Hanna A. Saadah. 1987.

Magazine: World War II, July 1995, Greatest Battle Never Fought. Ansil L. Walker, Page 22.

The Invasion of Japan: Men and Mission of the Manhattan Project. Linda K. Wood, Page 38.

Los Alamos: Beginning of an Era 1943-1945. Los Alamos History written by the staff of LASL's Public Relations Office. Reprinted in 1986 under the auspices of the Los Alamos Historical Society.

'We Pulled Together...and Won!," Personal Memories of the World War II Years...from over the Seas and Back at Home, as told through the words and snapshots of those who united for victory. From the readers of *Reminisce Magazine.* 1993.

"THE GOOD WAR" An Oral History of World War Two. Studs Terkel. Ballantine Books, New York.

The Los Banos Raid—the 1 Ith Airborne Jumps at Dawn. Lt. Gen. E. M. Flanagan, Jr. USA (Ret.). Published by Presidio Press.

Women in Resistance and in the Holocaust: THE VOICES OF EYEWITNESSES. Edited and with an introduction by Vera Laska. Contributions in Women's Studies, Number 37. Greenwood Press Westport, Connecticut. "London, England.

The Twenty-Sixth General Hospital, "A History of the Twenty Sixth General Hospital"; Bureau of Engraving, Inc. Minneapolis, Minnesota. 1945.

Infield, Glenn B. *Disaster at Bari.* Ace Books, New York City, N.Y. - 1971.

Infield, Glenn, "Disaster at Bari." *American Heritage.* October 1971, XXII, pp. 60-64, 104-105.

INDEX

Abbott, Hardy, 227
Ahpeatone, OK, 145
Alexander, Harold, 22
Almen, Dorothy, 20-27
Altus, OK, 4
Altus Air Force Base, 242
Anchor Ranch, NM, 126
Anderson, L.H., 227
Ardmore, OK, 242
Army Nurse Corps, 145-148, 180, 194-207, 247-248
Ashbridge, Colonel, 122
Atomic bomb, 17, 41, 55, 90, 113-130
Avenger Field, Sweetwater, TX, 164-165
Axton, Hoyt, 15
Axton, John, 15
Axton, Johnny, 15
Axton, Mae Boren, 15

Bachle, Elaine Marie, 6
Bachle, Mrs. L.L. See Bachle, Rosemary Eckroat
Bachle, Rosellen, 6
Bachle, Rosemary Eckroat, 4, 6, 79-84, 105-110, 113-144, 194-212
Baker, Captain, 123
Baptist Medical Center, Oklahoma City, 95
Bari, Italy, 195, 202-204, 207
Barrymore, Blanche, 28-34
Battle of the Bulge, 39-42
Berlin Airlift, 68-69, 100
Beneke, Tex, 106, 230
Bermant, Anna, 57-58
Bickford, Susan M., 191-192
Blackwell, OK, 49
Blanton, Becky, 66-75
Blanton, Cindi, 66-75
Blanton, Derrick, 67-75
Blanton, Duane, 66-75
Blanton, Jeffrey, 67-75
Blanton, Kari, 66-75
Blanton, Polli G., 66-75
Boland, John L., 8-11
Boland, Lillian C., 8-11
Borthick, Roy C., 43-47
Bradbury, Commander, 130

Bring Daddy Back Club, 4-7
Brown, Gordon, 13, 15-19
Brown, Opal Hartsell, 13-19, 242-245
Buetell, Captain, 239
Burge, Mable, 15
Bush, George, 242

Camp Lee, VA, 218-221
Camp Lejeune, NC, 191-192, 229
Camp Stoneman, CA, 55
Camp Shelby, MS, 51
Carlile, Glenda, 145-148
Cavanagh, Will, 42
Central High School, Oklahoma City, 95
Chapman, Nora E., 43-48
Chattanooga, OK, 145, 146
Chiang Kai-chek, 37
Chickasha, OK, 197
Claremore, OK, 95
Classen High School, Oklahoma City, 95
Cleveland County Health Department, 212
Cline, Dwane E., 49-55
Comanche County, OK 15-16
Cooperider, Everett, 227
Cosby, Stan, 189
Covington, Jack, 38
Cowboy Hall of Fame, 207
Cramer, Janiece Ritter, 85-90
Cramer, William L., 86-90
Crooch, Russell, 18

Dabney, Darlene, 124
Dabney, Jean Waiter, 120-124
Dabney, Jimmy, 124
Dabney, Nancy, 124
Dabney, Winston, 122-124
Dachau Prison, 159-160
Dailey, Victor, 227
Denman, Steven Grant, Jr., 100
Desert Storm, 96, 100, 242-245
Dickie, Dr., 43-44
Dodson, Elaine Mr., 163-166
Dog tags, 91
Donlevy, Brian, 232
Dougherty, Russell Chris, 77
Dougherty, Russel Ray, 76-78

Duke, Guadalupe, 9-10
Douglas Aircraft factory, Oklahoma
City, 106, 109-110, 113
Duncan, OK, 13

Edmond, OK, 5, 76, 77
Efate, 182-185
Eisenhower, Dwight D., 210, 238, 246
El Reno, OK, 4, 49
England, 20-23, 198-199, 213-215
Eufaula, OK, 43

Fairview, OK, 160
Forbess, Ruby, 18
Fort Sill, OK, 18-19, 120, 194-197, 206
France, 133-135
Franklin, Mrs. E.L., 6, 7
Froman, Darol, 122
Futch, Sue, 16

Gaither, David, 242-245
Gaither, Melba Jo, 242-245
Gene Autry, OK, 242
Germany, 79-84, 99, 149-160
Glann, Mary Louise Courey, 229-232
Gorrell, Dena R., 3
Grant County, OK, 218, 226
Graves, Alvin, 122
Green, Ida, 128-130
Groves, Leslie R., 126
Gummer, Donald F., 97-100
Gummer, Kathleen, 97-100
Gummer, Kay, 99
Guthrie, OK, 4

Ham, Bill, 89
Hamilton, Carol, 35-36
Hope, Bob, 232
Harper, Paul, 227
Harris, Bud, 149
Harris, Ora, 149-158
Hartsell, Aubrey, 15
Hartsell, Jesse, 13, 16-18
Hartsell, Nannie, 15
Hayes, Dan, 211-212
Hayes, Jean Williams, 208-212
Hefner, Robert A., 5
Henry Chapelle Cemetery, 42
Hickam Air Force Base, HI, 99
Hogan, Rosemary, 145-148
Hollister, OK, 148
Hott, Donald, 227
Hulbert, Mary, 164

Infield, Glenn B., 207

Italy, 133-135, 195, 202-204, 207

Jakovinak, Ivan, 18-19
Johnson, J.B., 13, 16-17
Johnson, Lyndon B., 64
Jones, Mary, 163-166

Karlebach, Dr., 151
Kay, Martha, 213-215
Keating, Cathy, vii-viii
Kelly, Carolyn, 144
Kelly, Paul J., 143-144
Kelly, Paul J., Jr., 144
Kennedy, John F., 67
Kernan, Estelle Knapp, 167-176
Kernan, Philip A., 173-176
Kernan, Philip A., Jr., 176
Kerr, George E., 145
Kerr, Robert S., 5
Kilian, Bennie, 227
Kirkpatrick Museum, Oklahoma City,
207
Koo, Kim Jin, 18
Korea, 205-206
Korean War, 17, 100, 205-206
Krikorian, Nerses H., 127
Krikorian, Pat, 125-127
Krittenbrink, Clarence, 227
Ku Klux Klan, 68

Kyser, Kay, 232

Laesione, OK, 13, 15-18
Laird, Bill, 49-55
Laird, Rosie E., 49-55
Lake, Veronica, 232
Lawton, OK, 194, 196
Lefebvre, Irene Sturm, 218-227
Lefebvre, Paul, 219-227
Leipzig, Germany, 149-158
Lette, Larry, 6
Lette, Mrs. R.C., 4, 6-7
Lewis, Ida Mae, 13
London, England, 20-23, 213-215
Los Alamos, NM, 111-130
Los Alamos School, 126
Los Baños Camp, 139-143
Luciano, Arnold, 148
Lucy, 133-136

MacArthur, Douglas, 16, 141, 224
Magurus, Mr., 155
Manhattan Project, 113-130
Marchant, Irby, 83-84
Marchant, Irmgard, 79-84.

Maria, 133-136
Marine Corps Women's Reserve, 191-192, 229-232, 246-247
Marsh, Billie, 12
MASH, 205-206
Mason, Flo, 56, 96
Matthews, Russ, 219
McAlister, Marj, 76-78
McBee, Estelle, 8-10
McCombs, Virginia Ridgeway, 177-188
McCoy, John J., 26
McDonald, Lee Gummer, 97-100
McDonald, William F., 99-100
Medford, OK, 218, 219, 226, 227
Medicine Park, OK, 5
Mehard, Douglas, 13, 16, 17
Mehard, Ida, 13
Mercy Hospital, Oklahoma City, 65
Miami, OK, 85
Midwest City, OK, 83, 84
Miller, Louise L., 101-104
Mojave Desert Marine Air Station, CA, 230
Money, Mrs. A.V., 6, 7
Monroney, Mike, 5
Mooney, Melba Jean, 6
Moore, E.H., 5
Myers, Dorothy, 228
Myrer, Anton, 188

Navy Nurse Corps, 177-188, 248
Naylor, Joan, 91
Newman, John Henry, 131
New Zealand, 185-187
Nordon Bomb Sight, 103
Norick, Jimmy, 105-110
Norick, Madalynne, 105-110
Norick, Ronald J., 105-110
Norick, Vicki, 110
Norman, OK, 41, 105
Northwest Classen High School, Oklahoma City, 95

Oakwood, OK, 49, 55
O'Connor, Irene, 220
Oklahoma, passim
Oklahoma (ship), 13
Oklahoma City, OK, 4, 5, 13, 39, 48, 49, 59, 61, 65, 89, 94-95, 100, 105, 106, 109, 110, 135, 144, 207, 227, 230
Oklahoma Education Association, 59
Oklahoma Library for the Blind and Physically Handicapped, 95
Oklahoma Military Academy, 105

Oklahoma State University, 45, 90
Oolagah, OK, 95
Oppenheimer, J. Robert, 114, 126, 129

Parsons, William S., 129
Philippines, 109, 137-148, 220-226
Pockavich, Dr., 51-52
Postlewait, Dilmond, 227
Postlewait, Evelyn, 227
Punchbowl Cemetery, HI, 38
Pyle, Ernie, 17

Red Cross, 10, 61, 62, 65, 139, 249
Riggs, Billie, 59-65
Ridgeway, Elmer, 178, 185-188
Ridgeway, Jessie Virginia Boling, 177-178
Ritchie, Ernest, 130
Riveting, 101-104
Rogers County, OK, 241
Rogers, Will, 95
Roosevelt, Eleanor, 21-22, 63-64, 178, 187
Roosevelt, Franklin D., 15, 17, 85, 125, 224, 235, 246
Russell Dougherty School, Edmond, 77

Saadah, Hanna A., 189
St. Luke's Methodist Church, Oklahoma City, 95
Santa Fe, NM, 113, 121-123, 128
Saudi Arabia, 242-244
Setterberg, Mildred L. Brezic, 233-235
Shoemaker, John, 16
Sold, Henrietta, 149
Soli, Sandra, 216-217
SPARS, 248-249
Spartan School of Aviation, Tulsa, 166
Steaks, Mr., 89
Stevens, Pattie Croft, 137-144
Stevens, Q.O., 144
Stillwater, OK, 45
Stockings, 91
Stohl, Dora J., 194-207
Sturm, Donald, 220
Sturm, Loyde P., 226
Sturm, Melvin, 223
Sturm, Raymond, 223
Sydner, Bernardine Buyez, 190

Taft High School, Oklahoma City, 95
Tanner, Theo, 148
Tarnakov, Wolodymire, 18
Taylor, Doris N., 94-95
Taylor, Glen Ray, 227

Temple, OK, 241
Thomas, Elmer, 5
Tinker Field, OK, 113
Truman, Harry S., 17
Truscott, Lucius, 211
Tulsa, OK, 5, 166
Turner, Lela N., 193

Ufnal, Henry, 18
United Nations, 20-23
University of Oklahoma, 11, 14, 39, 41,
   59, 64, 90, 167, 212
UNRRA, 209-211
USO, 94-95, 180

Victorian Order of Nurses, 208-210
Vietnam War, 17, 19, 46-48, 63-64, 66-
   75, 100, 206

WAACs. See WACs
WACs, 120-130, 218-227, 233-241,
   244, 246
Ward, Amos G., 236-241
Ward, Irene Isaacson, 236-241

Washington, D.C., 24-27, 66, 104, 129,
   171-175, 219, 235
WASPs, 163-166
WAVES, 129, 167-176, 230, 247
Wayne, John, 64
Wedel, Betty, 159-160
Weintroob, Al, 57-58
Western Union, 85-87
Wichita Mountain Wild Life Refuge, OK,
   18
Will Rogers Memorial, Claremore, 95
Will Rogers World Airport, Oklahoma
   City, 95, 100
Wiseman, Betty Butler, 37-42
Wiseman, Earl, 39-42
Woods, General, 143
World War II, passim
Wrey, Dorothy, 15
Wright, Mrs. Nelson, 7
Wyandotte, OK, 85

Yunker, Louis, 227

Zentz, Mina R., 92-93